ROSS FOR BOSS

SUNY series on the Presidency:
Contemporary Issues

John Kenneth White
editor

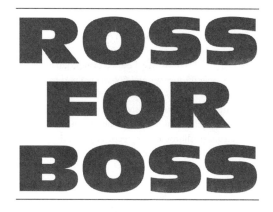

ROSS FOR BOSS

The Perot Phenomenon and Beyond

Edited by

TED G. JELEN

STATE UNIVERSITY OF NEW YORK PRESS

Published by

STATE UNIVERSITY OF NEW YORK PRESS, ALBANY

Printed in the United States of America

For information, address
State University of New York Press,
90 State Street, Suite 700, Albany, NY 12207

Production and book design, Laurie Searl
Marketing, Michael Campochiaro

Library of Congress Cataloging-in-Publication Data

Ross for boss : the Perot phenomenon and beyond /
edited by Ted G. Jelen.
    p. cm. — (SUNY series on the presidency)
    Includes bibliographical references and index.
    ISBN 0-7914-4853-3 (alk. paper) — ISBN
0-7914-4854-1 (pbk. : alk. paper)
    1. Third parties (United States politics). 2.
Presidents—United States—Election—1992. 3.
Perot, H. Ross, 1930- 4. Presidential candidates—United States. I. Jelen, Ted G. II.
SUNY series in the presidency.

JK2261 .R677 2001
324.973′0928—dc21
                             00-038764

10   9   8   7   6   5   4   3   2   1

Contents

Figures and Tables

Figures

Tables

Contributors

PAUL A. DJUPE
Denison University

CHRISTOPHER P. GILBERT
Gustavus Adolphus College

TED G. JELEN
University of Nevada, Las Vegas

TIMOTHY R. JOHNSON
University of Minnesota, Twin Cities

JEFFREY KOCH
State University of New York College at Geneseo

ANDREW D. MARTIN
Washington University, St. Louis

JEREMY D. MAYER
Kalamazoo College

KENNETH D. NORDIN
Benedictine University

DAVID A. M. PETERSON
Texas A & M University

JAMES SIMMONS
University of Wisconsin, Oshkosh

SOLON SIMMONS
University of Wisconsin, Madison

BRIAN SPANG
attorney-at-law, Chicago

CLYDE WILCOX
Georgetown University

Foreword

As this book goes to press in December of 2000, the presidential race between Al
Gore and George W. Bush has apparently been decided in Governor Bush's favor.
The final outcome of the election became apparent 36 days after votes were cast
on November 7, and was made final by a 5–4 decision of the United States
Supreme Court, which halted manual recounts in the state of Florida. The results
of the 2000 presidential election will be examined and re-examined by practicing
politicians, journalists, and academics alike for years to come. My purpose in this
foreword is to place the 2000 election in the theoretical context which motivates
this book: the aftermath of the Perot phenomenon of 1992 and 1996, and, more
generally, the role of third parties in U.S. electoral politics. Despite the fact that
minor party candidates, either individually or collectively, did not do as well as
Perot did in either 1992 or 1996 should not obscure the revealing, and perhaps
important, nature of contemporary electoral politics outside the two party system.

As I argue in the opening chapter of this collection, the main purpose of
minor party candidacies is not to gain office, but to advance a policy agenda. Third
parties in American politics typically measure their success by the extent to which
the major parties adopt their issues positions. In this sense of altering the course of
public policy, the Perot campaign in 1992 was partially successful in the sense of
achieving at least one of its policy objectives: deficit reduction. In his 1992 campaign for president, Ross Perot characterized a large budget deficit as being similar
to "a crazy old aunt in the attic" whose presence no one wished to acknowledge.
In the presidential campaign of 2000, candidates Gore and Bush debated the
question of what to do with an ever-increasing budget surplus. Partially in
response to Perot's strong showing in 1992, and his somewhat weaker but still
impressive importance in 1996, both parties advanced programs to reduce, and
eventually eliminate, the federal budget deficit. It is at least arguable that voters
who voted for Perot out of concern for the federal deficit cast extraordinarily
influential votes in 1992 and 1996.

The rest of Perot's agenda did not fare as well. Perot's concern with protecting American jobs from foreign competition did not qualify for the political
agenda of 2000. No serious candidate for president from either party (George
Bush and John McCain for the Republicans, Al Gore and Bill Bradley for the

Democrats) opposed free trade either in principle or in policy detail. Similarly, Perot's efforts to reform the political process did not bear fruit in 2000. As I write this in the aftermath of Governor Bush's narrow and contested victory, campaign finance reform remains a mere aspiration for members of both major parties. Further, while legislative term limits have been enacted in several states (perhaps most notably, Florida), the momentum of the term limits movement appears to have abated, as many recently elected citizen legislators have belatedly discovered the benefits of experience and incumbency.

The successes and shortcomings of the Perot movement provide a backdrop for the two most highly visible minor party candidacies of the 2000 election: those of Pat Buchanan and Ralph Nader. Each of these political insurgents added a central component of the Perot platform to his issue agenda: economic nationalism in the case of Buchanan, political reform in the case of Nader.

As the nominee of the Reform Party, which was Ross Perot's most enduring legacy, Buchanan did a great deal to destroy the Reform Party as a formal organization in U.S. politics. Based on Perot's 9 per cent showing in the 1996 election, the Reform Party qualified for nearly $13 million in federal funds. Buchanan's paltry showing of just under 1 per cent in 2000 ensures that the Reform Party will not qualify for federal campaign funds in 2004.

Could Buchanan have done better? After all, he advanced a view of economic nationalism, which was a crucial part of the Perot program, and, as noted earlier, was not adopted by any candidate of the major parties. Moreover, as the chapter in this volume by Simmons and Simmons shows, there still exists a constituency for this approach to international trade. However, it seems clear that Buchanan himself was an ineffective spokesman for this issue. I have conducted some preliminary analyses of exit polls of Republican primaries in 1992 and 1996, and the results of these studies suggest that Buchanan was perceived by the electorate primarily in terms of conservatism on social issues. Indeed, in the GOP primary contests of 1992 and 1996, the best predictor of a Buchanan vote was the respondent's attitude toward abortion. By contrast, in the 1996 primaries, Buchanan split the votes of Republican economic protectionists almost evenly with Bob Dole.

In 2000, Buchanan ran a number of commercials on television and (especially) radio, in which he emphasized the importance of closing America's borders to unfair foreign competition, illegal immigrants, and illicit drugs. However, most of these spots had a strong cultural component (one radio spot has a sound background of men laughing and speaking staccato Spanish) and did not directly address the economic concerns of many blue-collar workers. To the (limited) extent that such advertisements penetrated public consciousness, they may well have reinforced Buchanan's image as a cultural conservative, which stands in contrast to Perot's own social liberalism on such issues as abortion.

Conceivably, Buchanan could have made an impact with a strong, focused

Conceivably, Buchanan could have made an impact with a strong, focused campaign from the cultural right, with a particular emphasis on the abortion issue. At a minimum, such a campaign would have posed a strategic nightmare for Governor Bush, who sought to de-emphasize the salience of divisive social issues. Buchanan might well have drawn substantial support from voters who identify with the Christian Right, some of whom may have felt abandoned by Governor Bush. However, having won the nomination of the Reform Party after a divisive convention, and having accepted the federal funding which Perot had earned in the 1996 campaign, Buchanan apparently felt honor-bound to respect the platform and constituency of his newly acquired party affiliation.

In a very general way, the presidential candidacy of Green Party candidate Ralph Nader in 2000 reflected the populist message of political reform advanced by Ross Perot in 1992 and 1996. Nader also expressed deep concerns about the effects of "globalism" in economic affairs, but appears to have based these reservations on political, rather than economic, considerations. While Nader was clearly concerned about protecting American jobs, his principal objection to economic globalism seems to have been an opposition to making decision-making structures even more remote from the influence or understanding of the average citizen. Organizations such as the International Monetary Fund or the World Trade Organization are not directly accountable to American voters and represented to Ralph Nader a further concentration of economic and political power.

Despite a rather dismal 2 per cent showing in the presidential election, it seems likely that Ralph Nader did influence the outcome. While conclusive evidence for this claim must await more systematic inquiry, the circumstantial case that Nader cost Gore the presidency is rather impressive. If one makes the conservative assumption that only half of Nader's vote would have gone to Al Gore if Nader had not been running, Nader seems to have cost Gore the states (and electoral votes) of New Hampshire (four electoral votes) and Florida (twenty-five electoral votes). Either of these states would have given Gore an Electoral College majority, and therefore the presidency. Florida is a particularly egregious example. At this writing, Bush's winning margin in Florida is listed at 193 votes, out of over six million cast. In Florida, Nader received over 92,000 votes for President. Even a small fraction of these votes would have permitted Gore to win Florida's electoral votes.

Thus, if one assumes that even a plurality of Nader voters preferred Al Gore to George W. Bush, the Nader candidacy seems a classic instance of the "wasted vote" thesis. By voting for a minor party, a voter is effectively casting a vote for her worst alternative. As many Democratic leaders put it in the closing days of the 2000 campaign, "A vote for Nader is a vote for Bush."

Of course, rational choice theories of electoral behavior (discussed in more detail in the first chapter of this volume) suggest that such an outcome may be desirable for supporters of a minor party candidate, if the strategy of such voters is future-oriented. That is, a Nader voter whose preference ordering was Nader-Gore-Bush may have intentionally advantaged Governor Bush, in an effort to persuade the Democratic Party to offer a more palatable candidate in 2004. However, such an outcome in 2004 seems unlikely. While in principle Nader's appeal could coax a more "populist" candidate into the race for the Democratic presidential nomination in 2004, it seems probable that strategic actors in the Democratic Party (such as potential financial contributors, state and local party leaders, and members of Congress) will understand that Nader's impact on the 2000 election was the result of the preposterous closeness of the race between the major party candidates, and cannot be attributed to any mass appeal on the part of Ralph Nader. Unlike Perot, who received nearly one vote in five in 1992, a repeat of Nader's performance in 2004 is only likely to effect the outcome under highly unusual (indeed, perhap unique) circumstances which will almost certainly not be repeated. It thus seems improbable that the electoral or governing strategies of either major party will be affected by Nader's performance in the 2000 Presidential election.

In summary, minor party candidates occasionally perform an important agenda-setting function in American politics. In the presidential elections of 1992 and 1996, the candidacy of H. Ross Perot was formidable indeed, and threatened to affect the outcome of the race on both occasions. To a limited extent, Perot was successful in forcing his issues on the national political agenda, and achieved some success in persuading the major parties to adopt policies favored by his supporters. By contrast, although echoes of the Perot agenda were discernable in the 2000 candidacies of Pat Buchanan and Ralph Nader, it seems unlikely that either will affect the political agenda of the early twenty-first century. Despite the fact that Nader may have altered the outcome of the 2000 election, it seems improbable that the Nader candidacy will have any long-term impact on the Democratic Party. To this degree, then, the Perot phenomena of 1992 and 1996 represents a another instance of a recurring feature of electoral politics in the United States, rather than a permanent change in the shape of the contemporary party system.

Ted G. Jelen
Las Vegas, Nevada
December 15, 2000

1

The Perot Campaigns in Theoretical Perspective

Ted G. Jelen

The recent presidential campaigns of H. Ross Perot, and the subsequent events surrounding Perot's Reform Party, have posed political scientists with a fascinating set of intellectual issues. In 1992, nearly one vote in five in the presidential election was cast for Perot, making his showing the strongest for a candidate from outside the two party system since 1912. Four years later, Perot's support was cut nearly in half, but he was still able to attract about 9 percent of the popular vote for president. Moreover, the Reform Party (the vehicle for Perot's candidacy in 1996) appears to have an enduring role in contemporary American politics. In 1998, Reform candidate Jesse "The Body" Ventura (a former professional wrestler) was elected governor of Minnesota, and has since become a highly visible player in Reform Party politics. Further, the Reform Party presidential nomination for the 2000 election has become the object of vigorous competition. As I write this in the autumn of 1999, both former Republican presidential contender Pat Buchanan and financier Donald Trump are publicly considering seeking the Reform Party nomination. Thus, unlike other third party movements in the twentieth century (Rosenstone et al. 1996), the Perot movement, institutionalized in the Reform Party, may well survive the political viability of its original candidate. Thus, several years after the fact, political scientists and political pundits alike have not arrived at satisfactory accounts of the Perot phenomenon, nor is there an appreciation of the long-term potential of the movement Ross Perot appears to have put into motion.

This volume is intended to help explain Perot's meteoric rise and precipitous decline in contemporary American electoral politics, as well as the apparent persistence of the Reform movement into the twenty-first century. Perot's unusual success, and indeed, the very existence of Perot campaigns for the presidency, is difficult to explain. Almost uniquely among Western democratic systems, the United States is highly inhospitable to political challenges by movements that originate from outside the two-party system. The purpose of this introductory chapter is to review some of the formidable obstacles to American third-party movements, and to attempt preliminary explanations for Perot's ability to overcome some (but not all) of these barriers.

Institutional Barriers

Among the most well-known and well-established generalizations in the social sciences is "Duverger's Law," which states that two party systems are likely to develop in polities that use a single-member district, plurality system, such as that found in the United States (Duverger 1963). Most political offices in the United States are contested under plurality rules, in which the candidate receiving the largest share of the popular vote is declared elected, even if that share falls below a majority (50 percent).

It is not difficult to see why such an electoral system discourages third party candidates. Presumably, a voter who is contemplating a vote for a candidate from outside the two party system is likely to have a preference between the major party candidates. As the chapters by Simmons and Simmons, Koch, and Mayer and Wilcox show, Perot drew votes from both Democratic and Republican presidential candidates in 1992 and 1996. A voter whose first choice for president was Ross Perot, but who preferred George Bush (in 1992) or Bob Dole (in 1996) to Bill Clinton, was posed with something of a strategic dilemma: Does one cast a vote for her first choice (Perot), if that vote would advantage this voter's last choice (Clinton)? Would it not make more sense to vote for the Republican candidate, in an effort to deny the presidency to Bill Clinton? This dilemma, often termed the "wasted vote" thesis, has been an extremely formidable obstacle to minor party and independent candidates for most of American history.

The Electoral College, of course, magnifies the disadvantage under which third parties must compete. Under the Electoral College system, a successful candidate for president must garner a majority of the electoral votes (currently 270 of a possible 538). While, in principle, such a majority system might provide a minor party candidate with an opportunity to create an Electoral College deadlock (thereby requiring the president to be selected by the House of Representatives), such leverage can only exist if the minor party candidate in question actually received electoral votes. In most states (Maine and Nebraska are the exceptions), the state's electoral votes are assigned on a "winner take all" basis to the candidate receiving a plurality of the popular vote. Thus, in order to have any impact on the electoral vote, a minor party candidate typically must finish first in at least one state.

This sort of Electoral College deadlock has not occurred in the twentieth century. However, minor party candidates who have received electoral votes include Robert LaFollette (1924), Strom Thurmond (1948), and George Wallace (1968).[1] What these candidates have had in common is the fact that their popular support was geographically concentrated (in Wisconsin for LaFollette, and in the South for Thurmond and Wallace). Despite the fact that he ran better than any of these three former third-party candidates in 1992, and ran better than either LaFollette and Thurmond in 1996, Ross Perot received no electoral votes in either election. While Perot was able to finish second in several states in 1992, in no state did he obtain a popular vote plurality.

Thus, the practice of American elections tends to discourage both candidates and supporters of third parties quite strongly. Given the winner take all nature of elections in the United States, it is impossible for competitors from outside the two party system to make gains that are both gradual and tangible. While it is possible in principle for third parties to increase their popular support over a series of elections, the lack of tangible rewards (in terms of the election of public officials) has tended to reduce the lifespan of third party movements in the twentieth century.

Aside from the impact of electoral laws themselves, there are other institutional barriers to third party success in American elections. One of these is differential ballot access. The mechanics of conducting elections in the United States are generally regulated by state law, and no state or territory permits candidates to have unrestricted access to the ballot. Typically, most states impose some combination of petition signatures and filing fees, which vary substantially across states (Winger 1997; Dwyre and Kolodny 1997). While restrictions on ballot access have generally become less burdensome since the Wallace campaign of 1968, the existence of fifty-one (fifty states plus the District of Columbia) separate sets of regulations poses potential third party movements with a very high initial hurdle. Candidates and parties from outside the two party system must commit substantial resources to gaining admission to the electoral contest; something that is granted automatically to the Democratic and Republican parties.

The chapter in this volume by Martin and Spang, which describes the mobilization of the Virginia chapter of United We Stand, illustrates both the potential and limitations of such grass-roots movements. On the plus side, gaining ballot access did provide volunteers with an immediate, attainable goal in the early stages of the 1992 electoral cycle. This sort of activity may have created a psychological investment in the Perot campaigns, which could have sustained the commitment of Perot supporters during difficult times (such as Perot's untimely withdrawal in

July 1992). Conversely, movements such as United We Stand are unlikely to be popular with politically active citizens, who may have strong attachments to the existing parties. Third parties are often required to recruit from the ranks of people who are socially and politically isolated. The chapter by Gilbert, Johnson, Djupe, and Peterson on the impact of religion on the Perot campaigns suggests that third-party movements generally will lack the organizational support and political skills that often characterize active church members (Verba, Scholzman, and Brady 1995). This point can be generalized. The most fertile recruiting ground for third party supporters is likely to exist within those segments of the population that are not strongly politically or socially engaged. However, such people are also likely to lack the interest and skills necessary to participate in political activity.

Thus, the costs of admission to the electoral arena (in terms of time, money, and energy) are higher for the supporters of third party candidates than for those who support one of the two major parties. Moreover, these increased costs must often be borne by people whose ability to incur them is rather limited.

Attempts to "reform" campaign finance in the post-Watergate era have also limited the potential of some third-party movements. Under the regulations that have been in place since 1976, presidential candidates affiliated with the major parties are entitled to matching funds from the federal treasury during the primary season, and are entitled to federal financing during the general election. By contrast, the campaigns of John Anderson (in 1980) and Ross Perot in 1992 had to be financed privately (albeit under the same restrictions on fund raising imposed on major party candidates) with the possibility of reimbursement by the Federal Election Commission after the election. Further, the amount of such post hoc support for relatively successful third party candidates (e.g., those who qualify at all) is contingent on the level of electoral support such candidates receive. Again, third-party candidates typically have fewer resources with which to gain financial support, and must submit to more stringent requirements than those imposed on the major parties (Dwyre and Kolodny 1997).

Finally, certain federal regulations have often limited the media coverage available to third party candidates. Most conspicuously, third party candidates bear a substantial burden in order to be included in presidential debates. For the 2000 electoral cycle, for example, presidential candidates must achieve support of 15 percent or greater in one of the major national polls to be included in televised debates between presidential candidates (Clines 1999). Since these debates have become pivotal events in the conduct of general election campaigns since 1976, exclusion from debates can be a huge handicap for candidates from outside the two party system. A candidate such as Ross Perot in 1996 is faced with something of a Catch-22: In order to gain popular support, the candidate must participate in debates; in order to participate in televised debates, the candidate must demonstrate popular support.

Given these barriers to third party success, how did Ross Perot manage to fare as well as he did? It can easily be discerned that, despite the support of nearly one voter in five in 1992, Perot was unable to overcome in any way the bias imposed by the Electoral College. Despite a high expenditure of resources in two consecutive elections, Perot did not obtain a single electoral vote. Nevertheless, Perot was able to attract a very high level of support in 1992, and managed a fairly respectable showing in 1996. It has been argued (Rosenstone, Behr, and Lazarus 1996) that, in 1992, Perot was able to overcome many of the traditional obstacles to third-party success by using some of his substantial personal wealth. As the chapter by Kenneth Nordin illustrates, Perot was able to purchase large segments of television time for his "informercials" with his own personal fortune. Under the Supreme Court's 1976 decision in *Buckley v. Valeo,* personal expenditures by candidates on their own behalf cannot constitutionally be limited. Perot was apparently able to parlay the investment of his own money into adroit use of "free" media (most notably, frequent appearances on the Larry King show), which in turn generated sufficient popular support to allow Perot to be included in the presidential debates. The preceding discussion has suggested that third party candidates and movements face formidable start-up costs in order to enter the electoral competition. Billionaire Perot was able to bear these costs more easily than most other third party candidates, and was thus able to attract a relatively large popular following.

In 1996, and perhaps in 2000 as well, Perot was able to take advantage of some of the institutional provisions that have traditionally benefited the major parties. While 1996 witnessed another extended struggle for ballot access for the newly formed Reform Party, Perot himself qualified for (and accepted) $29 million in federal funds, based on his 1992 showing (Green and Binning 1997). Based on Perot's more limited demonstration of support in 1996, the Reform Party candidate for president in 2000 will be eligible for approximately $12.6 million in federal subsidies, which will be available during the campaign (Clines 1999). While this total will be dwarfed by the subsidies available to the Democratic and Republican candidates for president, the $12.6 million may provide a basis for garnering the popular support necessary to gain entrance to televised presidential debates. Thus, in 2000, the Presidential nomination of the Reform Party may well be worth having, since Perot's previous efforts have paid some of the start-up costs of third party activity in advance.

Strategic Considerations

Despite the impressive limitations on third party activity in the United States, the presentation of alternatives to the two major parties is a frequently occurring feature of American politics (Rosenstone et al 1996). Indeed, to suggest that Perot simply bought his way into contention in 1992 is to ignore features of the political environment in the late twentieth century that made Perot's approach particularly appealing to an important and politically consequential segment of the American electorate. While Perot's personal resources were perhaps *necessary* to his performance in the 1992 and 1996 elections, such resources would not have been sufficient under different circumstances. Thus, important questions for analysts of contemporary American electoral politics might be "Why Perot?" and "Why now?"

William Riker (1976) has proposed a dynamic theory, which can account for both the occurrence and decline of third parties in the United States. According to Anthony Downs (1956), parties in two party systems tend to converge toward the center of the left-right (or liberal-conservative continuum). As the major parties (such as the Republicans and the Democrats) come to resemble one another, voters on the extreme right or extreme left are likely to feel abandoned by the party closest to them, and increasingly indifferent to the differences between the two major parties. Thus, voters and candidates might well engage in a rational "future-oriented" strategy, in which votes in a present election are "wasted," in order to bring one or both parties closer to the optimal position on the extremes. As one of the major parties adapts to the challenge posed by the third party, by moving closer to the third party's positions, the rationale for the existence of the third party becomes weaker, and fewer voters are likely to be indifferent to the difference between the two major parties. Thus, in subsequent elections, the third party is increasingly unlikely to attract electoral support, even as its issue positions are adopted to some extent by the major parties.

At first glance, Riker's theory seems unlikely to apply to the Perot movement, since many accounts (including the Mayer and Wilcox piece in this volume) have suggested that Perot voters were "zealots of the center," who rejected the more strident issue positions of both major parties (see especially Miller and Shanks 1996). However, it does seem possible that, in the context of the 1992 election, it is the center of the liberal-conservative continuum that has been vacated by the major parties. Downsian analysis suggests that the logic of two party competition mandates that parties interested in electoral success will converge toward the center of the political spectrum. However, if the ideological movement of the Democrats and Republicans is constrained (perhaps by the internal dynamics of each party), the parties may leave vacant the center.

A recent analysis by Shafer and Claggett (1995) suggests that this is precisely what has happened in recent American politics. Schafer and Claggett have argued that public opinion in the United States is characterized by "two majorities": a conservative majority on "cultural/moral issues" involving personal morality and foreign affairs, and a liberal majority on issues pertaining to matters of economics.

The analysis further suggests that the former set of issues provide a context in which Republicans are likely to prevail, while Democrats have an advantage when the agenda concerns economic issues. However, both parties are, in a Downsian sense, acting irrationally in two distinct ways. In the first instance, each party in the late twentieth century has chosen to respond to internal constitutencies that advantage the competition. Thus, the Republican Party has emphasized its economic conservatism, despite the fact that this set of issues tends to favor Democrats. Conversely, Democratic candidates have tended to focus on issues of personal morality (such as gay rights, feminism, and civil liberties for unpopular expression) even though these issues tend to advantage Republicans. For reasons that have yet to be explained adequately, each party has tended to compete in the opposition's ballpark. Secondly, Shafer and Claggett argue that each party has wasted its potential majority, by taking more extreme positions than the majority will bear. Thus, the commitment of some Democratic candidates to "hard" versions of affirmative action and income redistribution has alienated the moderate economic liberalism of many former supporters (e.g., "Reagan Democrats"), while the stridency of some Republican candidates on issues such as abortion and gay rights has prevented the mobilization of many potential supporters (Wilcox 1992; Jelen 1991).

It is not entirely clear why political candidates in contemporary American politics behave "irrationally" in this narrow Downsian sense. Some analysts have suggested that party "reforms" begun after 1968 have made political parties more responsive to relatively extreme activists (Crotty and Jackson 1985; Ladd 1978; Lengle 1981; and Polsby 1983), but recent research (Wilcox 1995; Norrander 1989) has shown that primary electorates are no more extreme than general election voters. What does seem clear is that candidates of both major parties, whether as the result of conviction or miscalculation, have frequently acted in a manner that does not permit them to maximize their share of the vote.

If elites in the major parties regard themselves to some extent as captives of their extremist wings, it may follow that the "vital center" has been the area of the political spectrum that has been vacated. Analyses of the issue positions of Perot voters have shown that they are generally more liberal than those who supported Bush or Dole, and more conservative than those who supported Clinton, in 1992 and 1996. Moreover, Perot may be regarded as an aggressive centrist in other respects as well. As the essays in this volume by Nordin and by Martin and Spang make clear, two of Perot's major issue positions were opposition to the federal deficit and support for term limits. Moreover, Perot's "can-do" approach suggested that problems in U.S. politics are not about ends but means. For example, Perot's promise to "get under the hood" and fix the economy suggests that there exists general agreement on what "fixing the economy" might mean. Perot thus campaigned in part against the *idea* of partisanship, and indeed, against the idea that politics is a profession.

Seen in this light, Perot's campaign thus may fit Riker's account rather nicely. Perot, as do most relatively successful third party candidates, gained a measure of electoral support by occupying a portion of the political spectrum not held by the major parties. Paradoxically, the vacant space in U.S. politics may have been in the center.

Was Perot Successful?

Traditionally, third parties in the United States are rarely "successful" in the traditional sense of winning elections. Duverger's Law suggests that it is highly unlikely that the United States will ever sustain a stable multiparty system, and, in only one instance in American history—the ascendancy of the Republican Party in 1860—has a minor party succeeded in displacing one of the two major parties in the electoral system. Rather, the success or failure of third parties has generally been assessed in terms of their agenda-setting function (Rosenstone, Behr, and Lazarus 1996). That is, minor parties in the United States have often raised issues ignored by the two major parties, and the positions initially taken by minor parties on these issues are occasionally adopted by one or both of the major parties.

Given this policy-based criterion, how has the Perot movement fared? As the next chapter by Kenneth Nordin shows, Perot based his candidacies on three major themes: the need to reduce the federal budget deficit, reform of the political process itself, and the protection of American jobs from foreign competition. Specifically, the need for political reform was manifested in the term limits movement, which was endorsed by Perot, and an attack on NAFTA (the North American Free Trade Agreement) was the most visible aspect of Perot's economic nationalism.

In 1992, Perot characterized the federal budget deficit as being comparable to "a crazy old aunt in the attic," which neither party cared to discuss. By the end of the decade, both parties had endorsed plans to reduce the budget deficit, and, by 1998, the Federal Government was believed to be operating at a surplus. The Republican Party (the majority party in Congress since 1994) passed a series of budget reduction measures, and the Clinton administration has taken credit for a long period of economic prosperity which increased government revenues and lowered certain public expenditures. As this is being written in the final year of the Clinton administration, a major issue in public debate is the disposition of the budget surplus. Should government revenues that exceed expenditures be applied to the national debt, or does the surplus provide an opportunity for a major cut in federal taxes? The nature of the debate on a surplus in the federal budget suggests that both parties have responded to Perot's focus on the deficit as an important problem. For voters who placed a high priority on deficit reduction in 1992 and 1996, a vote cast for H. Ross Perot was as influential a vote as has ever been cast in an American election. Rather than being "wasted," as Duverger's Law would suggest, votes cast for Perot in 1992 and 1996 had a profound effect on the direction of American politics, and, ultimately, on policies adopted by both major parties.

The record on political reform generally, and on the specific issue of term limits, has been mixed. The idea that the number of terms to which public officials (particularly members of Congress) should be limited has come to symbolize opposition to the existence of a supposed "political class" of nearly permanent, electorally secure legislators. Such a class has been regarded as "out of touch" with the concerns of ordinary citizens, and Perot was a proponent of efforts to replace such entrenched officials with frequently changing "citizen legislators." Limiting an individual representative or senator's term to two or three terms is an idea that has gained widespread support toward this goal.

A promise to consider the issue of term limits was an explicit item on the GOP's "Contract With America," a statement of principles produced by Congressional Republicans for the 1994 off-year elections. The question was quite prominent as a campaign issue in the 1994 elections, and several long-term members of Congress (including House Speaker Thomas Foley) were defeated in part because of their opposition to formal term limits. Thus, proponents of term limits were quite successful in placing the issue on the public agenda, and it seems likely that Perot's high level of public support in 1992 was instrumental in achieving a high level of visibility for this issue.

However, the movement to limit the terms of elected legislators has, to date, been unsuccessful. Despite several attempts by several Republicans in the House of Representatives to enact legal term limits, measures that would mandate such limits have never been passed by either house of Congress. Moreover, several members of the House "Class of '94," who had promised to limit the number of terms for which they would run voluntarily have begun to reconsider their positions. Apparently, the experience of serving in the House of Representatives has introduced some recently elected members to the advantages of seniority and continuity of leadership.

Finally, Perot's efforts to protect American jobs through protectionist policies has not been particularly successful. As noted in the chapter by Kenneth Nordin, Perot debated Vice President Al Gore on the question of NAFTA in November 1993 on the *Larry King Live* show. Despite Perot's history and experience in using the medium of television, as well as his familiarity with the particular format of the King program, Perot was considered to have "lost" the NAFTA debate to Gore. Subsequently, NAFTA was ratified by the United States Senate, and the general issue of protectionism has generally disappeared from the public agenda of American politics. As this is written in the fall of 1999, it is perhaps noteworthy that no candidate for the presidential nomination of either major party has taken a position against free trade. The decision of House minority leader Richard Gephardt (a long time supporter of protective tariffs) not to seek the Democratic presidential nomination in 2000 meant that there would be no Democratic candidate for president not committed to the importance of free trade. Perennial Republican candidate and economic nationalist Pat Buchanan is, at this writing, considering leaving the Republican Party to seek the presidential nomination of the Reform Party. If the analysis presented in this volume by Simmons and Simmons is substantially correct, there may well be a constituency for such a message, which will apparently be unrepresented by either major party in 2000. While Buchanan's conservatism on social issues may not be attractive to many potential supporters of the Reform Party, the fact that the major parties appear to have left the issue of economic nationalism to the Reform candidate may provide a basis of support for a Buchanan candidacy.[2]

Thus, the consequences of the Perot candidacies for public policy appear substantial, but limited. While the major parties have responded promptly and profoundly to Perot's treatment of the issue of the budget deficit, the same cannot be said of the issues of political reform or economic nationalism.

Plan of the Book

This volume had its origins at a panel on "Third-Party Movements in American Politics," held at the annual meeting of the Midwest Political Science Association in Chicago in April of 1994. Versions of four of the papers included in this collection (those by Martin and Spang, Koch, Simmons and Simmons, and Gilbert et al.) were initially presented at that meeting. The idea of an edited volume emerged at a Dutch Treat lunch which immediately followed the panel session. As the project evolved (surviving a long delay during which the editor moved from suburban Chicago to Las Vegas), and as both Ross Perot and the Reform Party added to their respective histories, chapters were revised and added to describe and explain more recent developments. As this is being written, the Reform Party is being considered by several potential presidential candidates as a vehicle for articulating issue positions that may not be receiving much attention from the Democratic and Republican parties. The existence and persistence of the movement begun by Ross Perot in 1992 provides the rationale for this collection of studies.

The essays that comprise this volume provide sophisticated analyses of the Perot movement in 1992 and 1996, and may provide a basis for evaluating the potential of the Perot movement in the immediate future. The first two pieces deal with the Perot phenomenon at the elite level. Kenneth Nordin suggests that, to a large extent, Perot's 1992 success can be attributed to an adroit understanding of the medium of television, and of the sorts of themes likely to succeed in that arena. Perot's somewhat weaker performance is perhaps attributable to a loss of control over "the story," and reduced access to the electronic media. The chapter by Martin and Spang shows that the "volunteers" (an important practical and rhetorical device in the Perot movement) exhibited high levels of "social capital" (Putnam 1995), without strong political commitments. Martin and Spang remind us of a lesson originally taught by Alexis de Tocqueville (1945), in which he emphasized the important of "voluntary associations" in limiting the tyranny of the majority. The existence of a large number of politically skilled people without strong political commitments constituted an important "slack" resource on which Ross Perot was able to draw (Dahl 1961).

The next four chapters concern the nature of support received by Ross Perot on the part of the mass public. Most analysts (see Asher 1995) have not been able to discern major differences between Perot voters and supporters of other candidates. Simmons and Simmons show that Perot drew disproportionate support from a constituency inhabiting a particular economic situation, with a coherent set of grievances. Jeffrey Koch builds on this finding, by showing that, to a large extent, Perot's leadership was instrumental in creating the sense of grievance that he cultivated among his supporters, which in turn may have had important consequences for the historic Congressional elections of 1994. Gilbert, Johnson, Peterson, and Djupe show that Perot drew much of his support from religiously uncommitted (and perhaps socially marginal) citizens. The Gilbert et al. piece raises more general questions about the roles of social integration and social capital in the dynamics of third party support at the mass level. Wilcox and Mayer suggest that the decline in Perot's support between 1992 and 1996 was uniform across virtually all social strata, which in turn suggests that the roots of Perot's decline cannot be attributed to simple changes in individual attitudes or behavior.

A final chapter by Gilbert and Peterson compares the sources of Perot support in Minnesota with that gained by Gov. Jesse Ventura in 1998. The continuities and discontinuities between the two candidates in a state with a strong independent tradition suggest that there may be substantial limits to the long-term national viability of the Reform Party.

We hope that the essays in this volume will contribute to a deeper understanding of the Perot phenomenon, and indeed, to the dynamics of American electoral politics generally. The Perot campaigns have provided an unusual opportunity to observe change in American politics at the levels of popular culture, elite-level activism, and public opinion. The studies that follow constitute an attempt to exploit this intellectual opportunity.

Notes

1. This discussion, of course, excludes the election of 1912, in which the Republican candidate (William Taft) was an incumbent president, and the "Bull Moose" candidate (Theodore Roosevelt) was a former GOP president. Both candidates received electoral votes, but the split in the Republican ranks made Woodrow Wilson's relatively narrow popular vote victory an Electoral College landslide.

2. Preliminary analysis of selected exit polls for the 1996 Republican primaries suggests that Buchanan was much more successful in attracting the votes of social conservatives than economic nationalists. Indeed, the strongest predictor of Buchanan support in 1996 was the voters' attitude toward abortion, rather than the voters' position on issues of free trade or immigration. See Morrison 1999.

References

Asher, Herbert. 1995. "The Perot Campaign." In Herbert F. Weisberg, ed., *Democracy's Feast: Elections in America.* Chatham, N.J.: Chatham House, 153–175.

Clines, Francis X. 1999. "Counting Controversy as Blessing: Buchanan Exults in the Storm Before His Decision on a Party," *New York Times,* October 2, A8.

Crotty, William, and John S. Jackson III. 1985. *Presidential Primaries and Nominations.* Washington, D.C.: Congressional Quarterly Press.

Dahl, Robert. 1961. *Who Governs?* New Haven: Yale University Press.

Downs, Anthony. 1956. *An Economic Theory of Democracy.* New York: Harper and Row.

Duverger, Maurice. 1963. *Political Parties: Their Origin and Activity in the Modern State.* New York: Wiley.

Dwyre, Diana, and Robin Kolodny. 1997. "Barriers to Minor Party Success and Prospects for Change." In Paul S. Herrnson and John C. Green, eds., *Multiparty Politics in America.* Lanham, Md.: Rowman and Littlefield, 173–182.

Green, John C., and William Binning. 1997. "Surviving Perot: The Origins and Future of the Reform Party." In Paul S. Herrnson and John C. Green, eds., *Multiparty Politics in America.* Lanham, Md.: Rowman and Littlefield: 87–102.

Jelen, Ted G. 1991. *The Political Mobilization of Religious Beliefs.* New York: Praeger.

Ladd, Everett Carl. 1978. *Where Have All the Voters Gone?* New York: Norton.

Lengle, James I. 1981. *Representation and Presidential Primaries.* Westport, Ct.: Greenwood.

Miller, Warren E., and J. Merrill Shanks. 1996. *The New American Voter.* Cambridge: Harvard University Press.

Morrison, Jane Ann. 1999. "Expert Sees Buchanan Third-Party Bid as Harmful to GOP," *Las Vegas Review-Journal,* October 3, 11B.

Norrander, Barbara. 1989. "Ideological Representativeness of Presidential Primary Voters," *American Journal of Political Science* 33: 570–587.

Polsby, Nelson W. 1983. *Consequences of Party Reform.* New York: Oxford University Press.

Putnam, Robert D. 1995. "Bowling Alone," *Journal of Democracy* 6: 65–78.

Riker, William H. 1976. "The Number of Political Parties: A Re-examination of Duverger's Law," *Comparative Politics* 9: 93–106.

Rosenstone, Steven J., Roy L. Behr, and Edward H. Lazarus. 1996. *Third Parties in America*. 2nd edition. Princeton: Princeton University Press.

Shafer, Byron E., and William J. M. Claggett. 1995. *The Two Majorities: The Issue Content of Modern American Politics*. Baltimore: Johns Hopkins University Press.

Tocqueville, Alexis de. 1945. *Democracy in America,* ed. Phillips Bradley. 2 vols. New York: Vintage Books.

Verba, Sidney, Kay Lehman Scholzman, and Henry E. Brady. 1995. *Voice and Equality. Civic Voluntarism in American Politics.* Cambridge: Harvard University Press.

Wilcox, Clyde. 1992. *God's Warriors: The Christian Right in the Twentieth Century.* Baltimore: Johns Hopkins University Press.

Winger, Richard. 1997. "Institutional Obstacles to a Multiparty System." In Paul S. Herrnson and John C. Green, eds., *Multiparty Politics in America*. Lanham, Md.: Rowman and Littlefield, 160–171.

2

The Television Candidate

H. Ross Perot's 1992 and 1996 Presidential Races

Kenneth D. Nordin

Introduction

Texas billionaire H. Ross Perot twice ran for the American presidency, in 1992 and again in 1996. The campaigns were unorthodox because Perot relied almost exclusively on television appearances and commercials to attract voters. No other presidential candidate had ever attempted such a strategy. But Perot was no ordinary candidate. First, he had become one of the wealthiest and most famous men in America before he entered politics. Second, he knew how to market himself and his political agenda. Third, he understood the power of television and how to gain access to it. Perot exploited television sufficiently to attract millions of voters despite the fact that no major political party stood behind him. He became a viable presidential candidate because he could transmit his charisma to TV's audience. In 1992 Perot received nearly 19 percent of the popular vote. In 1996 Perot's problem-plagued campaign attracted only half the voter support of the 1992 race. But his vote tally in 1996 qualified his new Reform Party for future electoral financial support.

Ironically, television became both the making and the unmaking of candidate Perot. Two conflicting images of the Texas businessman emerged on the small screen. In one, a portrait that he himself created, he was a political Lone Ranger, a lonely hero able to ride into Washington and single-handedly clean up the mess. He was the successful entrepreneur prepared to bring his organizational skills and financial acumen into the White House and fix the nation's economy. This Ross Perot was a charming, witty, plain-speaking fellow who stood on a populist platform designed to help the common man. Perot nurtured this good guy image through his television commercials and his guest appearances on "soft news" or "alternative media" shows (Larry King, Oprah Winfrey, Joan Rivers, etc.). But another image of the Texas billionaire also emerged in the course of the two campaigns. It depicted a candidate whose behavior was erratic, whose political agenda was vague on specifics, who was testy with the press, and who had a reputation for being highly manipulative. Bad news about the candidate formed this negative profile, and Perot could not contain it. He tried to control his bad guy image by limiting face to face contacts with political reporters. But the dual image haunted Perot during the campaigns and cost him voter support. The purpose of this chapter is to review Ross Perot's sophisticated use of television in his two presidential campaigns and to trace the rise and fall of his candidacy before television cameras.

The 1992 Presidential Campaign: A Four Act Drama

Perot and his associates designed a well-conceived strategy that exploited a wide range of television programming for the 1992 campaign First, Perot would declare himself an unofficial candidate early in the year and put into play a nationwide voter petition drive to place his name on the presidential ballot in all fifty states. He would nurture this voter initiative through frequent guest appearances on television talk and news shows. Second, he would officially declare his candidacy when the petition drive was completed. This would take place in the fall before the presidential debates took place. To Perot, participation in the debates was crucial. They would validate his candidacy, and he could state his case before a national audience of eighty million people. Finally, in the last weeks of the campaign, Perot would unleash an advertising blitz in all the mass media—but mainly on television—that would feature both short commercials and longer "infomercials." Perot was prepared to spend more on his marketing campaign—up to $100 million, if necessary—than his major party rivals could afford (Posner, 253). Perot did not want to buy advertising time early in the campaign, because he believed commercials were most effective in the final stages of a race. An advertising blitz in the last weeks of a race could influence undecided voters and encourage supporters to actually cast their ballots. In short, Perot developed a simple, but potentially effective plan, which recognized the power of television in modern elections.

But the campaign did not unfold according to script. Unforeseen events and bad news about himself caused Perot to waver, even to abandon his candidacy for more than two months midway through the race. Instead of a carefully controlled media campaign, Perot's candidacy turned into a television drama. Indeed, the events of Perot's 1992 candidacy can be viewed as a four -act play during which the candidate first challenges the major parties, then withdraws from the race in a huff, reenters the contest with a flourish, and finally scrambles to restore his image and regain lost voter support.

Act I: Winning Popular Support

The curtain went up on Perot's presidential race when he appeared on CNN's *Larry King Live* show on the evening of February 21, 1992. The show's genial host asked the Texas billionaire that evening if there was any scenario under which he would run for president. Perot, who had previously maintained that was not a presidential candidate, replied, "If you want to register me in fifty states, number one, I'll promise you this: between now and the convention we'll get both parties' heads straight" (King, 149). While Perot's rhetoric was vague, his message was clear: "If enough people want me, I'll be their hero."

Perot had laid the groundwork for a presidential bid before his appearance on Larry King's show. Throughout 1991 he had made the rounds of TV talk shows in which he developed the populist themes he would carry into the campaign. He criticized the Republican administrations of Ronald Reagan and George Bush for not balancing the budget. He characterized American leadership in the Gulf War as "Super Bowl mentality." He argued that Washington was heavily influenced by lobbyists who worked for foreign interests. He portrayed the federal government as an institution caught in gridlock. But until his appearance on *Larry King Live,* the Texas billionaire had consistently rejected any suggestion that he might become a presidential candidate (Posner, 245–246).

In the weeks following his surprise announcement, Perot put together a campaign team and designed his campaign strategy. Then, on March 18, he gave a speech at the National Press Club entitled "We Own This Country," which was carried live on C-SPAN. It marked the beginning of Perot's made-for-television campaign. The candidate hustled from one television show to another, among them *This Week with David Brinkley, ABC News 20/20, The MacNeil/ Lehrer NewsHour, Talking with David Frost, 60 Minutes, Donahue,* and another *Larry King Live* show. Before the campaign ended, Perot appeared on thirty-three talk shows (Bennett, News, 176). Perot's rivals, especially Clinton, were also making the rounds of "soft news" television shows, leading analysts to conclude that presidential candidates had developed a new strategy for reaching out to voters. These talk show performances enabled Perot to create the illusion that he shared a personal relationship with each member of the TV audience. As Perot chatted in his folksy manner with a genial talk show host, viewers could place themselves vicariously into the conversation. Perot also viewed the talk shows, especially those with live audiences and viewer call-in segments as an electronic town hall meeting (Bredeson, 100–102, Kolbert, Political, A20). The high tech shows were modern-day forums reminiscent of the participatory democracy long practiced in New England town meetings. From February to June, Perot campaigned almost exclusively on television. He made few public appearances. While Perot worked the television talk show circuit, his campaign team, headed by Tom Luce, a Dallas lawyer and close friend, organized the petition drive state by state to place the independent candidate's name on presidential ballots. On March 31, Perot named Admiral James Stockdale, a former Vietnam prisoner of war and another old friend, as his vice presidential running mate. But Perot kept television viewers in suspense—and interested—by remaining an undeclared candidate.

The campaign message Perot developed in his television appearances revolved around populist, anti-Washington themes. He chastised the Republican administrations of Presidents Reagan and Bush for creating enormous deficits in the federal budget. He called for a fifty-cent-a-gallon automotive gasoline tax to offset the deficit. He argued that the American economy was in trouble because the country was losing industrial jobs to Third World countries. He asserted that the lobbyist system in Washington had become corrupt because former office holders and bureaucrats represented foreign governments and interests. He advocated reform of campaign finance laws. Perot's social agenda was surprisingly liberal. He was pro-choice on abortion, supported gay rights, believed gun control laws were necessary, and urged an increase in government spending for AIDS research.

On each talk or news show, Perot generated sound bites in the form of clever one-liners. For example on a *60 Minutes* show, he compared the federal deficit to "a crazy aunt you keep down in the basement. All the neighbors know she's there, but nobody talks about her" (Speaks, 9). On a *Larry King Live* show, Perot compared the tax system to "an old inner tube that's been patched by every special interest in the country" (Speaks, 31). Such "straight talk" rhetoric boosted Perot's popularity in the early months of the campaign.

In the first phase of the campaign, Perot encountered little negative criticism. His talk show hosts seldom challenged Perot on any part of his political agenda or his assertions. The candidate had full control over his message. But in mid-April 1992 on NBC's *Meet the Press,* Tim Russert challenged Perot's federal budget figures. Perot remained outwardly in control during the show but afterward was so infuriated that he threatened to quit the race (Posner, 255). Perot received further bad press when veteran TV journalist Barbara Walters questioned him on ABC's *20/20* show on May 29 on whether he would appoint a homosexual to his cabinet, if he became president. "I don't want anybody there that will be a point of controversy with the American people," Perot said. "It will distract from the work to be done" (Posner, 260). A negative press response forced Perot to recant the statement. These and other negative news stories were a foreshadowing of events to come. Perot chaffed under criticism by the press. Consequently, the only regular information his office gave political reporters during this phase of the campaign was a schedule of his television appearances (Posner, 259).

As the first act of Perot's television campaign drew to a close at the end of May 1992, Perot continued to work the talk show circuit. He made more appearances on *Larry King Live,* he toured the morning shows on the three networks, he faced reporters on the Sunday morning journalistic shows, and he made the rounds of such secondary talk shows as *Tom Snyder, Talk of the Nation,* and *Coast to Coast.* C-Span broadcast three speeches Perot delivered before the National Press Club, the American Newspaper Publishers Association, and the American Society of Newspaper Editors. Perot's television strategy was effective. Public opinion polls taken in late May indicated public support for his candidacy had climbed above 30 percent. His rating among voters was equal to Bush and Clinton, the front runners for the Republican and Democratic Party nominations. Although Perot had no established political party behind him, and had never held public office, he had established himself through the magic of television as a viable presidential candidate. But it was something of an illusion. Perot's image and his campaign began two unravel in Act II of his political venture.

Act II: A Sudden Exit

The second phase of Perot's television campaign extended across June and July 1992. What ensued had considerable melodrama, ending with Perot's withdrawal from the race. Act II of the political drama opened in early June on a high note when the candidate announced he had added Hamilton Jordan and Edward Rollins to his campaign team. Jordan, a Democrat, had been an important aide to Jimmy Carter; Rollins had served as a key Republican strategist for Ronald Reagan. The hook: Perot hoped his new appointments would attract voters from both major parties. Despite his desire for political diversity in his campaign, a conflict soon arose between the businessman candidate and his new advisors.

Jordan and Rollins proposed a $150 million publicity blitz featuring television ads and paid political messages in newspapers and magazines. They wanted the advertising campaign to begin before the end of June. Always the savvy businessman, Perot vetoed the idea on the grounds that their campaign strategy would be too costly. He also rejected the idea of running television ads in June, because he believed political campaigns were won or lost in the last thirty days of the race.

A frustrated Rollins, who never gained Perot's confidence, quit the campaign on July 15th (Bredeson, 94–96; Kolbert, Perot, A1; Posner, 262–285).

The following day, Perot, apparently disturbed by this turn of events and upset over mounting negative news stories, went before television cameras in Dallas and announced he was withdrawing from the race, a contest he had never officially entered. Perot explained that the Democratic Party had "revitalized itself," and, as a result, he feared the election would be decided in the House of Representatives if he stayed in the race.

Perot's action stunned the American public, especially his supporters. But his seemingly irrational behavior could have been a ploy to give his campaign a spark. Opinion polls in early July indicated that his voter support was beginning to slip. Perot once again became coy with the American public. A day after he publicly quit the race, he told ABC's Barbara Walters that he would not return to the race "unless I thought it was good for the country." That same evening Perot implied on *Larry King Live,* his favorite television venue, that his campaign was not completely dead. When King observed that Perot was "still sort of hanging that leaf out," Perot retorted, "That's the magic, Larry" (Posner, 286).

Perot's behavior undermined the good guy image he had carefully nurtured in the previous months. The press implied that Perot had a history of being a quitter. Reporters pointed to Perot's attempt to take an early leave from the Navy—which he had entered after graduating from the Naval Academy—his abrupt departure from IBM, following a dispute over the structure of his sales commissions, and other episodes as evidence of the candidate's tendency to bail out of tough situations. Other stories began to surface about Perot's propensity to have secret investigations conducted into the private affairs of employees and rivals (Kelly, A1). The negative press stories, coupled with Perot's sudden departure from the contest, caused his popularity in national polls to go into a tailspin. In early October, his base of popular support had fallen to a measly seven percent. But Perot's political quest was far from over.

Act III: A Dramatic Return

Perot remained aloof from the campaign for more than seventy days. His volunteer organization, however, continued the state-by-state petition drives to put the Texas billionaire's name on presidential ballots. By mid-September, the goal of placing Perot on the presidential ballots in all fifty states was met. The stage was now set for Perot's dramatic return to the race. Perot, who had become a master at exploiting television, devised an unusual media event to launch his return to the presidential race. The Republican and Democratic election teams served as dupes in his grand reemergence as a candidate.

On September 28, 1992, television's coverage of the presidential campaign focused on Dallas where delegations from the Republican and Democratic Parties had gathered at Perot's invitation. Each party delegation was to make a two-hour presentation before a convention of Perot's supporters. Reporters and television cameras were excluded from the sessions, but press conferences followed each presentation. The two major parties believed Perot intended to remain out of the race and had come seeking votes from his supporters. Larry King underscored the importance of the event by broadcasting his show from Dallas that evening. "We've come to the mountain," King told his audience that evening.

But Perot had no intention of throwing his support to either party. A day after the Republican and Democratic delegations had reached out to Perot's supporters, he reported to the press that his 800 telephone number had received 1.5 million hits urging him to become a candidate again. Perot, who understood the importance of a delayed stage entry, waited two more days—until October 1—to announce at a press conference that he was officially in the presidential race. His volunteers, he told the media, "have asked me to run . . . and I have accepted their request" (Posner, 290). He made clear to the press that he would run his campaign mainly through television and not on the campaign trail. Perot now put into play two major elements of his made-for-television campaign: advertising and the nationally televised presidential debates.

Perot's infomercials became one of the enduring images of the 1992 presidential race. Previously, presidential candidates had regarded as undignified the thirty-and sixty-minute paid-for air time, used mainly by advertisers of skin care products, fitness equipment, real estate schemes, psychics, and the like. But Perot saw informercials as an effective medium for reaching a national audience. Moreover, he possessed sufficient clout over the networks to buy prime time airspace. On the day Perot officially entered the race, he bought a half hour from CBS for $380,000 and an hour of prime time from ABC for $500,000. He aired his first show, *The Problems—Plain Talk About Jobs, Debt, and the Washington Mess*, on October 6, five days after he had become an official candidate.

To some jaundiced reporters, Perot's show appeared hokey (Zoglin, 70). The candidate sat behind a desk holding a pointer in one hand. With his other hand, he flipped through a stack of charts—at the rate of one a minute—that illustrated his talk on the nation's economy. The format was anything but amateurish. Perot maintained the persona he had carefully cultivated on the earlier talk shows. In his folksy manner, he reiterated the criticisms about the American economy that he had been making throughout the campaign. He argued, for example, that a declining job base was partly responsible for the federal budget deficit. He called for a partnership between government and business corporations to rebuild the nation's industrial base, which had once been "the world's greatest industrial engine." The commercial attracted 16.5 million viewers, outdrawing much of the prime time competition that evening, including a major league baseball playoff game (Posner, 291).

At the same time, the Perot team launched its first thirty- and sixty-second spot commercials of the race. Perot did not appear in these commercials. The ads took a soft message approach. They featured imagery such as a violent storm, a red flag, or a ticking clock to stress that America was facing a series of immanent disasters which only Perot could stop. The ads concluded with a narrator intoning, "The candidate is Ross Perot. The issue is leadership. The choice is yours." The first spot commercials aired on October 10 and appeared with increasing frequency throughout the remainder of the campaign.

But Perot knew that the campaign needed more than advertising and guest appearances on talk shows to boost his candidacy. He was eager to join Bush and Clinton in the forthcoming presidential debates. His presence on the debates, he realized, would set him apart from other third party candidates and establish in the minds of viewers that he had a realistic chance to win the presidency. However, Perot could not force his way onto the debate stage. He had to be invited by the two major parties. It turned out that both Bush and Clinton wanted Perot to take part in the debates. Both rivals believed Perot had the potential to cut into the vote of the other. Neither thought he was a threat to win. The Commission of Presidential Debates on a split decision approved Perot's participation in the three scheduled debates.

The format of the debates, in which the candidates fielded questions either from political reporters or an audience, worked well for Perot's down-to-earth style. He appeared at ease before the television cameras. He frequently scored points, as it were, with his sharp one-liners. He outperformed George Bush in all three debates and ran neck and neck with Bill Clinton according to post-debate network evaluations.

The first debate was held on October 11, on the campus of Washington University in St. Louis. Each candidate stood behind a podium. At one point in the debate, when Perot was questioned about his lack of government experience, he observed, "I don't have experience in running up a $4 trillion debt. (Bredeson, 97). Focus groups watching the debates for the networks thought Perot had been the most effective of the three candidates. They liked Clinton but placed Bush a distant third. Opinion polls following the debate indicated that voter support for Perot had nearly doubled from early October, climbing to around 14 percent. A *Newsweek* poll taken after the first debate indicated that 70 percent of the respondents regarded Perot more favorably as a presidential candidate.

On October 15, the three candidates met again in Virginia, on the campus of the University of Richmond. Carole Simpson of ABC News moderated questions from 209 people identified by the Gallup Organization as uncommitted voters. Their questions focused on such campaign issues as free trade, health care, gun control, and urban problems. The three candidates sat in the open on stools. During their responses, they sometimes wandered around the stage, giving the debate a talk show atmosphere. Perot zeroed in on the issues of the budget deficit and the gridlock in Washington, which the Democratics and Republicans blamed on each other. "It's not the Republicans' fault, of course, and it's not the Democrats' fault," he wryly observed. "Somewhere out there there's an extraterrestrial that's doing this to us, I guess." (Transcript of 2nd TV Debate, A14). News programs following the debate featured a statistical flub Perot made during the debate, but post-debate evaluators liked his overall performance. Opinion polls taken after the second debate indicated Perot's support ranged from 14 to 16 percent.

The third debate took place on October 19 on the campus of Michigan State University in East Lansing, Michigan. Perot challenged the Bush administration's policy on Iraq during the debate and suggested that Clinton's experience as governor of Arkansas was inadequate for the job in Washington. Post-debate polls indicated a further increase in Perot's voter support, up to 19 percent. The presidential debates, coupled with the candidate's television commercials gave Perot the momentum he was looking for. But then, he once again irreparably harmed his public image before television cameras.

On Sunday, October 25, Perot appeared on CBS's *60 Minutes* to give the "real reason" for his earlier withdrawal from the race. He told the show's national audience that in July he had received "multiple reports" of a Republican Party plot to disrupt the August wedding of his daughter, Carolyn, and to distribute a false computer-generated photo of her (Excerpts from Speech, A12). When Perot had pulled out of the race in July, the Federal Bureau of Investigation (FBI) had looked into the issue. But the FBI had found no evidence to support Perot's claims and had dropped its investigation. Perot, however, remained convinced of the reality of the Republican's "dirty tricks." He hoped that his comments on *60 Minutes* would give new life to the investigation. But CBS talked to the FBI in preparation for the show, and when correspondent Leslie Stahl advised Perot that the FBI had found no evidence to support his claim, Perot retorted, "We've got a squirrely situation in the FBI if that happened. Sounds like politics to me" (Posner, 321).

Perot's comments became the focus of media attention. He was widely ridiculed for making assertions he could not support with evidence. At a Dallas press conference the next day, Perot engaged in sharp exchanges with the press. Orson G. Swindel, a close friend and associate of Perot's, later called the candidate's appearance at the press conference "catastrophic" and observed, "He didn't look presidential" (Posner, 321). Perot's comments tarnished his image as a presidential candidate. His momentum in the opinion polls came to a standstill.

In retrospect, Perot's *60 Minutes* performance, and his behavior with the press thereafter, marked the climax of his 1992 campaign. During the last weeks of the race, Perot filled the airwaves with informercials and spot commercials to woo voters, but from a theatrical perspective, his campaign ended with the self-destruction of his image on *60 Minutes*. The advertising blitz became the falling action phase of Perot's TV drama, the final scenes in which all the issues in the play are resolved. In that sense, Perot 's multimillion dollar advertising blitz in the final weeks served to restore his image and to propel his budding political movement, which he labelled "United We Stand" beyond election day.

Act IV: An Advertising Blitzkrieg

In the last weeks of the race, Perot mounted the most expensive political advertising campaign in American history. In the first two weeks of October, he spent $24 million on commercials. In the next ten days he was to spend another $10 million. An hour-long infomerical, which aired on Monday night October 26, ten days before the national elections, cost close to an additional $1 million. The national press viewed Perot's spot ads and informercials as an effort to offset the negative news the billionaire candidate had generated in his campaign. For example, Elizabeth Kolbert observed in *The New York Times*, "Now the main question seems to be which media image will prevail: the Ross Perot of news stories ('Paranoid!' . . . 'Looney!') or the Ross Perot of the advertisements (down to earth, sober, pragmatic)" (A1).

Perot himself appeared in the new spot commercials in a manner designed to fix up his image. In one, the candidate sat behind an executive-sized desk—just as he appeared in many of his informercials—and appealed for voter support. The following excerpt from one of his scripts, which Perot read while looking directly into the camera, illustrates the direct appraoch of his new commercials:

> If you want to rebuild the job base, let your vote say so. If you want a government that comes from the people, instead of at the people, let your vote say so. If you want to reduce our $4 trillion national debt, let your vote say so. Look at the issues. Look at the facts. Look at all three candidates. And then vote your conscience. (Kolbert, Perot Spending, A1)

The New York Times found the independent candidate's purchase of local air time for his spot ads somewhat quixotic. For example, opinion polls indidcated that Clinton held a big lead in California in the final weeks of the race. Nevertheless, Perot's team purchased $750,000 worth of air time in the Los Angeles and spent another $600,000 in the San Francisco television market. By contrast, Perot spent only $180,000 for air time on three stations in the New York area. At the time, the race was much more competitive in New York, Connecticut, and New Jersey, the three states served by New York City television (Kolbert, Perot Spending, A1).

In the final days of the 1992 campaign, Perot attempted to blanket national television with his spot advertisements. They ran on both network and cable television. In addition, two of his ads were translated into Spanish and aired on Hispanic television. A survey of the three major networks, ABC, CBS, and NBC, near the end of October indicated that Perot had outspent both of his major rivals on television advertising. Perot, according to the survey, had paid $19.5 million—although much of that amount was for thirty- and sixty-minute informercials. Bush's advertising expenses, according to the survey, came to $17.5 million and Clinton was a distant third in network ads, $5.4 million. Overall, Clinton spent nearly as much as Perot on television ads, but his campaign focused more more on local markets (Berke, A19).

Perot also picked up the pace for airing his infomercials in the last weeks of the campaign. Between October 28 and the end of the campaign, he aired seven half-hour commercials at the cost of millions of dollars. ABC, for example, reported that Perot had bought $5.7 million worth of air time to cover the last two weeks of the campaign. Each infomercial drew surprisingly large audiences. Some attracted more than sixteen million viewers. The average audience size for all of the informercials was more than nine million people. The popularity of the informercials indicated that in the last weeks of the campaign Perot remained a fascinating media figure despite his loss of momemtum among voters (Kolbert, Perot Spending, A1).

In an effort to refurbish his image, one of Perot's new thirty-minute commercials became an autobiography. It featured Perot being interviewed by Martin Murphy, a former news anchorman who had become his media. In it, Perot talked about how he had started to work at age seven, his experience of breaking horses as a young man, his studies at the Naval Academy, and his service on the destroyer USS *Sigourney*. He stressed that he had worked hard all his life. Black and white photos of Perot's life appeared on screen as the two men chatted. In another hour-long commercial, Perot devoted thirty minutes of the program to introducing his family to the national television audience. These commercials helped viewers to believe that they knew Perot and had a personal relationship with him. These commercials were highly effective in a campaign in which opinion polls indidcated American voters had grown increasingly disconnected from the electoral process.

In response to criticisms raised throughout the campaign that he was vague on solutions to economic problems, the candidate also developed new chart-talk infomercials in which he became more specific. Most of his ideas were in his paperback book, *United We Stand; How We Can Take Back Our Country,* which he had recently published. Perot proposed higher income tax rates, fewer exemptions on expensive mortgages and business expenses, higher tobacco taxes, and a fifty-cents-per-gallon gasoline tax increase. He claimed his plan would save taxpayers $754 billion and eliminate the deficit in the federal budget within six years.

In most of his informercials, Perot made no attacks on his rivals, Bush and Clinton. But on November 1, he aired a thirty-minute informercial in which he attacked Bush's record as president and Clinton's performance as governor of Arkansas. He suggested neither had the wherewithal to run a small business, let alone the nation. He belittled Clinton's claims for creating new jobs in Arkansas: "One out of five jobs in the last twelve years has been created in the poultry business," Perot noted. "Now this is not an industry of tomorrow. This is honest work. It is hard work. The people who do it are world-class people, but if we decide to take this level of business creativity nationwide, we'll all be plucking chickens for a living" (Holmes, A14).

On election night, Perot received 19 percent of the popular vote, more than any third party candidate had received since Theodore Roosevelt's campaign on the Bull Moose ticket in 1914. He exited off stage before television cameras in Dallas with a smile on his face and a promise that he would make another run for the White House if his supporters asked him to. However, his running mate, Admiral Stockdale, in a brief speech that same night, suggested that the most enduring aspect of Perot's campaign may have been his unconventional use of television to skirt political reporters and speak directly to the American people: "Ross showed you don't have to talk to [ABC's] Sam Donaldson to get on television," he said. "Ross has shown that American candidates can now bypass the filters and go directly to the people" (Sack, Leaving Door Open, B5).

The 1996 Race: The Sequel

The 1996 presidential race has been described as a "listless campaign" involving two candidates, President Clinton on the Democratic ticket and Senator Bob Dole on the Republican side, who generated little enthusiasm among voters (Mashek, 2–3). Ross Perot's entry into the fray generated little public interest and the media virtually ignored him. Recent studies, in fact, have demonstrated that the press marginalized Perot in the 1996 campaign. Perot attempted, in vain, to run a television-based campaign similar to his 1992 race. He appeared on talk shows, developed new commercials, and sought to join the televised presidential debates. But his efforts were futile. He made fewer guest appearances on the news and talk shows. The networks resisted his efforts to buy prime time for his infomercials. His effort to be included in the presidential debates ended in lawsuits and failed. According to opinion polls, Perot's popular support throughout the race remained below 10 percent. From a theatrical perspective, Perot's 1996 race was a dud.

Perot's 1996 campaign, the sequel to his 1992 political drama, can be viewed as a one-act play with brief three scenes. The first scene takes place in August, when Perot faces a challenge to become the Reform Party's presidential nominee. The second scene takes place two months later when Perot fails to be included in the presidential debates. The third scene finds Perot staging another advertising blitz while he travels the country making stump speeches. Perot's second bid for the White House ended poorly. But the advent of his Reform Party suggested the future production of yet another sequel in Perot's political quests.

Scene One: The New Party

On September 25, 1995, Ross Perot went on *Larry King Live,* his favorite television show for making important statements, to announce he was organizing the Reform Party. "We're at a critical time in our country's history," Perot said, "and tonight we're going to start the process of starting a new party" (Posner p. 337). In the months that followed, Perot and his supporters initiated petition drives to gain official recognition of the Reform Party in all fifty states. By the summer of 1996, the process was completed, and the party prepared to chose its presidential contender. Richard Lamm, the former Democratic governor of Colorado, announced his candidacy on July 9. A day later, Perot went on *Larry King Live* to announce his candidacy. Speculation had been building throughout the spring whether he would enter the race. On August 18, Perot won the nomination in a controversial ballot process. Lamm claimed the vote was undemocratic and rigged against him. He refused to endorse Perot's presidential candidacy (Mashek, 45). The contest between the two Reform Party candidates drew some media attention to the new third party, but it did not enhance Perot's public image. His status as a potential presidential candidate was already tarnished before he entered the 1996 campaign.

Another poor television performance had futher damaged Perot's image before he entered the 1996 campaign. It had occurred in 1993. In the months following the 1992 race, Perot's popular appeal had soared once again. He became the cover story in the *U.S. News & World Report* issue of May 17, 1993, which stated on its front cover that "Ross Perot may be the most important force in American politics." He appeared on talk shows, aired more infomercials, gave interviews to selected journalists, and co-authored an inexpensive paperback, *Save Your Job, Save Our Country: Why NAFTA must Be Stopped Now.* The other author was Pat Choate, a conservative economist. Perot opposed the North American Free Trade Agreement because he believed it would cause America to lose industrial jobs to the cheaper labor market in Mexico. The Clinton administration, which was attempting to gain Senate approval of the treaty at the time, became alarmed at Perot's opposition. The White House challenged the Texas businessman to a public debate.

On the evening of November 9, 1993, Vice President Al Gore and Perot debated the treaty on *Larry King Live*. Gore proved to be the more forceful debater (Valentine, 85–86). He forced Perot on the defensive throughout the debate. Perot became sarcastic and testy. Gore remained firm and calm throughout the debate, which attracted the largest audience in cable television history. The news media was highly critical of Perot's performance and a Gallup Poll taken a week later indicated that his favorable rating—which had soared upward after the 1992 race—plunged from 66 percent to 29 percent. It was a drop comparable to the public's reaction to Perot's charges of Republican "dirty tricks" on the *60 Minutes* show during the 1992 campaign (Posner, 327–330).

That negative image still haunted Perot when he entered the 1996 presidential race. Governor Lamm's charges gave the press new fodder for criticizing or satirizing Perot's candidacy. But Perot, who tried to ignore political reporters as much as possible, pressed on with his campaign. Always the master of suspense, he did not announce his choice for his vice presidential running mate until several weeks after the Reform Party's convention. Finally, on September 11, Perot announced that Pat Choate, co-author of the NAFTA book, would be his running mate. Characteristically, Perot announced his choice of Choate at the end of a thirty-minute informercial. Perot presented a brief video presenting Choate's background, then the two men chatted while sitting in wing chairs. Later that night, Choate was interviewed by Larry King.

Five days later, Perot aired a thirty-minute commercial on the Fox network in which he again chastised President Clinton and Congress for passing the North American Free Trade Agreement. In an "I told you so" presentation, he reiterated his claims that the treaty had led to thousands of jobs being lost to Mexico: "Yes folks, we predicted it," Perot told his audience, " there is a giant sucking sound coming out of Mexico. They're sucking our dollars down there and both parties were locked arm in arm and bound at the hip to make that happen" (Tollerson, A11). Pat Choate took part in the video lecture.

The new Reform Party and its candidates, however, failed to galvanize public interest At the end of the first phase of the 1996 campaign, Perot's support in the polls remained at the single digit level. He hoped to jumpstart his stalled campaign in the forthcoming presidential debates. He wanted to appear before television cameras on the same stage with Clinton and Dole. But his desire did not materialize.

Scene Two: The Quest to Debate

On September 17, 1996, the Commission on Presidential Debates decided that Perot should not participate in the forthcoming presidential debates on the grounds that he did not have a realistic chance of winning the election. The commission was made up of representatives of the two major parties. Dole and the Republican leadership did not want Perot in the debates, because they believed that any rise in the Texas businessman's popular support would siphon votes away from them. The Clinton team also thought Perot could capture Republican votes; for that reason, they wanted him in the debates.

The commission's decision against Perot was a crushing blow to his campaign strategy. In a speech before the Commonwealth Club of California a day after the decision, an angry Perot labelled his exclusion from the debates as "a blatant display of power by the Republicans and the large donors who fund their campaign" (Brooke, A1). Perot noted that the presidential debates in 1992 had attracted audiences as large as eighty million people. "Any candidate who is excluded from these debates cannot present his views to the eighty million voters under any other method," he said.

Perot also criticized in the same speech the television networks for refusing to sell him the prime time he wanted for his infomercials. In particular he and his campaign team wanted to buy time immediately after each presidential and vice presidential debate. "They [the networks] think they're forcing us to our only recourse: being to buy one-minute television ads. And that's what they want. They don't want you to understand these problems in detail," he told a San Francisco audience.

Six days after the commission's decision, the Perot team went to court to challenge their candidate's exclusion from the debates. A few days later, on October 1, Federal Judge Thomas F. Hogan rejected Perot's suit on the grounds that the courts did not have the authority to determine who should participate in the debates. The judge further ruled that Perot had no rights under the First Amendment to join the debates (Lewis, A1). Two days later, the Perot team appealed the lower court's decision, arguing that the commission's criteria for deciding who could take part in the debates was subjective and illegal. The Perot team's court papers also accused the commission of irreparably harming the Reform Party and its candidate by stating that he had not have a realistic chance of winning the election (Perot, in Court Brief, A10).

The legal action gave Perot some front page media attention but no increase in popular support. As the second scenario of Perot's 1996 political drama came to an end, the Reform Party candidate was forced to develop a new strategy outside television to salvage what he could of the race.

Scene Three: The Conventional Candidate

When Perot opened his 1996 presidential campaign, he intended to repeat his 1992 strategy of promoting his candidacy through infomercials. He planned to buy fifteen blocks of time for his long commercials before Election Day. But the television networks refused to sell him prime air time. By the end of September, Perot had aired only five long commercials, none of them in desirable time slots. In early September, for example, Perot's team reluctantly bought two thirty-minute time slots on ABC. One of them was paired against CBS's highly popular *60 Minutes.* The other ran after midnight on a Thursday morning following ABC's *Nightline.* A spokesman for Perot's team, Russ Verney, noted at the time that Perot would have to buy more short commercials. Verney lamented this development. "Short commercials are great for manipulating the public in the way negative advertising is used," he observed, "but are not a means of communicating the detailed information necessary for the American people to cast informed votes in November."

Less available air time was only one of the problems Perot's infomercials faced in 1996. The other was poor audience response. *The New York Times* reported that Perot's long commercials were drawing only half the audience they had in 1992 (Perot's TV Audience, A13). By mid-October 1996 it was clear Perot's strategy for blanketing the networks with infomercials had disintegrated. That failure, coupled with his exclusion from the presidential debates, forced Perot into a radical change in campaign strategy.

In the final weeks of the 1996 campaign, Perot became a conventional candidate. He barnstormed across the nation. He often delivered two speeches a day, mainly on college campuses, because he wanted to attract young voters to his Reform Party. The content of his speeches also represented a change in strategy. In the 1992 campaign and throughout most of the 1996 race, Perot had more or less eschewed personal attacks on his opponents. But in the last weeks of the 1996 contest, he attacked Clinton on his party's campaign financing, the president's lack of military experience, and his rumored womanizing.

On election eve, Perot once again returned to the airwaves. In a last-minute blitz, the Texas billionaire spent more than $2 million to buy thirty minutes of time each on NBC and CBS and a full hour on ABC; all three commercials aired the night before Election Day. Perot's infomercials on ABC and NBC ran against each other in the 8:00 P.M. Eastern time slot. His commercial on CBS ran at 8:30 P.M. Perot had told an audience earlier that day at Stanford University that his commercials would be "two hours of saturation bombing before you go to the polls" (the infomercials, which Perot also promoted in full-page newspaper ads, stressed Perot's viability as a candidate and urged people to vote. The commercials also alleged that President Clinton faced "serious criminal charges" for irregular campaign financing and other sins. Perot had offered to scrap the commercials if President Clinton would join him in a live program to debate ethical issues surrounding the Oval Office. The White House did not respond to Perot's offer.

On Election Day, Perot received only 8 percent of the popular vote. The vote tally may have ended Perot's aspirations to be an American president; but, by gaining more than 5 percent of the vote, his Reform Party became eligible to receive federal funding for the race in the year 2000. In retrospect, formation of the Reform Party was Perot's major achievement of the 1996 campaign. His personal image now diminished, Perot faced serious barriers against any futher political campaign.

Conclusion: Campaigning in the Age of Television

Ross Perot's two presidental campaigns illustrate several significant developments in the role television now plays in presidential elections. These include the continuing importance of advertising, the rise of "soft news" talk shows as an important forum for candidates, the potential of television and other mass media formats to create an electronic town hall, and finally, the potential that television offers Ross Perot–type candidates to make serious bids for the presidency even if they have little political power. Each development, as manifested in Perot's campaigns, warrants a closer review.

Perot's costly investment in commercials underscores Kathleen Hall Jamieson's observation that "Political advertising is now the major means by which candidates for the presidency communicate their messages to voters" (89). Such ads, Jamieson points out, help candidates to build name recognition, reveal their personalities and abilities, and frame the political agenda they consider important in an election. The intent of such ads is to put candidates in a favorable light conducive to attracting voters. Perot demonstrated that he was particularly adept in campaign marketing. He pioneered the use of thirty- and sixty-minute informercials for laying out in detail the political issues he considered important. He also utilized the long commercials to nuture a favorable image of himself. His spot commercials, by contrast, tended to focus on the message that Perot was a viable candidate. Perot also knew when advertising would have its greatest impact in a campaign. Ads at the end of a campaign, he believed, could sway undecided voters and galvanize supporters into casting their ballots on Election Day.

A second aspect of Perot's campaign was his use of talk shows. Perot's objectives for his talk show appearances were similar to those in his marketing strategy. Talk shows such as *Larry King Live* gave Perot free air time in which he could promote his image and spell out his political agenda. Perot preferred this forum over meet-the-press news shows because he disliked the confrontational atmosphere of the latter programs. Moreover, he had less control over their content. By contrast, the up-close camera angles used on talk shows, the genial conversation with nonadversarial hosts, and call-in questions from viewers helped Perot to establish an impression with the television audience that they knew the candidate personally and could trust him. Both Clinton and Perot fully exploited the talk show curcuit in 1992 , less so in 1996. Talk shows, however, are not available to all candidates. Only those with high public profiles can gain access to that forum.

Perot's vision of campaigning within the context of an electronic town hall, in which modern communication technology allows considerable interaction between voters and candidates, drew considerable attention during his campaigns. The concept held powerful appeal to Americans who want direct contact with their candidates and fit well with the populist agenda Perot put forth. However, the ideal concept of participatory democracy never came into being in Perot's two campaigns. On shows such as *Larry King Live,* few viewers actually talked to Perot, their calls were screened by a producer, and the candidate had full control over how much time he wanted to devote to a particular subject. It's an idea, however that holds promise for the future.

Finally, Perot demonstrated that disaffected voters will support a candidate even if there is no powerful political structure behind him. Perot utilized television programming to become an overnight political hero. His skillful use of television convinced many Americans to become emotionally involved with him. He became their hero. Voters took him on his word that he could personally go to Washington and clean up the mess without taking into account the realities of the political process in which power accounts for everything. W. Lance Bennett has pointed out that this personalized form of politics is a "fantasy world, and like those of play, sport or fiction, it can involve people intensely on the basis of catharsis, escape, hope, or sheer entertainment" (Bennett, News, 51). But the realm of television is a world of fantasy, and fantasy is ephemeral. Bad news about a political hero, Bennett points out, can turn yesterday's hero into tomorrow's fool. That is what happened to Perot. Bad news arising in the course of his campaigns robbed Perot of his hero's image. Much of his popular support subsequently disappeared.

A question, then, remains: had bad news not undermined Perot's image, could his television campaigns have propelled him into the American presidency? That is a question some future candidate who possess the wealth, public fame, and political ambition of a Ross Perot might seek to answer.

References

Bennett, J. 1996. "Political Ads Leap from the TV Landscape," *New York Times,* October 14, A1, A11.

Bennett, W. L. 1992. *The Governing Crisis: Media, Money, and Marketing in American Elections.* New York: St. Martin's Press.

Bennett, W. L. 1996. *News: The Politics of Illusion* 3rd ed. White Plains, N.Y.: Longman.

Berke, R. 1992. "Perot Leads in $40 Million TV Ad Blitz," *New York Times,* October 27, A19.

Bredeson, C. 1993. *Ross Perot: Billionaire Politician.* Springfield, N.J.: Enslow Publishers.

Borger, G., and J. Buckley. 1993. "Perot Keeps Going and Going...," *Newsweek* (May 17), 37–47.

Brooke, J. 1996. "Perot Assails His Exclusion from Debates," September 19, A1.

Carter, B. 1992. "Perot Gave Networks a Race, at Any Rate," *New York Times,* November 3, A14.

Diamond, E., M. McKay, and R. Silverman. 1993. "Pop Goes Politics: New Media, Interactive Formats, and the 1992 Presidential Campaign (Reflections on the Nature and Role of the Print and Electronic Media in the 1992 Campaigns), *American Behavioral Scientist* 37: 257–261.

Dickson, S. H., C. Pilsen, and S. Hanners. 1997. *A Cynical Press: Coverage of the 1996 Presidential Campaign.* Paper presented at the annual meeting of Association for Education in Journalism and Mass Communication. Chicago.

Goodman, W. 1992. "In a 'Lone Ranger' Role, Perot Builds an Audience," *New York Times,* April 23, A23.

Holmes, S. A. 1992. "Perot Buys More Ads and Plans Appearances," *New York Times,* October 18, A25.

———. 1992. "Candidate Perot Might Learn from Strategist Perot," *New York Times,* October 30, A22.

———. 1992. "In Half-hour, Perot Details Plan for Cutting Deficit," *New York Times,* October 17, A7.

———. 1992. "Perot Assails Rivals as Unfit to Run a Small Business," *New York Times,* November 2, 14.

———. 1992. "Perot Buys More Ads and Plans Appearances," *New York Times,* October 18, L25.

———. 1992. "Perot Hires Pair of Top Managers to Run Campaign," *New York Times,* June 4, A1, A18.

———. 1992. "Perot in Wide-Ranging TV Interview," *New York Times,* May 19, A19.

———. 1992. "Perot Wraps up His Campaign Where He Mostly Ran It: on TV," *New York Times,* November 3, A1, A14.

Jamieson, K. H. 1996. "Packing the Presidency." In J. Hanson and D. J. Maxcy, eds., *Sources: Notable Selections in Mass Media.* Guilford, Ct.: Dushkin Publishing Group.

Kelly, M. 1992. "Perot Stresses Homey Image, but the Image Is No Accident," *New York Times,* May 26, A1, A14.

King, L. 1995. *The Best of Larry King Live: The Greatest Interviews.* Atlanta: Turner Publishing.

Kolbert, E. 1992. "Perot Vision: Consensus by Computer, Using TV," *New York Times,* June 6, A1, A8.

———. 1992. "Perot Spending More on Ads than Any Candidate Before," *New York Times,* October 28, A1, A17.

———. 1992. "Political Candidates and Call-in Shows: When the People Want to Be Heard," *New York Times,* June 10, A20.

Krauthammer, C. 1992. "Ross Perot and the Call-in Presidency," *Time* (July 13), 84.

Lewis, N. A. 1996. Judge Rejects Suit by Perot to Join Presidential Debates," *New York Times,* October 2, A1, C23.

Mashek, J. W, L. T. McGill, and A. D. Powell III. 1997. *Lethargy 96: How the Media Covered a Listless Campaign.* Arlington, Va.: The Freedom Forum.

McNulty, T. J., and S. Daley. 1992. "Call-in TV Provides Candidates Opportunity to Avoid the Press, *Chicago Tribune,* June 14, 3.

Nagourney, A. 1996. "Perot Chooses an Economist for His Ticket," *New York Times,* September 11, 1.

"Perot: Arguing He's a Viable Candidate." 1992. *New York Times,* October 28, A17.

"Perot, in Court Brief, Faults Debate Group." 1996. *New York Times,* October 4, A10.

"Perot Presents His Autobiography, Part II, in 30-Minute TV Program." *New York Times,* A20.

"Perot's TV Audience." 1996. *New York Times,* September 12, A13.

Perot, R. 1995. *We Must Save Medicare and Medicaid Now.* New York: HarperPerennial.

Posner, G. 1996. *Citizen Perot: His Life and Times.* New York: Random House.

Rich, F. 1992. "Perot, Like 'Twin Peaks,' Started Strong and Went Downhill," *New York Times,* November 2, A13.

Robinson, J. W. 1992. *Ross Perot Speaks Out: Issue by Issue, What He Says About Our Nation—Its Problems and Its Promise.* Roclin, Cal.: Prima Publishing.

Sack, K. 1992. "For TV, Perot Spends Heavily on Wart Removal," *New York Times,* October 25, A28

———. 1992. "Leaving Door Open, Perot Exits Dancing," *New York Times,* November 4, B5.

———. 1992. "Perot Intensifies His Ad Campaign," *New York Times,* October 22, A21.

———. 1992. "Perot Scores in 3d Debate, Then Opens Fire on the Press," *New York Times,* October 21, A18.

Tollerson, E. 1996. "Politics Re-emerges as the Favorite Foe of Perot Campaign," *New York Times,* September 26, A1, A14.

———. 1996. "Trying Different Approach, Perot Takes to the Campaign Trail and Goes on the Attack," *New York Times,* November 1, A13.

Toner, R. 1992. "Issues, Not Attacks, Dominate as Audience Guides 2d Debate," *New York Times,* October 16, A1, A10.

Transcript of 3d Debate Between the Presidential Candidates. 1992. *New York Times,* October 26, A21, A22.

Valentine, M. D. 1995. *An Argumentative Analysis of the Ross Perot—Albert Gore NAFTA Debate.* Unpublished M.S. thesis. Bloomington, Ill.: Illinois State University.

Verhovek, S. H. 1996. "Perot's New Campaign Propels Unanswered Questions Back to Surface," *New York Times,* September 16, A10.

Worthington, R. 1996. "Perot Uses TV Blitz for Final Pitch," *Chicago Tribune,* November 5, 1:12.

Zoglin, R. 1992. "It Just Wasn't That Simple," *Time* (November 16), 70.

3

A Case Study of a Third Presidential Campaign Organization

Virginians for Perot

Andrew D. Martin
Brian E. Spang

C itizens are the driving force in democratic governance. Indeed, it is the citizens who go to the ballot box to select their leaders, from the president of the United States down to the local dog catcher. But the role of the citizen extends far beyond elections. Indeed, citizen volunteers are at the heart of retail politics when they volunteer for campaign organizations. These volunteers have many responsibilities, which run from benign office work to fund raising and consulting. Volunteering for already established Democratic and Republican campaigns has taken place for more than one hundred years in the United States. But the with entry of Ross Perot into the 1992 presidential campaign, volunteers played a more important role; they helped build a campaign organization from the ground up. In this chapter, we take a close look at Perot's campaign organization in Virginia, and seek to explore who these volunteers were and what motivated them.

After Perot made his announcement, campaign organizations rapidly formed in all fifty states. This chapter examines Perot's 1992 campaign organization in Virginia—Virginians For Perot (VFP). In VFP (as well as with Perot's other state-level campaign organizations) a large group of volunteer activists helped run Perot's campaign at the state and local levels. Although much of the existing political science literature focuses on Perot voters (see Peterson, Johnson, and Gilbert 1995), we take a different approach to the Perot phenomenon by analyzing the leaders of Perot's state-level campaign organization in Virginia.

Using a survey of the VFP leadership, we seek to answer the following questions:

- Who were the people leading VFP?
- What did they think about important political issues and politics?
- How did they behave politically both before and during the 1992 election?
- Why did they get involved in the Perot movement?
- What future do they see for the Reform Party (formerly United We Stand America)?

The History of Virginians for Perot

Soon after Perot's announcement of his willingness to run for the presidency in February 1992, activists in all fifty states began to form campaign organizations. The VFP leaders we interviewed reported that the enthusiasm among volunteers in Virginia was as intense as in any other state. Why would a declaration from a man with little political experience create such activity among thousands of people across the country? Probably because Perot provided millions of Americans who harboring feelings of anger and alienation toward the government a seemingly viable alternative to the major party candidates. Indeed, Perot underestimated the consequences of his announcement, and it soon became apparent that he was ill-equipped to deal with the sudden outpouring of support. He responded to the initial wave of support by pulling in several people from the Perot Group, the real estate arm of his corporation, to help coordinate the petition drive across the country. However, few of these employees had any political experience, and while they served a significant role in Perot's antigovernment advertising and propaganda campaigns, their involvement in the political campaign became a serious drawback to the efficiency of the organization.

In Virginia, a great wave of enthusiasm and activity began after the first *Larry King Live* episode. As one core activist described it, the petition movement "erupted . . . it just kind of happened." However, this great amount of early interest in Virginia, combined with the aforementioned lack of a cohesive or experienced national organization in Dallas, led to the haphazard creation of a state organization with little centralized direction. After the first Virginia rally for Perot was held in early March in Tyson's Corner, a group of five individuals incorporated Virginians for Perot and established themselves as the board of directors. Around the same time, other volunteers also organized themselves into local, district, and county groups all across the state somewhat independently of the new board of directors. With the exception of two people, all those we interviewed had no previous political or activist experience, and several admitted to not fully understanding exactly how to fulfill their leadership roles. One activist remarked, "Everything we did was something new to us. We didn't have sense to know what would work." This initial disorganization in Virginia should not be a surprise, given the haphazard way the national organization was initially put together. In fact, it was the ability of VFP to achieve any degree of cohesion that must be analyzed.

Despite its difficult beginnings, VFP did soon establish itself at both the state and local levels. Simply stated, the alienation many volunteers felt from the two major parties was strong enough to bring them together in order to get the requisite number of petition signatures to get Perot on the presidential ballot. Many activists were surprised by the overwhelming response to their early effort, especially the thousands of volunteers that mobilized across the state. Nancy Rodrigues, the former state media director for VFP, placed this energy in perspective by comparing it to her other political experiences. "Volunteers were just beating down the door wanting to know how they could help. I still marvel at the [energy and enthusiasm]. After working on later campaigns, I have seen nowhere near the intensity." It was this incredible enthusiasm and motivation for change that pulled these activists together and got VFP off the ground.

Nevertheless, as VFP state and local positions were created and occupied, new organizational problems began to develop, both within the state and between the state and the national organization. In fact, one former district coordinator described the early relations between the state officials in Richmond and the individual districts as "terribly flawed," and the stories of those intimately involved in the campaign reveal a consistent theme of confusion and misunderstanding in the communications between the state and local levels. For example, several district and local volunteers complained that the original structure vested too much control within the board of directors. These volunteers believed that because the organization had been founded as a grass-roots organization, those who were out in the community with the petitions should have had more influence at the state level. Conversely, others argued that there was not enough central control in VFP. According to one volunteer in the latter camp, "Petty arguments occurred because there was no central leadership. A campaign should be a totalitarian effort . . . democracy just doesn't work in a political campaign." These basic philosophical differences were compounded by the political inexperience of many of the organization's leaders at both the state and local levels.

Another problem that plagued the early organization was opportunism. Unfortunately, a number of people simply saw involvement in VFP as an opportunity to increase their own personal or business power and prestige. The goals of any organization are obviously more difficult to meet when some members of the organization are looking out only for themselves, and every single person we interviewed, including several district coordinators and two former state coordinators, conceded that this opportunist element existed at all levels of VFP during the early months. However, just as the organization had come together out of nowhere, so did the intrastate relations improve. The most vocal protesters and opportunists were weeded out, district coordinators were given positions on the board of directors, and Robert Schumaker—a strong-willed, no-nonsense state coordinator—accepted the challenge to bring order and stability to the organization. By early July, many of the major in-state disagreements had been settled and the entire organization looked forward to two major events: a large rally in Williamsburg, and a ceremonial presentation of the ballot petitions in Richmond.

Meanwhile, VFP was concurrently experiencing problems in its relations with the national organization in Dallas. As a practical matter, the volunteers found it difficult to communicate the ideals and positions of Perot to the public when their candidate refused to endorse or relate any specific plan of action. VFP encountered even more serious problems in communicating with the national organization. As mentioned earlier, the national organization had not anticipated the tremendous nationwide response to Perot's candidacy. It responded by staffing the national office with politically inexperienced personnel who, according to those we interviewed, amplified their political naivete by attempting to maintain an overly strict control over the state organization. One leader was "puzzled by the friction between [the national and the state offices]. Perot styled himself as an organizational guy, but he had little organization." Tellingly, the two former state media directors we spoke with remarked on the lack of communication they had with Dallas, and many echoed the observation that "nationals didn't have a clue as to what they were doing." One particularly illuminating story was provided by one of the former state media directors, who asked Dallas to provide a number of photographs of Perot for use in media releases, promotional advertisements, and the like. She received one small picture of Perot with strict instructions that it not be used for any promotional reason, but was only to be placed on her desk to be gazed upon for inspiration. Our interviews also provided evidence of the paranoia and penchant for ultra-tight security that was attributed to Perot in highly publicized media accounts of the background checks he ordered on his workers and family (Gillespie 1993). Several activists described Perot as a "control freak" and complained that their directives from Dallas represented attempts to micromanage the campaign. According to most interviewees, VFP's relationship with Dallas continued in this disjointed manner into July and through the summer with no appreciable change for the better.

Then, on July 16, 1992, Ross Perot abruptly dropped out of the presidential race.VFP was caught by total surprise; no one in the organization had any inkling that Perot was ready to abandon the campaign. Indeed, Perot's sudden withdrawal from the race left VFP with many substantial outstanding bills, including one for the ten thousand tee-shirts stacked in the Williamsburg office in anticipation of an upcoming statewide rally on the campus of The College of William and Mary. The effect on the morale within the organization was even more damaging, as feelings of anger and betrayal overwhelmed some VFP activists, while others just became depressed and dejected. The fading morale and general disaffection with organizational goals caused many of the original core activists to leave the organization. Nevertheless, soon after Perot's stunning announcement a meeting took place among several state officers and a decision was made to press on with VFP. Those who remained worked to keep the organization functioning, and in fact many of the state organizations throughout the country remained in place.

As we know, Ross Perot changed his mind and decided to return to the presidential race on October 1, 1992—thirty-three days before the election. Although approximately half of the original core activists chose not to rejoin the organization, Perot's reentry into the presidential race revitalized those who remained. They carried the campaign through to election day, which saw Perot win 13.7 percent of the popular vote in Virginia but no electoral votes nationally.

It is important for the purposes of this chapter to briefly discuss the issues Ross Perot advocated in 1992. The issues he most vocally supported were congressional term limits, a pro-choice position on abortion, and an increase in the gasoline tax (Perot 1992). Perot also favored decreased military spending, a decreased military involvement overseas, a national health care plan, and opposition to international trade agreements (which after the election turned into his staunch opposition to the North American Free Trade Agreement [NAFTA] and the General Agreement on Tarriffs and Trade [GATT]).

After the election the initial interest of VFP—working to get Perot elected President—no longer existed. However, out of the presidential campaign grew the organization United We Stand America (UWSA), which included among its early leadership many people who had leadership roles in the presidential campaign. The Virginia state organization, United We Stand America-Virginia (UWSA-VA) was actually first envisioned at a meeting of remaining state volunteers during the period Perot dropped out of the presidential race, in which they decided upon a mission statement and adopted the idea of a permanent nationwide organization.

By January 1993 state directors for UWSA-VA were in place and a blueprint for the organization had been formulated. UWSA-VA held its first state convention in Charlottesville on July 16–17, 1993, and became the first state to receive a charter from the national organization. In early February 1994 representatives from UWSA chapters in all fifty states attended the organization's first national leadership conference. Some two years after the 1992 presidential election close to 50 percent of the VFP original core activists remained active in UWSA-VA, but it is important to remember that UWSA is not a political organization. It is a nonpartisan citizens action education group, and therefore it cannot run or endorse candidates for any elected office. Its main goal is the education of the American people, so they will can better make informed decisions about their government. However, USWA's visibility over the last few years has been closely tied to political events, including the NAFTA debates in the fall of 1993 and the 1996 presidential campaign.

Theories of Elite Behavior

Before we proceed to investigate the elites in the Perot movement, it is important to provide a theoretical framework from which to generate predictions about activists in the Perot movement. Although the literature is rich with theories of mass behavior (see Peterson, Johnson, and Gilbert 1995 for a review), little has been written about theories of elite behavior. Existing theories of interest groups are a notable exception. In this section, we review extant theories of interest groups and make predictions about the activists in VFP. We proceed to evaluate these predictions in the following section.

Virginians for Perot clearly fits the description of an organized interest group. VFP possessed an instrumental interest—to get Ross Perot elected president. The fact that the organization had a defined structure points to the usefulness of theories of interest groups to study organizational behavior. Of course, organizational questions of many kinds can be answered using interest group theories; thus, a study of individual behavior within a political party organization would be appropriate for interest group analysis. As an interest group, VFP's resources came from two sources: contributions by members and Perot. These resources were used to pursue the attainment of a collective good (the election of Perot) and to provide incentives for individuals to get involved. Finally, VFP possessed a patron and an entrepreneur with significant resources: Perot himself. Therefore, VFP possesses the characteristics of an interest group and is ripe for applying theories of interest group formation and maintenance.

Lawrence Rothenberg (1988, 1992) applies the economy of incentive growing from the interest group literature (see Olson 1965; Salisbury 1989; Moe 1980; Walker 1983, 1991) to study the retention decision of members—whether individuals choose to remain with an interest group or not. Rothenberg indicates that the individual decision to join an interest group can be explained as a learning process. This is contrary to Moe (1980), who argues that individuals are poorly informed about the benefits to be gained from joining a group. According to Moe (1980), individuals therefore make mistakes when performing cost/benefit calculations. The implication of this argument is that when individuals become completely informed about benefits, they will leave the group. Rothenberg answers this argument by indicating that once members join a group, they learn about both the selective benefits and the collective goods the group provides. This, along with imperfect information about costs, explains why individuals join. In short, once people join, they learn the value of the benefits provided, and then decide to continue with the group based on that new information. Rothenberg analyzes some implications of this line of reasoning, and shows with his membership survey of Common Cause that experiential learning does take place. However, by not questioning the individuals who left the group, he cannot definitively conclude that the learning that took place actually motivated people to leave. He indicates that collective benefits and solidary benefits are significant in the retention decision as well as the initial decision to join.

In his later publication (1992), Rothenberg applies this logic to the behavior of two types of activists: checkbook activists and temporal activists (127). Temporal activists are further subdivided into a group of core activists—those who are leaders of local and state organizations—and occasional activists—those individuals who become active when the group calls. What motivates these core activists? Rothenberg indicates that they are passionately devoted to group ideals—this passion for ideals is the benefit that exceeds their temporal costs. In Common Cause, Rothenberg examines the decision group members make when choosing to escalate their level of commitment. In this case, since VFP was constructed so quickly, the core activists learned about the group just as other members did. Thus, many activists may initially not have known much about the organization, especially the purposive benefits offered by the political expression of policy goals.

Using Rothenberg's theory, we develop the following hypotheses about the activists in VFP. The primary cost borne by the activists in VFP is their time. To offset this significant cost, we expect that those individuals who became involved in VFP did so to obtain expressive benefits by voicing their political opinions. For such benefits to have any value, we also expect dissatisfied, alienated individuals to be involved in VFP. This follows from the fact that individuals who are greatly dissatisfied with American governance gain benefits not only from attempting to help elect Ross Perot president, but also from participating in an organization that (in their view) is changing the face of American politics. A similar expressive benefit comes from the policies advocated by Perot regarding such as NAFTA, on which both Bush and Clinton took the same stance. We therefore expect those individuals who were activists in VFP to strongly agree with the policy positions take by Ross Perot. A final implication of this literature deals with the retention decision of the core activists. Rothenberg's theory of experiential search predicts that after individuals learned about VFP and realized that the organization was not pursuing goals they agreed with they chose to leave the organization. This conclusion is revealed in our previous research in a multivariate statistical analysis of our survey of VFP activists (Martin and Spang 1995). Before proceeding to discuss our methodology and results, it is important to note that the results we present here are not an empirical test of interest group theories. Rather, we are interested in describing the leadership of the organization demographically, behaviorally, and attitudinally.

Methodology

When conducting any case study, the question arises about the typicality of the case under study. Are there reasons to believe that Virginia is uniquely different with regard to the Perot phenomenon? Our answer to this question is no. Indeed, Virginia seems to be a very representative case. In the 1992 presidential election, while slightly more Republican than the national outcome, Virginia had approximately 5 percent of Perot voters. In the 102nd and 103rd Congress, the Virginia House delegation was two-thirds Democratic, with one senator from each party. Both of these mirror the national representation in these institutions. Finally, in looking at the Democrats and Republican party elites from Virgina (see the discussion below), we find that these people from Virginia look very much like those from other states. For all of these reasons, Virginia looks to be a typical case by which to study the Perot movement. To best understand the construction of a particular campaign organization, it is necessary to narrow our focus to this single case.

The data used to answer our research questions was generated using a mail questionnaire sent to all individuals on the initial VFP list of statewide activists. The list was obtained from Nancy Rodrigues, the former media director of VFP. Every state position is represented on this list—including executive positions of the organization and the state, finance, legal, and strategy coordinators. We also include media directors for each congressional district in Virginia, electors from each district, and district, county, and city coordinators and treasurers. Also included in this list was a page of names from the eighth congressional district, which includes Arlington County in Northern Virginia. In fact, close to one-third of the total surveys sent out went to people from the eighth district. However, this seeming overrepresentation of the eighth district does not diminish the fact that the sample represents the entire leadership of the Virginians For Perot statewide organization, particularly since a large number of the original activists came from northern Virginia. Each mailing included a questionnaire, a postage-paid return envelope to the author, and a cover letter that explained our project and asked each respondent to complete and return the questionnaire. One-hundred and eight questionnaires were initially sent out. One initial respondent provided us with a list of the statewide administration of Virginians For Perot dated April 21, 1992, which contained several names not included on our original list. A second mailing of twenty-six was then sent out to include these new names and acknowledged address corrections from the first mailing. A third mailing was then sent to all those people not responding to the first two mailings. Of the 134 total mailings sent out, nineteen were returned unopened with no forwarding address. Out of the 115 questionnaires that reached their destination, eighty-six were returned for an exceptional return rate of 74.8 percent. This response rate in itself tells us something about the activists of VFP—they are quite politically aware and remained interested in sharing their opinions with others. The number of observations in the data set is quite small, with just 86 usable questionnaires. However, that number is large enough to make meaningful comparisons.[1]

Our survey was carried out through the fall of 1993 and early months of 1994, more than a year after the Perot presidential campaign. As a result, we must acknowledge that many responses—such as those dealing with the evaluation of Perot himself—may have changed from the time of the campaign due to influences of the intervening year not detectable in the survey. Even so, the high percentage of surveys received, coupled with the information obtained through our personal interviews of those holding the highest positions in the organization, should help to paint an accurate picture of the leadership of Virginians for Perot.

At the time of writing we were unaware of any comparable data set of Perot volunteers from any other state. However, in an effort to put the responses to our VFP questionnaire in context, we compare them with data from two other sources. First, we use data from the "Activists in the United States Nomination Process 1980–1988" study conducted by Abramowitz et al. (1994), which provides comparisons of the VFP activists to activists in the Democratic and Republican parties. See Abramowitz et al. for a description of these data (1994), which are available through the Inter-University Consortium for Political and Social Research (Study Number 6143). Although the data are from 1988, both the Democrats and the Republicans underwent few significant changes between 1988 and 1992. Thus, this study allows comparisons of elite behavior in Perot's organization to the behavior of the elites in the two major political parties. To facilitate comparisons of the VFP activists to the American voting public, we also use data from the "American National Election Study, 1992" (Miller 1993). Data from the National Election Study can also be obtained from the Inter-University Consortium for Political and Social Research (Study Number 6067). This study includes many questions that parallel the questions in our survey, enabling us to make comparisons between the VFP activists and the voting population.

Data and Results

In this section, we present the data obtained from our survey of the leadership of VFP. We present our raw data, and comparisons between VFP, the other political parties, and the American voters generally.[2] We return to the questions posed in the introduction:

- Who were the people leading VFP?
- What did they think about important political issues and politics?
- How did they behave politically both before and during the 1992 election?
- Why did they get involved in the Perot movement?
- What future do they see for the Reform Party (formerly United We Stand America)?

Our analysis begins by examining some simple demographic data. Summary statistics are reported in Table 3.1.

Table 3.1. Demographic Description of VFP

	VFP Leadership	National Electorate	Democratic Leadership	GOP Leadership
Education				
High School or Less	4.7%	51.9%	19.9%	22.9%
Some College	26.7%	24.6%	21.2%	29.8%
College Graduate or Postgraduate	68.6%	23.5%	58.9%	47.3%
Age				
Under 30	3.5%	19.6%	6.6%	8.1%
30-50	50.0%	43.4%	42.6%	38.3%
51-60	23.3%	12.1%	18.1%	9.2%
Over 60	23.3%	24.9%	32.7%	34.3%
Female	36.0%	53.4%	50.1%	40.6%
Nonwhite	4.7%	15.3%	5.9%	1.3%
	n=86	n=2487	n=764	n=385

From Table 3.1, it is apparent that the VFP leadership is well educated. In fact, this leadership group is better educated than the Democratic and Republican leadership. Surprisingly, the VFP activists are younger than we might expect. Certainly many of Perot's supporters are senior citizens, but the elites in VFP are younger than elites in both the Democratic and Republican parties. The VFP leadership is only 36 percent female, substantially less than the percent female in the Democratic Party (50.1%) and slightly less than the percent women in the Republican party (40.6%). Finally, as is the case with the leadership in the two primary parties, the VFP leadership is comprised of mostly whites. In sum, the VFP leadership seems to be better educated and younger than leaders in the other parties, and includes fewer women.

While this demographic description is an important starting point, it is also important to see how the leadership of VFP characterize themselves politically. In Figure 3.1, we present the partisan identification of the VFP leadership as well as that of the American electorate.

From this figure, it is clear that the electorate is evenly spread among the seven classifications, with a slight skew toward the Democratic party. As expected, the VFP leadership is primarily independent; in fact, more than 30 percent identify themselves as independents. The second largest category for the VFP leadership is "leaning Republican." This alludes to the fact that Perot was drawing many individuals who might have been willing to get involved with George Bush's campaign. A similar and even more startling fact is apparent in Figure 3.2, where we present the responses to a question dealing with political philosophy.

Looking first at the national electorate, it is apparent that most Americans consider themselves middle of the road. Although the national electorate is moderate, there are more people who identify themselves as conservative than as liberal. The responses of the VFP leadership, on the other hand, indicate a different trend. The modal category for the VFP leadership is middle of the road, but the remaining individuals are primarily conservative. In Virginia, there were few liberal (or for that matter liberal-leaning) core activists. There was a large number of individuals who were conservative. This again points to the conclusion that the Perot movement took activists away from conservative Republican campaigns (including George Bush's campaign) instead of liberal Democratic campaigns (including Bill Clinton's campaign). Thus, we can claim that the VFP activists are primarily moderate to conservative.

To investigate this self-identification a bit further, we also asked a series of questions about specific issues. We present the level of support for certain policies among the leaders of VFP in Figure 3.3.

The VFP leadership was in agreement with Ross Perot on many core issues of the Perot candidacy: Perot's opposition to a constitutional amendment prohibiting abortion, his opposition to affirmative action, his advocacy of an increase

46

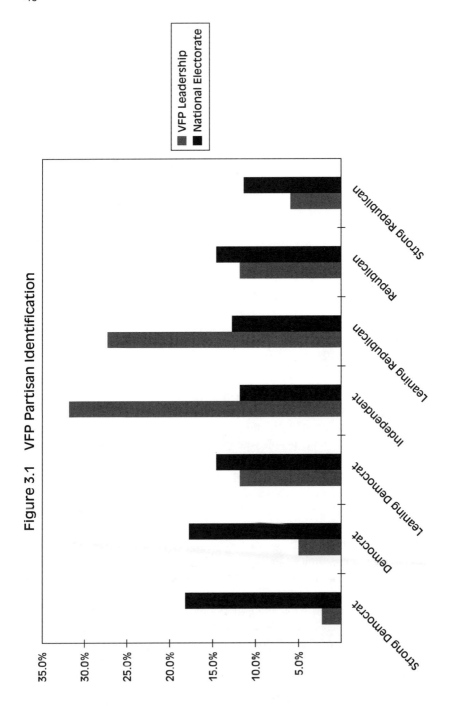

Figure 3.1   VFP Partisan Identification

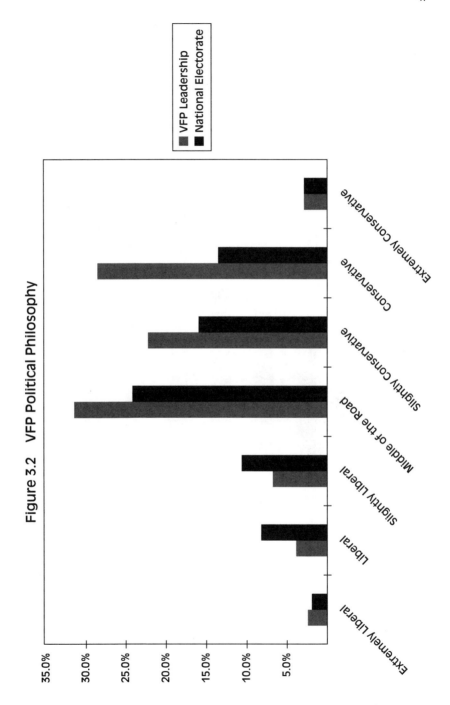

Figure 3.2   VFP Political Philosophy

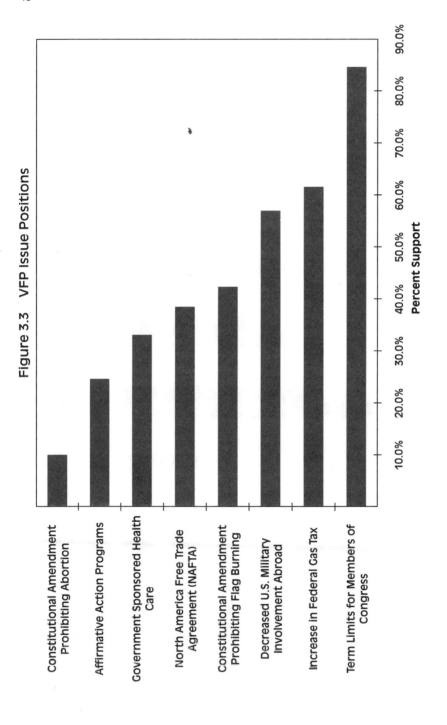

Figure 3.3   VFP Issue Positions

in the federal gas tax, and his support for term limits for members of Congress. The issues on which Perot and his leadership in Virginia did not agree is surprising. Although Perot strongly opposed NAFTA, only 60 percent of the leadership in Virginia supported him on this issue. Again, only 60 percent of the VFP leadership supported Perot on a decreased U.S. military involvement abroad. Most interesting is the fact that only 40 percent of the leadership supported Perot's endorsement of a national health care system. Although Clinton and Perot were in agreement on this issue, the fact that the activists were alienated from the other candidates leads us to the conclusion that they held overwhelming opposition to Bill Clinton. This led these individuals to commit their time to Ross Perot while it also led them to oppose the issue most strongly advocated by Bill Clinton—health care reform. In sum, the VFP leadership falls in line with Perot on most issues.

Part of the theory we outlined in the previous section predicts that the VFP leadership gained expressive benefits not only from their issue preferences discussed above, but also from their perceived opportunity to change the structure of American politics. To investigate this, we posed a series of questions dealing with the structure of American politics. Figure 3.4 presents the opinions the VFP leadership hold about the two party system.

Not surprisingly, not one of the VFP activists felt that the two party system is good for the country and works well. Nearly 35 percent felt that the two party system is not perfect, but better than any other system. More than 65 percent felt that the two party system is problematic and should be changed. This is not surprising given the fact that the one major goal of VFP was to change the structure of American politics by injecting a new party into the mix. In Figure 3.5 we present the feelings of the VFP leadership about government.

For this question, no activists indicated that they always trust government. Just over 10 percent trust government occasionally, while nearly 90 percent trust government sparingly. This also points to a severe disaffection with American governance, which led these individuals to get involved with the Perot movement (for similar findings dealing the Perot voters see Gilbert, Johnson, and Peterson 1994). Do these activists feel that they could do better than current elected officials? We posed this question to the VFP leadership. Figure 3.6 indicates that almost 70 percent of the sample feel that they could do better in public office than most current elected officials.

This indicates that the Perot activists in Virginia possessed high levels of political efficacy. Thus, while the VFP leadership was critical of the current state of affairs, they also felt that they could fix them.

This attitudinal description tells us quite a bit about the Perot organization. We now move our attention to describing the behavior of the VFP activists. First, in Table 3.2 we present the previous group activity in which the VFP leadership engaged.

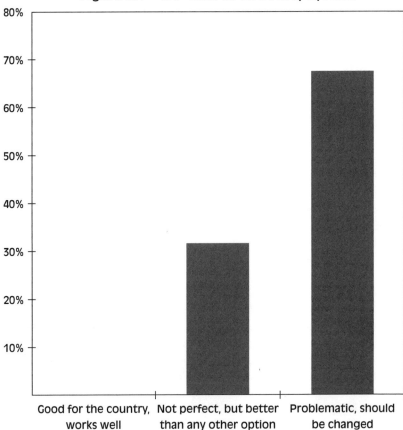

Figure 3.4   VFP View of Two Party System

From this table, it seems that the VFP activists were not as involved in interest group activities as their Republican and Democratic counterparts. The activists were highly active in two areas: business groups and neighborhood/education groups. This leads us to conclude that the VFP elites were not active in traditional interest groups (including ideological interest groups, labor groups, and veterans groups). They were, however, active in community-based groups. These individuals were tied into organizations in their communities, but were not as involved in national political organizations.

In Table 3.3 we provide statistics that document other political behavior of the VFP activists.

We first asked the VFP activists about their previous political involvement. Our results indicate that about one-quarter of the activists were involved in

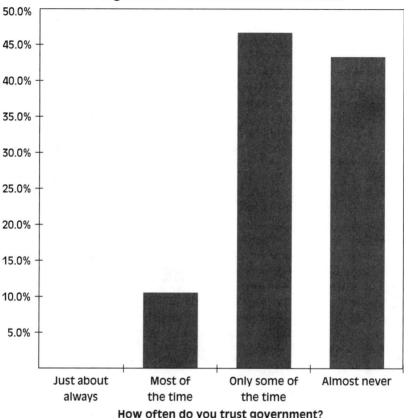

Figure 3.5   VFP Trust in Government

politics year after year. The remainder, just over three-quarters, get involved only when they perceive there is a worthwhile candidate—such as Ross Perot. This again confirms our suspicion that the VFP leadership was so disillusioned with the status quo that they were willing to bear the costs to attempt to change the system. We also posed questions to see how the elites would have behaved if Perot were not involved in the presidential race. To provide a baseline, we asked each activist about her vote in the 1992 presidential election. Almost 73 percent of our sample cast their vote for Perot, while 19 percent voted for Bush and 8 percent voted for Clinton. Had Perot not been in the race, our respondents who voted for Perot indicated that 35 percent of them would have voted for Bush and 35 percent would have voted for Clinton. This indicates that as far as this sample is concerned, the injection of Perot in the presidential race would have not altered the final outcome. We also asked the VFP activists about the Republicans and

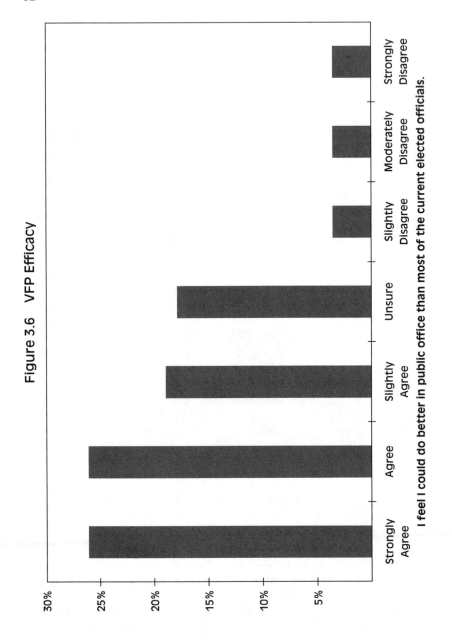

Figure 3.6   VFP Efficacy

I feel I could do better in public office than most of the current elected officials.

Table 3.2. VFP Group Activity

Group	VFP Leadership	Democratic Leadership	GOP Leadership
Business Groups	44.2%	22.1%	34.1%
Veterans Groups	10.5%	17.0%	19.7%
Environmental Groups	26.7%	35.6%	10.9%
Nonpartisan Political Groups	19.8%	32.8%	18.2%
Labor Groups	4.7%	29.7%	16.8%
Abortion Groups	8.1%	N/A	N/A
Conservative Ideological Groups	10.5%	2.2%	21.7%
Liberal Ideological Groups	4.7%	20.7%	1.3%
Religious Right Groups	4.7%	0.7%	21.0%
Women's Groups	9.3%	21.1%	5.8%
Neighborhood/Education Groups	47.7%	N/A	N/A
Teachers Organizations	4.7%	N/A	N/A
MIA/POW Groups	3.4%	N/A	N/A
Farm Organizations	4.7%	N/A	N/A
	n=86	*n=764*	*n=385*

Democrats running for the nomination. Not surprisingly, most of the VFP activists preferred George Bush for the Republican nomination. The results for the Democratic candidates are more interesting. Exactly 45 percent of the sample would have liked to have seen Paul Tsongas get the Democratic nomination; only 16.3 percent preferred Bill Clinton. Since Perot and Tsongas agreed on many key issues and both were perceived as outsiders, this result is intuitive. These findings again indicate that the VFP activists were disaffected with the candidates in the race, leading to their activism in the Perot campaign.

To further investigate the reasons for activist involvement in VFP, we asked each activist why he or she got involved in VFP. We present results from these questions in Figure 3.7.

These questions were asked in a series, thus allowing each activist to indicate all of their reasons for getting involved in the organization. Very few of the activists joined because they were recruited or because they signed a petition. Perot's great television exposure, including the frequent appearances on *Larry King Live* was a primary reason for many activists getting involved. Thus, it appears that without this media exposure it would have been very difficult for activists anywhere to form such a vast organization. This primary reason for activist involvement

Table 3.3. VFP Political Behavior

Political Involvement	
Involved in Politics Year after Year	*24.4%*
Involved in Politics Only When Worthwhile Candidate or Issue	*32.6%*
Newcomer in 1992	*43.0%*
	n=86

Vote in 1992 Presidential Election	
Bush	*18.8%*
Clinton	*8.2%*
Perot	*72.9%*
	n=85

Vote in 1992 Presidential Election If Perot Not Running (Perot Voters Only)	
Bush	*34.9%*
Clinton	*34.9%*
Not Voted	*15.9%*
Other Candidate	*9.5%*
	n=63

Preferred GOP 1992 Nominee	
George Bush	*36.1%*
Pat Buchanan	*13.3%*
Jack Kemp	*4.8%*
Other	*1.2%*
None	*44.6%*
	n=85

Preferred Democratic 1992 Nominee	
Paul Tsongas	*45.0%*
Bill Clinton	*16.3%*
Jerry Brown	*8.8%*
Bob Kerry	*7.5%*
Tom Harkin	*2.5%*
None	*20.0%*
	n=83

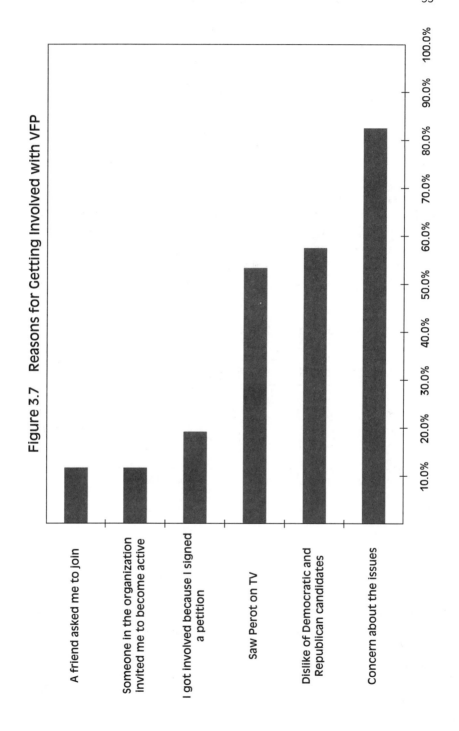

Figure 3.7 Reasons for Getting Involved with VFP

confirms our hypotheses and is consistent with our previous results—concern about the political issues. As we discussed above, many of the activists did not agree with Perot on all of the issues; however almost 90 percent of the activists found at least one issue on which they agreed with Perot. The second most important reason for getting involved in VFP was the dislike for the Democratic and Republican candidates, again pointing to a disaffection with the status quo.

The final set of results we present deal with the future of the Perot movement. Although this survey was taken in the fall of 1993 and the spring of 1994, it nonetheless provides insight into the mindset of the individuals who worked during the 1992 election. We present these results in Table 3.4.

First, only 25 percent of the sample anticipated that they would be involved in the 1996 campaign. After experiencing the organizational difficulties of VFP, it is not surprising that many activists did not plan to work during 1996. Two years after the election, however, more than 48 percent of activists would still vote for Ross Perot. Only 16 percent would support Bill Clinton, reflecting their initial lack of support for Clinton and their evaluation of the first two years of the

Table 3.4. Future of the VFP Leadership

Anticipated activity in UWSA-VA during 1996 campaign	
Yes	25.0%
No	50.0%
Not Sure	25.0%
	n=80

Vote in Perot / Republican / Clinton 1996 election	
Perot	48.2%
The Republican (e.g., Jack Kemp or Robert Dole)	35.8%
Clinton	16.0%
	n=81

Preferred direction for USWA in the next four years	
Form a political party (like the Patriot Party)	27.7%
Endorse GOP and Dem candidates, but not run own candidates	20.5%
Stress important issues, but not endorse candidates	37.4%
Other	14.4%
	n=83

Clinton presidency. We finally asked the activists what direction they wanted the organization to take. More than 37 percent wanted the organization to stress important issues, but not to endorse candidates. Another 21 percent wanted the organization to endorse GOP and Democratic candidates, but not to run their own candidates. Only 28 percent wanted UWSA-VA to form its own political party—a party now in existence called the Reform Party.

From our survey, we can make some of the following generalizations to answer our questions posed at the beginning of this section:

- The leaders of VFP were well educated, white, and male. For the most part, the leaders of VFP had little political experience, and participated infrequently in national interest groups.
- The VFP activists identified themselves as independents, and they were ideologically conservative. They also agreed with the issue positions taken by Ross Perot, except for Perot's support for a national health care system.
- Not surprisingly, the Perot leadership primarily voted for Ross Perot in the 1992 presidential election. They also supported Paul Tsongas over Bill Clinton for the Democratic nomination.
- The VFP activists got involved in the campaign to get expressive benefits; they wanted to change the two party system and support the issue positions of Ross Perot.
- Most of the original VFP activists were so disillusioned with the outcome in 1992 that they did not plan on participating in the 1996 election, even if Ross Perot were again a candidate.

Conclusion

In this chapter, we have painted a picture of Ross Perot's campaign organization in Virginia—Virginians for Perot. This adds to our knowledge of third party presidential candidacies by providing a detailed organizational history and describing the activists in the organization. Without an effective organization, even a political candidate with strong public support may not get a presidential campaign off the ground. Thus, when studying past third presidential candidates or making predictions about future third presidential runs, both social scientists and interested citizens must look at both the possibility of gaining votes (an ideological dimension) as well as the possibility of constructing an effective campaign organization (an organizational dimension). Although Ross Perot certainly had the possibility of garnering many votes, his inadequate campaign organization and his flipflop on his promise to run for the presidency caused him to lose many votes across America.

In Virginia after the 1992 election, the Virginia Independent Party (VIP) was created as a political organization to further the goals and ideals of Perot's 1992 candidacy, the former VFP, and the present UWSA-VA. Not surprisingly, many members of the VIP are members of UWSA-VA, and seven of the eleven VIP district chairpersons were involved in Perot's 1992 campaign organization in Virginia. At the grass-roots level, the VIP boasted a mailing list of 60,000 in 1996. The VIP was awarded ballot status by the State Board of Elections in February 1996, becoming the first new political party to become so certified in decades, and gained all the rights and privileges of the Democratic and Republican parties. Most importantly, this meant that the VIP presidential candidate would not be required to collect petition signatures and jump through all the other procedural hoops that Ross Perot encountered in 1992.

Soon after state certification, the VIP and the Reform Party agreed to cooperate in backing a presidential candidate in 1996. In addition to campaigning for Perot at the top of the ballot, the VIP ran their own candidates in three congressional elections, and endorsed candidates in another congressional race as well as Virginia's senate race. George R. Wood in the fifth district, Ward Edmonds in the eighth district, and Thomas Roberts in the ninth district ran for the House of Representatives under the banner of the VIP. They all faced traditional obstacles to third party candidates—a lack of money and exposure—and none seriously challenged the major party candidates. Senate Democratic candidate Marl Warner and fourth district Republican candidate Anthony Zevgolis received endorsements from the VIP. These endorsements went to these candidates primarily because they took the time to respond to a questionnaire and accepted a pledge to reform the government, while their opponents did not.

By 1996 the VIP and the Reform party were more mature organizations, and while lacking the resources of the major parties, organizational structures similar to the major parties were in place. The purpose of this paper has been to study organizational development, and we have documented one important challenge that third parties face—building and maintaining effective campaign organizations. Indeed, there exists an important organizational dimension to the possibility of success for third party candidates that should not be ignored by either political scientists or citizens. The study of Virginians for Perot in 1992 provides a unique opportunity to understand how citizens can build a campaign organization at the grass-roots level.

Notes

1. A hard copy of the questionnaire and an electronic copy of the data set can be obtained from the authors.

2. In the results presented, columns labelled "National Electorate" refer to the respondents of the "1992 American National Election Study." Those columns labelled "Democratic Leadership" and "GOP Leadership" come from Democratic caucus participants in Virginia and Republican caucus participants in Iowa surveyed by Abramowitz et al. (1994). For all figures presented in this section, n=87.

References

Abramowitz, Alan I., John McGlennon, Ronald B. Rapoport, and Walter Stone. 1994. *Activists in the United States Presidential Nomination Process, 1980–1988.* Ann Arbor: Inter-University Consortium for Political and Social Research. Study Number 6143.

Gilbert, Christopher P., Timothy R. Johnson, and David A. Peterson. 1994. "Patterns of Support and Defection for Third Party Presidential Candidates: A Comparison and Anderson, Perot, and Wallace Voters." Paper presented at the 1994 Annual Meeting of the Midwest Political Science Association, April 1994, Chicago.

Gillespie, J. David. 1993. *Politics at the Periphery: Third Parties in Two Party America.* Columbia: University of South Carolina Press.

Hugick, Larry. 1993. "Perot's Own Actions Determined His Fate," *The Public Perspective* 4: 17–18.

Knoke, David. 1990. *Organizing for Collective Action: The Political Economies of Associations.* Hawthorne, N.Y.: Aldine de Gruyter.

Martin, Andrew D., and Brian E. Spang. 1995. "An Empirical Examination of the Retention Decision of Core Activists in Virginians for Perot." Paper presented at the Annual Meeting of the Southern Political Science Association, November 1995, Tampa.

Miller, Warren E., Donald R. Kinder, Steven J. Rosenstone, and the National Election Studies. 1993. *American National Election Study, 1992: Pre- and Post-Election Survey.* Ann Arbor: Inter-University Consortium for Political and Social Research.

Moe, Terry. 1980. *The Organization of Interests.* Chicago: The University of Chicago Press.

Olson, Mancur. 1965. *The Logic of Collective Action.* Cambridge: Harvard University Press.

Perot, Ross. 1992. *United We Stand: How We Can Take Back Our Country.* New York: Hyperion.

Peterson, David A., Timothy R. Johnson, and Christopher P. Gilbert. 1995. "Voter Preference in American Presidential Elections: A Comparison of Two-Candidate and Three-Candidate Races." Paper presented at the 1995 Annual Meeting of the Midwest Political Science Association, April 1995, Chicago.

Rothenberg, Lawrence S. 1988. "Organizational Maintenance and the Retention Decision in Groups," *American Political Science Review* 82: 1129–1152.

———. 1992. *Linking Citizens to Government: Interest Group Politics at Common Cause.* Cambridge: Cambridge University Press.

Salisbury, Robert. 1969. "An Exchange Theory of Interest Groups," *Midwest Journal of Political Science* 8: 1–32.

Walker, Jack. 1983. "The Origins and Maintenance of Interest Groups in America," *American Political Science Review* 77: 390–405.

Walker, Jack L. 1991. *Mobilizing Interest Groups in America: Patrons, Professions, and Social Movements.* Ann Arbor: The University of Michigan Press.

4

Attitudes Toward Government, Partisan Dispositions, and the Rise of Ross Perot

Jeffrey Koch

Introduction

I n 1992, H. Ross Perot surprised most political observers by receiving 19 percent of the popular vote, a proportion not reached by a third party candidate since Teddy Roosevelt's Bull Moose Party received 27 percent in 1912. In 1996, running under the banner of the newly created Reform Party, he received a diminished but still respectable 9 percent of the vote. In this chapter I examine the conditions that led to the emergence of H. Ross Perot's 1992 and 1996 third party challenges and the effect of his third party challenge on the American electoral order. Specifically, I examine Americans' affect and orientation toward the major parties, their government, and political leaders in the 1980s and 1990s, and analyze how these characteristics contributed to Perot's 1992 and 1996 showing. Moreover, I investigate the changes in Perot supporters' attitudes and predisposition toward the American political parties, the American political system, its leaders and government as a result of his historic third party challenge. Scholars consider each of these—partisanship and orientations toward the government and its leaders—some of the most important political attitudes for a democratic political system. Mentoring citizens in their issue concerns and prefer- ences is one of the most important functions of political parties in a democracy.

Unfortunately, little attention has been directed toward understanding the effect of third parties on citizens' behavior and attitudes in this area. While a large body of scholarly research examines the mentoring functions of the major political parties, little effort has been devoted to understanding how this role might be performed by a third party.[1]

Due to the prominence of charges of corruption, incompetence, and unresponsiveness by elected officials in third party movements' campaign themes, scholars have been particularly interested in the public's attitudes toward the integrity and competence of government and its leaders as a key determinant of third party support. Aggregate-level empirical research documents that third parties are more likely to arise when citizens are particularly exercised about the competence and ethics of the government and the contemporary political leaders (Rosenstone et al. 1996; Gold 1995). Accordingly, theoretical works posit that, *ceteris paribus,* the most politically skeptical citizens are the ones most likely to abandon the major parties for a third party candidate. Unfortunately, scholarly efforts have failed to investigate the extent to which a third party candidate shapes the political cynicism of his or her supporters rather than advances positions that reflect those of the supporters. A very large body of empirical research on the issue positions of the mass public assumes that citizens at least partly derive their preferences on contemporary policy issues from the political party with which they identify. Nonetheless, empirical models of third party support assume that causality flows from political cynicism to candidate support. It is reasonable to suspect, however, that third party candidates, acting as outsiders and severe critics of both the political process and contemporary leaders, serve to increase citizens' political skepticism. To the degree that this is true, it indicates that third party movements are not only the beneficiaries of high levels of public cynicism but that they help instill it in the citizenry as well.

A second goal of this chapter is to document the partisan orientations of Perot supporters. One of the most widely watched political characteristics of the general public is their partisan identification. Party identification receives unusually high levels of attention from journalists, political scientists, and politicians because it is a very powerful predictor of vote choice; a party gaining identifiers is a party increasing in electoral strength. In this research I examine the partisan orientations of Perot supporters before and after the 1992 elections.

Four questions motivate the empirical analyses of this research. First, what were the electoral conditions in the 1980s and 1990s that led to Perot's third party emergence? At the aggregate level, were a set of conditions in place that reveal that a third party challenge was likely to enjoy a reasonable level of success? Second, did cynicism toward the contemporary political process and its leaders induce citizens to cast a third party vote in 1992 and 1996? Or, contrariwise, did Perot's rhetorical attacks on the contemporary political process and its leaders sharpen the differences between his supporters and those who voted for one of the major party candidates with respect to their political trust and external efficacy? Theoretical works on political parties contend that they help their identifiers understand the political process. Is there evidence that Perot performed a similar function for his followers in 1992, persuading them to adopt his vision of the contemporary political process?

Third, did support for Perot in 1992 shape citizens' political orientations in 1994, two years after his historic candidacy? If Perot's political rhetoric influenced his followers' views in 1992 and 1996, was the effect still present afterward, thereby attesting to the power of his influence? Fourth, what were the partisan orientations of Perot supporters prior to the 1992 election and afterward? In light of the strenuous efforts made by the major parties to attract those who voted for Perot in 1992, did one party prove more successful than the other in its efforts to expand its electoral coalition by absorbing the Perot supporters?

The Response of Major Parties Following the 1992 Presidential Election

Typically, the emergence of a serious third party challenge signifies change in the electoral landscape; usually, one party successfully enlarges itself by absorbing the supporters of the third party candidate. Following H. Ross Perot's 1992 electoral performance, each of the major parties mapped out and implemented a strategy to absorb the supporters of Mr. Perot. Newly elected President Clinton's 1993 budget achieved a substantial reduction in the size of the national deficit through a variety of spending reductions and tax increases. Moreover, Clinton introduced a new set of guidelines for lobbying activities for aides once they leave the White House to return to the private sector.

The Republican Party was no less diligent (and, it turns out, more successful) in its efforts to win the support of those who had voted for Perot in 1992. The Republicans depicted Clinton's attempts to change the American health insurance system as an effort that would result in substantial increases in taxes and enhance government control over an important aspect of Americans' lives; thereby echoing Perot's complaint that the government performs poorly, wastes valuable resources, and is in need of radical change. Most importantly, the 1994 Republican Contract with America contained several provisions that were specifically aimed at securing the support of Perot voters. For example, the Contract called for bringing to a vote a constitutional amendment to impose a limit on the number of terms served by members of Congress, passage of a balanced budget amendment, applying the laws passed by Congress for the private sector to Congress itself, "fiscal responsibility," open committee meetings in Congress, legal reform, reducing the number of congressional staff, and limiting the terms of committee chairs. All of these efforts were an attempt to have the Republican Party perceived as interested in achieving important reforms of the political process, and thereby to receive the support of the reform oriented Perot voters. In addition to these activities, there were a number of other reasons to believe the Republicans' effort to attract Perot voters might prove more successful than that of the Democrats. As the party that typically displays a general antipathy to government and as the out-party following the 1992 elections, the GOP was well positioned to serve as chief critic of government and all that was wrong with Washington, usurping Perot's role as master faultfinder of the American political system.[2]

In a number of respects the third party challenge headed by Mr. Perot was unique. The third party movement spearheaded by Perot in 1992 was followed by a 1996 run; many third party movements disappear after one challenge. The movement headed by Perot and aided by his tremendous wealth created a formal political party organization—the Reform Party—in an attempt to ensure contin-uation beyond Perot himself. Although his 1996 showing was less impressive than that recorded in 1992, it was still sufficiently strong to guarantee the Reform Party both a place on the ballot for the 2000 presidential election and federal funding. In future elections the Reform Party intends to recruit and sponsor candidates for offices in addition to the presidency, develop a grass-roots organizational base that may put it on equal footing with the major political parties, and take stands on salient issues and concerns in American politics.

Citizens' Trust in Government and
Partisan Evaluations in the 1990s

Typically, third parties emerge when there is an issue or concern that the major parties have failed to address to the satisfaction of a significant proportion of the electorate. For the Perot movement, their candidate focused unrelenting attention on what was wrong with the contemporary political process. The principal condi-tion giving rise to the Perot movement was the deep dissatisfaction of a significant proportion of the electorate with the political process and the political parties. To document these conditions that presented the opening for a serious third party challenge I examine the American National Election Studies (ANES) time series for citizens' views regarding the competence and integrity of the government and its leaders as well as their attitudes toward the major political parties.

Figure 4.1 presents the percentage of the public who agreed with the state-ment, "Public officials don't care what people like me think" for those years from

1952 through 1996 that ANES asked the question. Consistent with the findings of other scholarly studies and popular commentary, the 1990s are a period of deep cynicism toward the government and its leaders (Craig 1996). After a steady rise in political cynicism through the 1960s and 1970s, the level of cynicism appeared to peak in the 1980s, with approximately 50 percent voicing a cynical view toward the responsiveness of the political leaders. Following a brief decrease in cynicism in the mid-1980s due to an economic resurgence (Citrin and Green 1986), another sharp upturn in citizens' distrust of those elected to serve them occurred in 1990, prior to the 1992 election. Note that in 1996 citizens' trust in government registered a modest improvement, suggesting that the electoral landscape when Perot made his second run was less favorable to his attempt than in 1992.

Measures of political trust, presented in Figures 4.2 and 4.3, reveal a similar picture. Since 1958 respondents have been asked how much of the time the federal government can be trusted to do what is right. In the 1990s, 70 percent of the public believed that the government rarely handles public policy matters with even a minimal level of competence. Only 30 percent believed the government would handle its affairs in a reasonably proficient manner on a consistent basis. With regard to the honesty of elected officials, the proportion of the public believing government officials were corrupt was also fairly high, albeit short of a majority. Generally, about 40 percent of the public believed that quite a few of those running the nation's affairs were crooked.

Thus, one of the important conditions necessary for third party emergence, the presence of widespread discontent with the political process, was clearly in place in the 1990s. Many Americans viewed the government as incapable of satisfactorily dealing with the nation's problems, and its leaders as corrupt and unresponsive to the concerns of the common citizen. Again, it is worth noting that by 1996 citizens' views regarding the competence of the nation's leaders and their ethics became more positive, indicating a less favorable political environment for a third party challenge.

A second condition that enhances the likelihood of a viable third party challenge is the presence of a large proportion of the citizenry lacking strong attachments to the major political parties. A fairly lengthy body of scholarly and journalistic works define the contemporary American electoral period as one of weak political parties with respect to their relevance for the general public (Wattenberg 1990, 1991). Thus, this important condition has been in place for some time. What is striking, however, is that not only do many citizens possess weak ties to the political parties but a large number of citizens in the contemporary period find the parties irrelevant for dealing with the nation's important problems.

Since 1972 ANES has asked respondents what they consider the most important problem facing the United States to be. Following this question, respondents

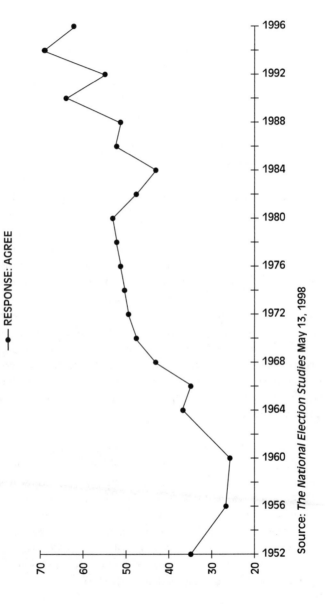

Figure 4.1   Public Officials Don't Care What People Think
1952–1996
●— RESPONSE: AGREE

Source: *The National Election Studies* May 13, 1998

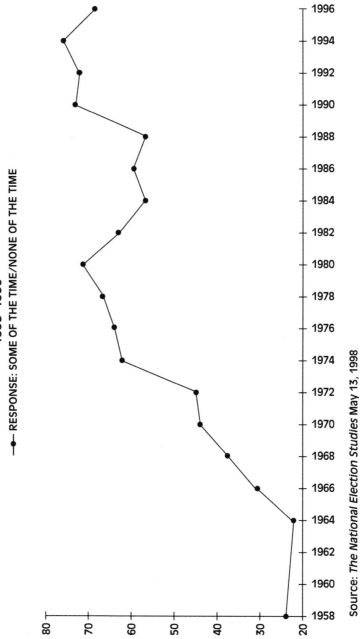

Figure 4.2 How Much of the Time Do You Trust the Federal Government? 1958–1996

—●— RESPONSE: SOME OF THE TIME/NONE OF THE TIME

Source: *The National Election Studies* May 13, 1998

68

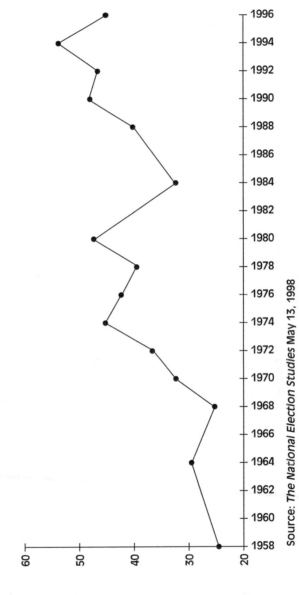

Figure 4.3   Are Government Officials Crooked?
1958–1996
—●— RESPONSE: QUITE A FEW

Source: *The National Election Studies* May 13, 1998

were asked which party was better able to handle this particular problem. Figure 4.4 presents the percentage of respondents who did not see a difference between the parties or who said they did not know which party could deal most effectively with what they considered the most important problem. Approximately 50 percent of the respondents typically could not discern a difference between the major parties in their ability to deal with what they considered the country's most important problem. In 1996 more citizens believed that one of the major parties could address the problem than in 1992, again portending a weaker showing by Perot.

Not only did many citizens fail to distinguish between the major parties in their ability to solve the nation's problems in the early 1990s; they were not particularly enthusiastic about them either. Since 1980 ANES has asked respondents to indicate their degree of affect toward the major political parties on the "feeling thermometer," where zero indicates the coldest possible feelings toward the parties and one hundred the warmest. The mean score for each year is slightly above fifty degrees, the midpoint on the scale. Thus, although not expressing outright hostility toward the major parties, the public has certainly not been wildly enthusiastic about them either.

In sum, in the 1990s a considerable segment of the public did not find either major political party particularly relevant for dealing with the nation's most pressing problems and, relatedly, did not express a great deal of enthusiasm for them. In the early 1990s most of the public believed the American political system was not working very well, and levels of cynicism were exceptionally high. It was into this context that H. Ross Perot launched his 1992 third party run for the presidency. By 1996, however, citizen trust in government had improved modestly and citizens expressed more confidence in the major parties' ability to address important problems, foreshadowing Perot's diminished vote totals.

Individual-Level Model of Third Party Support

Theoretical works on support for third parties contend that citizens who are disaffected with government and politics are most likely to consider an alternative candidate (Rosenstone et al. 1996). Given the fact that Perot tied his candidacy to the need for radical change in the way politics is conducted and since some research demonstrates a relationship between trust in government and support for Perot (Abramson et al. 1994; Gold 1995; Hetherington 1999), citizens' beliefs in the responsiveness, ethics, and competence of political leaders and their faith in the American political system are examined. The ANES data contain several measures of citizens' trust in government and their sense of external efficacy. I seek

Figure 4.4   Which Party Is Best Able to Handle the Most Important Problem?
1972–1996

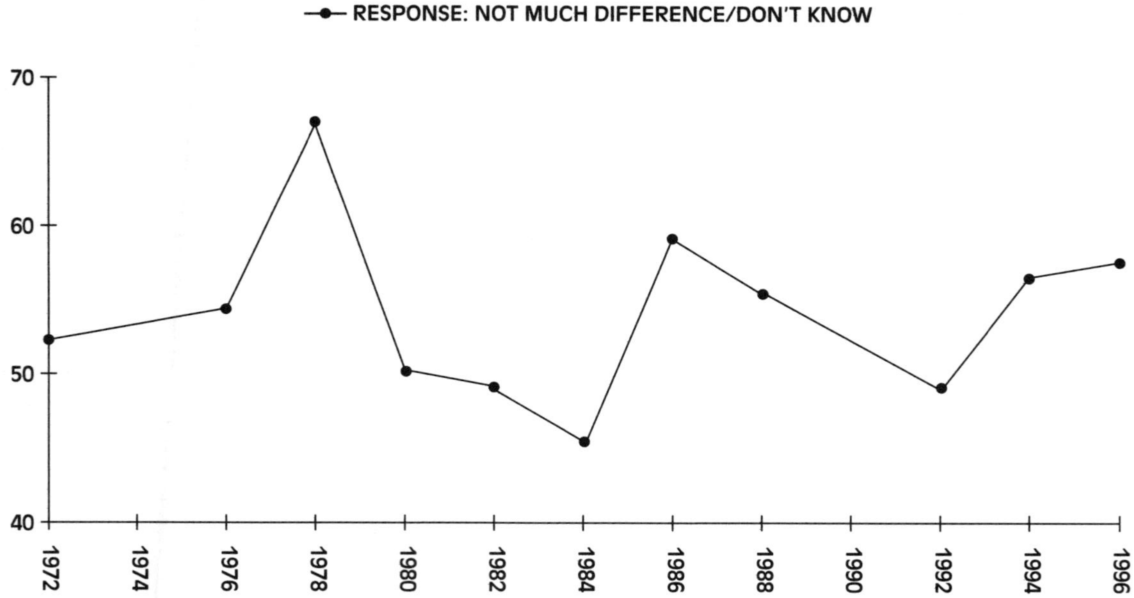

● RESPONSE: NOT MUCH DIFFERENCE/DON'T KNOW

Source: *The National Election Studies* May 13, 1998

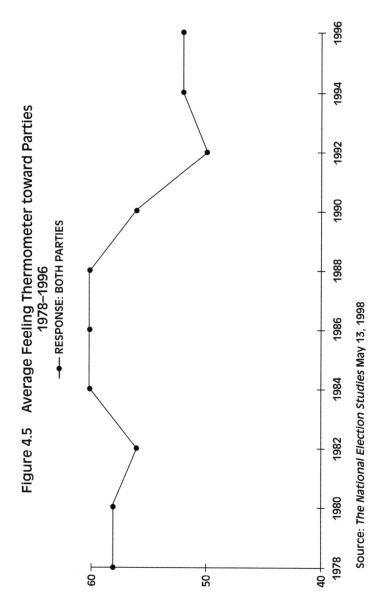

Figure 4.5   Average Feeling Thermometer toward Parties
1978–1996

RESPONSE: BOTH PARTIES

Source: *The National Election Studies* May 13, 1998

to determine if citizens' political cynicism led to their support for Perot, or whether their levels of trust and psychological support for the political system were changed or made politically salient by the Perot candidacy.

The data presented in Figures 4.1, 4.2, and 4.3 make clear that one of the conditions that gives rise to third party challenges was present in the general electorate in the early 1990s: citizens were deeply cynical about the established political order. Empirical research documents that trust in government was related to support for Perot in 1992, that those with greater political distrust were more likely to support Perot than those who felt more positively about the federal government (Abramson et al. 1994; Asher 1995; Atkeson et al. 1996; Gold 1995; Hetherington 1999; Zaller and Hunt 1995).

Previous studies on third party voting were unable to determine to what extent the issue positions or concerns of third party supporters that distinguish them from major party supporters were present prior to the emergence of the third party candidate (for example, see Gold 1995). This is a common problem in the study of voting behavior: the complex and potentially reciprocal nature of the choice process makes determining the direction of causality between issue concerns or positions, partisanship (or, in the case of third party voting, the lack of), and candidate choice problematic. Did an individual cast a vote of support for a candidate because of the congruity between her political concerns and positions and those advocated by a particular candidate? Or did that individual change her political orientation and positions, bringing them into line with the message of the candidate she preferred for reasons other than the political orientation under study? The existing empirical research on attitude persuasion and third party voting suggests that the effect of third party candidates on political cynicism is minimal. Theoretical works on third party voting contend that citizens' cynicism is an important determinant of candidate support (Hetherington 1999; Rosenstone et al. 1996) and empirical research on attitude change demonstrates that salient political attitudes are most resistant to change (Markus and Converse 1979). Utilizing a unique data set and appropriate statistical techniques, I have been able to determine the extent by which Perot supporters' cynicism toward government and the political process moved them to support Perot in 1992 and 1996; and the degree to which their attraction toward Perot shaped their cynicism toward the government and the contemporary political process and its leaders. Moreover, I analyze the effect of 1992 citizen support for Perot on his followers' attitudes toward government and its leaders in 1994, two years following his initial candidacy.

To understand the relationship between political cynicism and support for Ross Perot in 1992 and 1996, a model of third party candidate support has been developed and tested. The dependent variable is dichotomous, scored one if the respondent voted for Perot, zero otherwise. Prior research suggests a number of other determinants of third party support (Abramson 1994; Gold 1995; Rosenstone et al. 1996), and thus measures of age, political independence, race, gender, region, and citizens' overall evaluations of the candidates are included in the model. Let me briefly discuss each of these independent variables. The weaker a citizen's attachment to one of the major political parties the lower the psychological cost for that individual of casting a third party vote. To measure the strength of an individual's attachment to the major political parties, the 7-point ANES summary measure of partisanship is folded, so that the higher an individual's score on this 0–3 scale the weaker her attachment. Additionally, those individuals who perceive no difference between the major political parties in their ability to solve what they consider the nation's most important problem should be more willing to cast a third party vote than those who do perceive a difference. A dichotomous variable is included whereby zero indicates that the respondent believes one of the major parties is more able than the other to solve the problem he deems the nation's most important, and one that he does not. Unfortunately, due to the split-ballot design of the 1996 ANES only half the respondents were asked this question, reducing the cases available for analysis considerably.

Prior analyses of support for the Perot movement indicate that in 1992 Perot drew disproportionately from whites, males, and nonsoutherners (Abramson et al. 1994; Gold 1995). Thus, dummy variables measuring each of these characteristics are included in the model. Younger citizens, who generally have less defined voting propensities due to their limited political experience, typically provide third party candidates with a disproportionate level of support (Rosenstone 1996). Age, coded in years, is also included in the model. Classic models of vote choice demonstrate that citizens' global evaluations of the candidates powerfully influence their decision (Markus and Converse 1979). In these models citizens' global evaluations are measured by taking the differential in the feeling thermometer scores for the two candidates. The model of third party candidate choice, however, includes three candidates, making that procedure impossible. Therefore, a simple dummy variable is created that is scored one if the respondent gave a higher feeling thermometer score to Perot than to Bush and Clinton.

The variables at the center of this analysis are measures of citizens' political cynicism. The 1992 and 1996 ANES contains four measures of citizens' trust in government and two of their external efficacy. All sets of the measures for each concept are added together and then divided by the total number of measures, forming indexes of external efficacy and political trust. The results of a multivariate probit model of third party support are presented in Table 4.1.[3]

The variable measuring political trust is positively signed and statistically significant, indicating that the more negatively a citizen felt toward the current leaders the more likely she was to vote for Ross Perot in 1992 and 1996. The coefficient for external efficacy is correctly signed as well; its t-stat just misses the .05 cutoff (one-tail test) in 1992. In 1996 the coefficient for this variable failed to

Table 4.1. Determinants of Third Party Voting, 1992 and 1996

Independent Variables	1992	1996	
Political Trust	*.16****	*21***	*.12*
	(2.83)	*(2.22)*	*(.896)*
External Efficacy	*.063*	*.05*	*.03*
	(1.60)	*(.693)*	*(.261)*
Age	*-.012****	*-.01****	*-.003*
	(4.66)	*(2.50)*	*(.610)*
Intensity of Partisanship	*.23****	*.30****	*.09*
	(5.07)	*(3.77)*	*(.700)*
Party Differences	*.70****		*.77****
	(3.05)		*(3.04)*
Male	*.28****	*.20*	*.006*
	(3.27)	*(1.40)*	*(.031)*
Nonsoutherner	*.32****	*.06*	*.07*
	(3.19)	*(.395)*	*(.321)*
White	*1.15****	*.49**	*.53*
	(4.63)	*1.70*	*1.26*
Prefer	*.90****	*1.62****	*1.99****
	(10.54)	*(9.61)*	*(8.03)*
N =	*1441*	*1009*	*512*
R²=	*.20*	*.30*	*.36*

Entries are probit coefficients, T-stats are in parentheses.

* signifies $p < .10$ (one-tail test)
** signifies $p < .05$ (one-tail test)
*** signifies $p < .01$ (one-tail test)

reach statistical significance. Before concluding that citizen distrust of government and its leaders led to support for Mr. Perot in 1992 and 1996, an alternative direction of causality needs consideration. Perhaps those who were inclined to support Perot, for whatever reason, adopted the views of their preferred candidate toward the contemporary political process and its leaders. The problem is that both variables may be independent and dependent variables of each other.

A number of differences between determinants of Perot's 1992 and 1996 deserve comment. In 1992 partisanship yielded modestly weaker effects than in 1996, suggesting that the major parties did a better job of holding onto their supporters. Moreover, being male, white, and southern residence produced either no effects or considerably smaller effects on Perot support in 1996 than in 1992. The base of Perot's support, in terms of the electorate's demographic characteristics, was less distinctive in 1996 than in 1992.

To determine whether Perot persuaded his followers to adopt his particular views of the contemporary political process and its leaders I first estimate multivariate models of external efficacy and political trust. The determinants of political trust and external efficacy are less well understood than those of third party candidate support.[4] Nevertheless, regarding political trust, it is known that older citizens tend to be more cynical about politics than their younger counterparts and that those with higher levels of educational attainment are less trusting than those who received more education.[5] Additionally, prior research establishes that trust is shaped by citizens' assessments of the national economy[6] and the frequency with which an individual receives political information from newspapers. Thus, variables measuring assessments of the nation's economy and frequency of newspaper reading are included in the model. Since it is also of concern whether support for Perot increased political cynicism after the effects of these other variables had been controlled, the measure of third party candidate support used in the models is also included. Whether a citizen was a Perot supporter is measured with a simple dichotomous variable (one indicating a vote for Perot, zero a vote for a major party candidate). For external efficacy, only educational attainment and income are known determinants; each has a positive relationship. Unfortunately, the split-format design of the 1996 ANES results in a significant loss of cases, only one-half of the respondents were asked some of the questions, reducing the efficiency of estimating a nonrecursive model. Therefore, analysis is limited to the 1992 data. Separate analyses are conducted for external efficacy and political trust; the results of the analysis are presented in Table 4.2.

As expected, the coefficient for support for Perot is positively signed and statistically significant for both political trust and external efficacy. Thus, at this stage of the analysis it is impossible to determine whether political distrust and low levels of external efficacy led to support for Ross Perot in 1992, or if those who already supported Perot were persuaded to adopt his political views. Unravelling the direction of causality between these variables requires estimation of a simultaneous equation model. To estimate a simultaneous equation model one must locate a set of variables that are related to the relevant independent variable but not to the dependent variables. These variables are then used to create a measure "purged" of the effects of the dependent variable. Only then can it be determined whether support for Perot led to citizens becoming more cynical, or

Table 4.2. Determinants of External Efficacy and Political Trust, 1992

Independent Variables	External Efficacy	Political Trust
Education	-.085***	.01*
	(6.84)	(1.78)
Age		.006***
		(4.41)
Perot Voter	.22***	.21***
	(2.96)	(3.80)
Assessments of National Economy		.10***
		(5.01)
Income	-.01**	
	(2.16)	
Frequency of Newspaper Reading		-.015*
		(1.90)
Constant	4.06***	3.25***
	(26.68)	(18.23)
N =	1450	1441
R^2=	.05	.03

Entries are OLS coefficients, T-stats are in parentheses.

* signifies p < .10 (one-tail test)
** signifies p < .05 (one-tail test)
*** signifies p < .01 (one-tail test)

whether citizens' political skepticism induced them to support Perot in 1992. For external efficacy and political trust, the 1992 panel component of the ANES contains identical measures of each of these concepts. From these clearly exogenous measures, plus the demographic variables, instrument variables for political trust and external efficacy are created.[7] For an instrument variable of third party candidate support, all of the variables used in the model of third party support presented in Table 4.1 are employed. The results of the instrument variable analysis for third party candidate support, political trust, and external efficacy are presented in Tables 4.3 and 4.4.

Table 4.3. Determinants of External Efficacy and Political Trust, 1992, Instrument Variables Analysis

Independent Variables	External Efficacy	Political Trust
Education	-.08***	.01
	(6.35)	(1.02)
Age		.006**
		(4.49)
Perot Voter	.44**	.28*
	(2.17)	(1.95)
Assessments of National Economy		.09***
		(4.49)
Income	-.009*	
	(1.66)	
Frequency of Newspaper Reading		-.02***
		(2.58)
Constant	3.99***	3.39***
	(22.84)	(15.99)
N =	1342	1349
R² =	.04	.03

Entries are OLS coefficients, T-stats are in parentheses.

* signifies p < .10 (one-tail test)
** signifies p < .05 (one-tail test)
*** signifies p < .01 (one-tail test)

The results are very clear. The coefficient for third party support is still statistically significant for the models for political trust and external efficacy, indicating that those who were inclined to vote for Perot in 1992 were persuaded to adopt his political views. The coefficients for political trust and external efficacy, however, are no longer statistically significant in the model for 1992 third party voting, revealing that in both cases citizens' orientations toward the current officeholders, the political process, or government in general had little effect on the likelihood they would cast a vote for Ross Perot in 1992.[8]

Table 4.4. Determinants of Third Party Voting, 1992
Instrument Variables Analysis

Independent Variables	Instrument for Trust	Instrument for External Efficacy
Political Trust	-.0008	.07***
	(0.02)	(2.94)
External Efficacy	.01	-.05
	(1.13)	(1.26)
Age	-.002***	-.002***
	(2.63)	(3.09)
Intensity of Partisanship	.058***	04***
	(3.59)	(2.88)
Party Differences	.018**	.02**
	(2.20)	(2.25)
Male	.06**	.07**
	(2.12)	(2.50)
Nonsoutherner	.09***	.10***
	(2.81)	(2.98)
White	.10*	.09*
	(1.90)	1.76
Prefer	.20***	.21***
	(6.67)	(6.83)
N	666	664
R²=	.14	.13

Entries are OLS coefficients, T-stats are in parentheses.

* signifies p < .10 (one-tail test)
** signifies p < .05 (one-tail test)
*** signifies p < .01 (one-tail test)

Having established that support for Perot shaped citizens attitudes' toward government and contemporary political leaders, I now explore whether having supported Perot in 1992 affected citizens' attitudes toward government in 1994. To do so I construct multivariate models of external efficacy and political trust, using the same set of independent variables employed in the analysis of the 1992 data. The dependent variables are again indexes of external efficacy and political

Table 4.5. Determinants of External Efficacy and Political Trust, 1994

Independent Variables	External Efficacy	Political Trust
Education	-.18***	.015
	(9.64)	(.97)
Age		-.0003
		(.23)
Perot Voter	.25***	.23***
	(3.34)	(3.81)
Assessments of National Economy		.13***
		(4.97)
Income	.01**	
	(2.31)	
Frequency of Newspaper Reading		.002**
		(2.24)
Constant	3.97***	3.51***
	(32.52)	(21.07)
N =	1213	1168
R²=	.11	.03

Entries are OLS coefficients, T-stats are in parentheses.

* signifies p < .10 (one-tail test)
** signifies p < .05 (one-tail test)
*** signifies p < .01 (one-tail test)

trust developed from questions identical to those used in the 1992 ANES. These results are presented in Table 4.5. For both political trust and external efficacy, citizens' orientations in 1994 were still shaped by whether they had voted for Mr. Perot in the 1992 presidential election.

The picture that emerges is of a group of citizens who were generally similar to other voters in 1990 and 1991 in terms of their discontent with the contemporary political process and its leaders, but who became notably more cynical during the 1992 election as a result of the Perot candidacy; support for Perot resulted in lower levels of political trust and external efficacy. The Perot candidacy served to polarize the electorate in terms of their assessments of the responsiveness and competence of government and its elected leaders. Not only did the Perot candidacy serve to differentiate his supporters from those who voted for a major party candidate in 1992, but also these distinctions endured beyond that particular election. In 1994, those who had supported Perot in the 1992 presidential contest still retained the political cynicism which had been shaped by the 1992 campaign.

Partisan Orientations

Due to its powerful effects on the voting decision, no set of political predisposition is of more interest to scholars of elections than those that measure partisan orientations and general affect for the major political parties. In the aftermath of a third party movement the major parties typically attempt to position themselves to absorb the third party supporters, thereby expanding their electoral coalition. Following the 1992 election, both the Democrats and Republicans attempted to attract Perot supporters. President Clinton's first budget made signficant reductions in the deficit, and Clinton instituted a new set of standards for White House lobbying. Meanwhile, the Republicans tried to one-up the Democratic president by calling for a balanced budget amendment and significant reductions in the size and scope of government. The Contract with America, the name itself containing not-too-subtle populist overtones, included several provisions specifically aimed at attracting Perot voters to the Republican Party. Indeed, much of the Republican Party's 1994 campaign rhetoric parroted Perot's: they complained about the mess in Washington and the need to return government to the people. As the out-party, the GOP was in an excellent position to criticize the party in control of government. Due to their antigovernment stance, the Republican party seemd like natural inheritors of the Perot supporters. Moreover, some characteristics of the Perot supporters themselves suggested that, all other things equal, they would be likely to find the GOP a more hospitable home than the Democratic Party. As the analysis of third party support makes clear, Perot supporters were generally white and male, two characteristics that have predisposed citizens to identify with the Republican Party in recent years.

The 1990, 1991, 1992, 1993, 1994, and 1996 ANES surveys contain several measures of citizens' feeling and orientations toward the major political parties: respondents' feeling thermometer scores toward the Democrats and Republicans and (for 1990, 1994, and 1996) political parties in general, the ANES seven-point summary measure of partisan identification, and vote choice for House and Senate seats for 1990, 1992, 1994, and 1996. To provide a richer portrait of Perot supporters their attraction to Perot himself— as measured on the feeling thermometers— for 1992, 1993, 1994, and 1996 are also examined. The mean scores for Perot

Table 4.6. Partisan Orientations of Perot Voters

	1990	1991	1992	1993	1994	1996
Partisan	*3.08*	*3.11*	*3.18*	*3.19*	*3.37*	*3.20*
Identification	*(172)*	*(153)*	*(301)*	*(91)*	*(238)*	*(205)*
Republican Party	*56.41*	*57.70*	*50.91*	*57.25*	*57.28*	*53.93*
Feeling Thermometer	*(165)*	*(151)*	*(298)*	*(91)*	*(239)*	*(204)*
Democratic Party	*56.70*	*58.33*	*52.91*	*50.95*	*48.01*	*52.18*
Feeling Thermometer	*(165)*	*(150)*	*(298)*	*(91)*	*(239)*	*(204)*
Political Parties In	*49.44*	–	–		*44.35*	*46.18*
General Feeling	*(162)*				*(239)*	*(203)*
Thermometer						
Perot Feeling	–	–	*75.69*	*67.04*	*63.56*	*55.58*
Thermometer			*(300)*	*(91)*	*(239)*	*(204)*
% House Vote	*57%*	–	–		*37.6%*	*38.03*
Democratic	*(93)*				*(141)*	*(142)*
% Senate Vote	*55.4%*	–	–		*32.3%*	*35.53*
Democratic	*(56)*				*(124)*	*(76)*

voters for each measure, except vote choice, are calculated; for vote choice the percent voting for the Democratic candidates are presented. These data are presented in Table 4.6.

In 1990, 1991, and 1992 Perot supporters exhibited neutrality toward the major political parties. For example, the mean score for the Perot voters on the ANES summary party identification measure (the variable ranges from 0 to 6, 3 is the midpoint) in 1990 is 3.08, 3.18 in 1992. The mean score on the feeling thermometer for the Democratic Party in 1990 is 56.7, 56.4 for the Republican Party. As expected, Perot supporters do not express strong support for political parties in general; their mean score on the feeling thermometer for political parties is 49.44. Only for vote choice in 1990 is there evidence suggesting an advantage for one of the political parties, and here the advantage is fairly small. Fifty-seven percent of Perot supporters had voted for a Democratic House candidate in 1990; 55 percent had supported a Democratic Senate candidate. However, neither proportion is statistically significant from 50 percent at the .10 level. Thus, the overall impression formed of the partisan inclinations of the Perot supporters in 1990, 1991, and 1992 is one of partisan independence.

In 1993, one year after the Perot candidacy, evidence of movement by Perot supporters toward the Republican Party emerges. The ANES seven-point party identification scale still indicates political independence for the Perot supporters, but the feeling thermometers for the political parties reveal signs of strength for the GOP. The mean score for the Republican Party among Perot supporters is 57.25; while that expressed for the Democratic Party is 50.95. Perot himself is less esteemed in the eyes of those who cast a vote for him in 1992. In 1992, his supporters give him a mean score of 75.7 on the ANES feeling thermometer, by 1993 the score has dropped to 67.0.

In 1994 Perot voters moved even closer to the GOP. Their mean score on the ANES seven-point partisan identification measure is 3.37, statistically distinct from the 1992 score at the .01 level. Feeling thermometer scores also indicate a preference for the Republican Party. The mean feeling thermometer score of Perot supporters for the Democratic Party has fallen to 46.93; the score for the Republican Party stands at 57.52. Perot supporters affect for their 1992 presidential candidate continues to decline; in 1994 it stands at 63.5. Even though Perot supporters as a group have become more partisan, their support for political parties has not become more positive; in fact, it has become more negative. The mean feeling thermometer score for political parties in 1994 is 41.53, down from its 1990 value of 49.44.

Perot voters who participated in the 1994 congressional elections overwhelmingly cast their votes for Republican House and Senate candidates. The proportions are statistically distinguishable from 50 percent at the .05 level, and approximate those reported in exit polls that relied upon respondents' recall of their 1994 vote.[9]

By the 1996 presidential election, when Perot attempted to continue and expand the movement begun in 1992, those who had supported him during his initial run for office continued to move toward the Republican Party. Moreover, the amount of esteem directed toward Perot himself by his 1992 supporters diminished considerably by 1996. Only 25 percent of those who voted for Perot in 1992 cast a ballot for him again in 1996. A plurality—30 percent—of the 1992 Perot supporters went to the Republican nominee, Bob Dole. Approximately 24 percent of the 1992 Perot vote went to President Bill Clinton, while the balance of the Perot voters—22 percent—chose to sit out the 1996 contest.

Perot supporters' admiration for their candidate of choice in 1992 continued to decline, dropping to 55 on the 1996 Perot feeling thermometer—shedding additional light on why his vote share dropped from 19 percent in 1992 to approximately 9 percent in 1996. Additionally, as the data for 1996 presidential candidate choice suggest, 1992 Perot voters had moved closer to the GOP, albeit the ties weakened somewhat from 1994. The mean score for 1992 Perot voters on the ANES 7-point party identification summary measure stood at 3.20. Perot supporters' attraction to the Republican Party, as measured by the feeling thermometer, dropped to 54, only slightly above the score they gave the Democratic Party (52.18). When it came to vote choice in congressional elections, however, the gains registered by the Republican Party in 1994 were still in place in 1996. Approximately 62 percent of the 1992 Perot voters voted for a Republican House candidate, 64 percent for a Republican Senate candidate.

Two points can be made regarding the evolution of partisan inclinations of 1992 Perot voters through 1996. First, the Republican Party was more successful than their Democratic counterparts in enlisting the Perot supporters into their ranks. Second, the level of affection of 1992 Perot voters for Perot himself diminished considerably by 1996; the movement was unable to hold onto those who had supported it at its origin.

Historically, the most serious threat posed to third parties has been the ability of the major parties to absorb the third party's supporters by appropriating its issue positions or concerns. Like a large conglomerate eyeing a share of the market where a small firm has carved out a niche, the major parties possess huge resources that make it difficult for third parties to maintain a hold on the electorate for a lengthy period of time. The tremendous resources of the major parties—ballot access laws, media attention, money, patronage, the proportional representation system, grass-roots organizations—enable them to assimilate the third party supporters. From 1992 through 1996 Perot lost many of his adherents; the primary beneficiary of these desertions was the Republican Party.

Conclusion

One of the most important roles performed by political parties in a democratic polity is mobilization and mentoring. By serving as a mentor, political parties help citizens understand the political process, identify their interests, and formulate their preferences. A large body of research, beginning with *The American Voter* (Campbell et al. 1960), documents that citizens are likely to adopt the political positions of the political party with which they identify. Recent scholarship expands on this notion, positing that partisanship functions as a heuristic device citizens employ to understand the political process (Hamill et al. 1985). The empirical analyses presented here enhance our view of political parties as mentors in the United States by investigating the effect of third party candidacies on citizens' trust in government and external political efficacy. In 1992, third party candidate Ross Perot portrayed the contemporary America political system as inefficient, undemocratic, and corrupt; his followers were persuaded to accept this view as their own.

Prior research on third party movements and those that focused on the Perot candidacy in particular link third party support with citizens' discontent with the political system and its leaders. Generally, this research argues that citizens' cynicism about politics leads them to support the third party candidate, who usually distinguishes himself by his relentless attacks on the political process. The evidence, however, at least for H. Ross Perot's 1992 candidacy, suggests that those who supported Perot were persuaded to adopt his cynical view of American politics. Lacking the moorings provided by strong attachments to the major political parties and lengthy experience with the political system, these citizens' were a group especially vulnerable to Perot's message.

Political cynicism and the emergence of the Perot candidacy display a complex relationship. Although high levels of societal political cynicism provided for the emergence of the Perot movement, he did not draw support disproportionately from those most disgruntled with the American political system. Although I argue that Perot's rhetoric intensified citizens' political cynicism, rather than that their cynicism induced them to support Perot, it is worth noting that I do not believe that political cynicism was unrelated to the emergence of the Perot movement. During a period of good will toward the government and its leaders a third party candidate's message decrying political incompetence and corruption is likely to fall on deaf ears. The defining characteristic of Perot supporters that led them to embrace Perot was their partisan independence, but their political cynicism meant that Perot's message was one they would not easily dismiss. Having become entangled in the Perot movement these citizens found their political cynicism increased.

Third party efforts are likely to come a relatively frequent occurrence in contemporary American politics. Two characteristics of the American public—a weak attachment to the political parties and high levels of cynicism toward the government and its leaders—indicate that a set of conditions are in place in which third party challenges are likely to continue. Given the political predispositions of the American electorate in the 1990s it is expected that if the Reform Party and Perot disappear from the contemporary American political scene, another third party will emerge to fill the vacuum. Thus, the Perot supporters themselves may represent an elusive target for the major parties. Although in 1994 the GOP was more successful at drawing the support of the Perot voters, holding onto that support over time may prove a difficult task. In the contemporary period most elections remain candidate centered rather than party centered contests, making it difficult for either party to entice enduring commitments from those who have supported a third party candidate.

Notes

1. For examples of scholarly work on the mentoring functions of political parties see Campbell et al. 1960 and Jacoby 1991.

2. For an account of the 1994 midterm elections and the Contract with America see Wilcox 1995.

3. The following survey items were used to measure external efficacy; each was measured on a five-point scale: 1) People like me don't have any say about what the government does. 2) Public officials don't care much what people like me think. A high score indicates high cynicism. Trust in government was measured with the following survey questions: 1) How much of the time do you think you can trust the government in Washington to do what is right—just about always, most of the time, or only some of the time? 1 = just about always, 3 = most of the time, 5 = some of the time. 2) Would you say that the government is pretty much run by a few big interests looking out for themselves or that it is run for the benefit of all the people? 1 = for the benefit of all, 5 = few big interests. 3) Do you think the people in government waste a lot of the money we pay in taxes, waste some of it, or don't waste very much of it? 1 = not very much, 3 = some, 5 = a lot. 4) Do you think quite a few of the people running government are crooked, not very many are, or do you think hardly any of them are crooked? 1 = hardly any, 3 = not many, 5 = quite a few. High scores indicate high political distrust.

4. For a review of the determinants of political trust see Citrin and Green, 1986.

5. Age is coded in years, education on a 17-point scale where each value indicates an additional year of schooling.

6. Assessments of national economic conditions were coded on a five-point scale: a high score indicate more negative assessments. Frequency of newspaper readership is coded on a seven-point scale, each value indicating the number of days the respondent regularly reads a paper.

7. For a discussion of instrument variable analysis see Hanushek and Jackson (1977).

8. 1992 Perot voters were identified through a recall question.

9. See the *New York Times,* November 5, 1994, and November 10, 1994.

References

Abramson, Paul R., John H. Aldrich, Phil Paolino, and David W. Rohde. 1994. "The Problem of Third-Party and Independent Candidates in the American Political System: Wallace, Anderson, and Perot in Comparative Perspective." Paper delivered at the 1994 Annual Meeting of the American Political Science Association, New York.

Asher, Herbert. 1995. "The Perot Campaign." In Herbert W. Weisberg, ed., *Democracy's Feast: Elections in America.* Chatham, N.J.: Chatham Press.

Atkeson, Lonna R., James A. McCann, Ronald B. Rapoport, and Walter J. Stone. 1996. "Citizens for Perot: Assessing Patterns of Alienation and Activism." In Stephen C. Craig, ed., *Broken Contract.* Boulder: Westview Press.

Campbell, Angus, Philip E. Converse, Warren E. Miller, and Donald E Stokes. 1960. *The American Voter.* New York: Wiley Press.

Citrin, Jack, and Donald P. Green. 1986. "Presidential Leadership and the Resurgence of Congress," *British Journal of Political Science* 16: 431–453.

Converse, Philip E., and Gregory B. Markus. 1979. "Plus ca Change….' : The New CPS Election Study Panel," *American Political Science Review* 73: 2–49.

Craig, Stephen. 1996. *Broken Contract? Changing Relationships Between Americans and Their Government.* Boulder: Westview Press.

Gold, Howard J. 1995. "Third Party Voting in Presidential Elections: A Study of Perot, Anderson, and Wallace," *Political Research Quarterly* 48: 751–773.

Hetherington, Marc J. 1999. "The Effect of Political Trust on the Presidential Vote, 1968–96." *American Political Science Review* 93: 311–326.

Hamill, Ruth, Milton Lodge, and Frederick Blake. 1985. "The Breadth, Depth, and Utility of Class, Partisan, and Ideological Schemata," *American Journal of Political Science* 29: 850–70.

Hanushek, Eric A., and John E. Jackson. 1977. *Statistical Methods for the Social Scientists.* New York: Academic Press.

Jacoby, William G. 1991. "The Impact of Party Identification on Issue Attitudes," *American Journal of Political Science* 32: 643–661.

Markus, Gregory B., and Philip E. Converse. 1979. "A Dynamic Simultaneous Equation Model of Electoral Choice," *American Political Science Review* 73: 1055–1070.

Rosenstone, Steven J., Roy L. Behr, and Edward H. Lazarus. 1996. *Third Parties in America: Citizen Response to Third Party Failure.* Princeton: Princeton University Press.

Wattenberg, Martin P. 1990. *The Decline of American Political Parties, 1952–1992.* Cambridge: Harvard University Press.

———. 1991. *The Rise of Candidate-Centered Politics.* Cambridge: Harvard University Press.

Wilcox, Clyde. 1995. *The Latest American Revolution? The 1994 Elections and Their Implications for Governance.* New York: St. Martins Press.

Zaller, John, and Mark Hunt. 1995. "The Rise and Fall of Candidate Perot: The Outsider versus the Political System—Party II," *Political Communication* 12: 97–123.

5

The Politics of a
Bittersweet Economy

Economic Restructuring, Economic Stories, and Ross Perot in the Elections of 1992 and 1996

Solon Simmons and James Simmons

> It is because we are in the grip of a failed economic theory. The decision you are about to make better be about what kind of economic theory do you want. Not just people saying I want to fix it. What are we going to do?
> —Bill Clinton (10/15/92)

> The one thing I have done is lay [the deficit reduction plan] squarely on the table in front of the American people. . . . At least you'll understand it. I think that is fundamental in our country that you know what you're getting into.
> —Ross Perot (10/19/92)

Introduction

The presidential election of 1992 is remembered for at least two of its prominent features. The first was its extraordinary focus on the state of the economy. The second was the surprising role played in it by the nonpartisan businessman Ross Perot. It is less than a surprise that these features of that campaign are remembered together. The reason for this is straightforward. Ross Perot was a major force behind the economic focus in 1992, and the limited but impressive success he enjoyed was largely a result of that focus. Moreover, the continued presence and influence of Perot and the Reform Party is a product of that campaign and discursive forces set in motion in that period.

1992 was the year of the slogan, "It's the economy stupid!" The slogan was the product of the Clinton "war room," but could as easily have sprung from Perot's imagination. The election of 1992 was a battle of interpretations of the economic system in a way that few elections are and no election since then has been. What should be remembered about this election is not that it was characterized by an excessively economic focus, but that it acted as a forum for rival stories about how the economy worked and what should be done to fix it.

Although the election is long past, the fundamental conditions that generated its energy are largely unchanged. This claim may seem strange given that 1999 would be characterized by most as a season of high praise for the American economy. Unemployment and inflation rates are low, corporate profits and prospects continued growth are generally considered to be good. The American economy has seldom been so lauded by so many diverse figures around the world. It would have been difficult to have found anyone willing to employ this description in 1991 and 1992. Then, the country was coming out of a recession that had seriously disrupted the labor market with high unemployment and worker displacements. Inflation was moderate and a lack of collective optimism was reflected in a bear market that had continued in the wake of the 1987 crash. Nevertheless, the forces that propelled Bill Clinton into office and Ross Perot into the history books are common to both periods.

The American economy is certainly prospering in the aggregate today, but it is arguable whether the well-being of a common American worker has changed much from 1992. It is now a well-established fact that the median wage of an individual worker in this country declined steadily from about 1973 to the early 1990s and has climbed only slightly since that time (Mishel, Bernstein, and Scmitt 1999). The fact that the lowest wages have risen little in the face of strong growth in the economy as a whole suggests that material inequality is on the rise. The fact is corroborated by the standard indices as well as novel methods (Morris, Bernhardt, and Handcock 1994).

Such an economy could be characterized as bittersweet. To the median wage earner, the economy is strong on the whole. Inflation and unemployment are both low, but as a concrete matter measured in terms of wages, job security, and employment benefits (Olsen 1995; Rose 1997), things are relatively disappointing. It seems fair to say that the structure of the economy is changing in such a way to distribute rewards upward to those with the most desirable assets, skills, and connections and away from reliable, common people (Dresser, Mangum, and Rogers 1998; Frank and Cook 1996; Mishel, Bernstein, and Scmitt 1999). The causes of economic restructuring are complicated, involving, among other things, spatial, financial, political, and functional dimensions (Sassen 1990), but the reality of major change is difficult to question.

For those interested in elections and political phenomena, it is interesting to speculate about what impact economic restructuring might have on the political system. One perspective, dominant in studies of economic voting, might not take this kind of long-term development very seriously. The literature devoted to investigating the relationship between the state of the economy and political outcomes is extensive and varied and many questions remain unanswered (for reviews see Lewis-Beck 1988; Monroe 1978). It is not certain if voters behave rationally with respect to their interests or if they use information efficiently (Lewis-Beck 1988), or if politicians successfully manipulate policy to their advantage. However, it is clear that voters are not as narrowly self-interested as some early studies that detailed a phenomenon known as "pocketbook voting" indicated (Downs 1957; Kramer 1971). Voters seem to be more responsive to the general state of the economy than they are to changes in their own personal fortunes, which has been called "sociotropic voting" (Kinder and Kiewiet 1979; Lewis-Beck 1988).

It is also apparent that when voters choose to vote in their own interest they seem not to clearly understand how to go about it. Anthony Downs and V. O. Key (Downs 1957; Key 1966) suggest that, given that campaign information is costly in terms of time and energy, voters might not attempt to come to a full understanding of the political options available to them. Instead, they will either vote out an elected official who has done poorly or support one who has done well in the recent past. Recent debates on prospective voting (MacKuen, Erickson, and Stimson 1992) suggest a more complicated process in which voters use media cues to resolve their uncertainty about the prospective actions of individual candidates. Little conclusive evidence exists here (Clarke and Stewart 1995; Lewis-Beck 1988).

It seems that the link between the voter's actual financial experiences and his or her candidate choice remains an open question. What has received less attention than it might, is the impact of long-term trends in the distribution of rewards across groups and the way that these trends are interpreted by the members of those groups. The following quote from Yankelovich suggests why we might be interested in paying attention to the character of the public mood relative to economic downturns.

> Over the past year the public's level of anxiety has been rising steadily. What worries Americans is that the economy is growing stagnant or declining (75%), that Japan is ahead of the United States in terms of the ability to compete (77%) and that as a consequence the American standard of living is in grave danger. The main source of voters' anxiety is not the recession as such, but their interpretation of its meaning. There is a big difference between the public's reaction to this

recession and the last one. The public experienced the recession of 1981–1982 as if it were a giant traffic jam: once it was over the nation could resume normal speed. People are not reacting to the present recession in the same way, as if it were part of the normal business cycle. Even though they cannot quite put their finger on it, they fear that something is fundamentally wrong with the U.S. economy. They look to their leaders to pinpoint what is wrong and what to do about it. When their leaders fail to respond well, the anxiety deepens and spreads. (Yankelovich 1992, p. 2)

His emphasis on the meaning of the recession and the concern that the competitive advantage of the U.S. economy had declined relative to major competitors implies a longer-term interpretive calculus among his respondents. The conventional wisdom in economic voting studies suggests that voters tend to respond to short-term economic signals, which are taken to mean similar things to similar rational actors. A long wave of redistribution would not be expected to have a measurable influence beyond that which had already manifested in previous elections.

There is little reason to doubt that voters might make tactical/short-term decisions, that immediate concerns might explain a significant portion of the variance election outcomes. However, it seems reasonable to suppose that voters might well behave in strategic/long-term ways as well. A strategic focus might consider wider architectures of economic and political institutions that take long periods of time and significant political, financial, and ideological momentum to change. If voters are rational enough to think about institutional change in this way, the portion of the electorate whose well-being has persistently declined over the past thirty years should be behaving in ways left heretofore invisible by the dominant theories of the economic voting literature.

Given the fact that this group is comprised of less-educated voters of moderate income, we might expect that their strategic response would be both less organized and less expertly targeted than that of more affluent actors. It might also be fair to expect that there would be a great deal of confusion over what could be done to reverse the established trend. Under these conditions, there might be erratic movements one way and then another as voters energetically try to generate momentum in any direction until something sticks, much like geese flying around a pond during migration season. This description fits the political context of the 1990s very well, which is best characterized as volatile (Teixeira and Rogers 1996).

Examples of such volatile behavior are not hard to find. One needs only look at Perot's strong showing in 1992, the right turn to a Republican congress in 1994, the strong, class-based movement of Pat Buchanan in 1996 (Kohut 1996), the carnevalesque elevation of Jesse Ventura in 1998, or the current scramble for the endorsement of the Reform Party by figures such as Donald Trump. Clearly, something new is happening in American politics, or perhaps it is instead something cyclical that happens in American politics whenever innovation and entrepreneurial activity encourage new patterns of reward to emerge. Perhaps, in such periods, economic inequality becomes a constant problem for American political culture that can only be solved when someone tells the right story at the right time to the right people.

Bearing in mind the coincidence of volatile voting behavior, long-term restructuring of economic rewards, and Yankelovich's insight into the meaning of the 1990–1991 recession, it is possible to develop a perspective on how voters make sense of their own economic prospects. This will be the first step toward an understanding of how they go about deciding on policy preferences and the candidates who promote them on the basis of the economy. The perspective developed here focuses on the mediating role of economic stories that provide voters with a plausible link between the means proposed and the ends desired. Given that a great majority of the population is poorly educated on economic matters (Walstad 1994), when it comes to great and complicated decisions such as electing a president to reverse economic inequality, average people must either rely on some expert interpretation (Giddens 1991; Kinder and Mebane 1983; Roemer 1994) or make decisions blindly.

The stories that candidates tell become an extremely important feature of their campaign. Therefore, to understand how economic conditions affect election outcomes, we must also examine the particular spin a candidate introduces. Stated in a more elevated way, the theoretical orientation of the candidate to free markets, collective bargaining, low interest rates, trade agreements, and a host of other possible areas of concern is potentially of central importance to the voting decision.

To understand the Perot phenomenon and the current electoral volatility, we must first examine what stories Perot told in 1992 and how these helped him to capture nearly 20 percent of the vote in that year, and, second, determine whether these themes and emphases continued to explain support for him in the 1996 election. In the following chapter we propose to test these possibilities empirically using exit poll data from both years.

Perot's Economic Stories

As stated above, if the themes developed by a candidate can be specified, it should be possible to test for their effectiveness by assessing how people who accepted their importance voted. If support is stronger among voters who accept the candidates' themes than among those who do not, it is reasonable to believe that the story was influential. In this section we draw on campaign sources, the televised debates, and Perot's own publications to develop a picture of the economic themes particular to Perot in 1992.

Perot's economic message can be divided into three major themes. For purposes of analysis we have called these Fiscal Conservatism, Market Reformism, and jobs-based Economic Nationalism, referring to his discussions of the deficit, bureaucratic reform, and trade policies respectively. Nearly any public comment made by Perot in the 1992 season contained at least two and usually all three of these elements.

Among Perot's campaign stories, none was more successful than the budget deficit alarm. According to Stanley Greenberg, "The federal deficit is a powerful symbol of the mess in Washington and has a great deal of meaning to Perot Voters. They use the deficit to talk about a broad range of things that are wrong in the country." After even a casual analysis of the 1992 campaign, this is hardly a surprise. The budget issue was the primary focus of Perot's campaign, claiming more air time and witty formulations than any other topic. Moreover, more than any other issue, it was the basis of his success. At one point in the second televised presidential debate a woman from the audience asked the candidates to describe how the deficit had affected them personally. In order for George Bush to make sense of what she meant he needed a clarification from the moderator: "I think she means how has the recession affected you personally." The deficit had become the symbol of all of the economic problems facing the country.

Why the deficit symbol was so powerful is not immediately clear. It may be that it was a latent problem that had been around and in the press for many years but had never been articulated as a barrier to future economic prosperity. Deficit spending had been a staple of Washington politics since the Vietnam era. Perot's approach attached a commonsense and moral tone to what had before been seen to be a technical budgeting issue. By drawing parallels between the government budget and personal budgets, Perot was able to incite the public to moral indignation in a way that others had failed to do previously. The quotes in the following section can all be found in Perot's *Not for Sale at Any Price* (Perot 1992).

> We've allowed ourselves to be lulled into thinking that the bill would never come due. We've been led to believe we could keep on borrowing our children's money to finance a lifestyle we haven't earned and can't afford. It can't go on. (p. 13)

The metaphor may have resonated for a variety of reasons. Consumer debt, driven by the expanded use of credit cards, had been on the rise while real income was declining. Like today, many people were financing a lifestyle they could not afford, but the phenomenon was less salient then. The issue had also been covered by the media for several years. Reagan's rampant deficit spending had long drawn fire from congressional Democrats and presidential contenders such as Walter

Mondale. Perhaps most importantly, the debt was really at a historically extreme height and most people were aware of this fact. Whatever the reasons for its success, the deficit issue was a crucial piece of the 1992 campaign agenda. To some extent it is the key public economic issue to this day. On the basis of the strength of Perot's message in this area, we would have expected voters to be more likely to support Perot if they believed that the deficit was the greatest problem facing the country and that it should have been a national priority to reduce it.

Perot was not only a fiscal conservative, he was also an organizational reformer. Nearly as characteristic of Perot's overall message was the idea that business in Washington was corrupt and mired in bureaucratic gridlock. He became famous for his opinion that Washington was a "bad system filled with good people." Borrowing ideas from his extensive business experience, he developed a coherent story that described how government had become bloated and inefficient. He argued that the incentives that were in place had reduced accountability among office holders and that reform would require making government run more like a business.

> The United States is the largest and most complex business enterprise in the history of mankind. Elected officials like to say that government can't be run like a business. I can see why. In business, people are held accountable. In Washington nobody is. (p. 11)

Not only was government really a big business in disguise, it was too big a business and was attempting to do things that it should not do. His argument, which was in some ways already current at the time, was, "[W]e were led to believe government could solve our problems. It couldn't and it made some problems worse." Solutions should mirror those of a business restructuring, involving cost cutting and redirection of activities and organizational innovations:

> Drastically cut the White House and executive staff. . . . What do all these people do? From my experience, their main mission is to insulate executive officers and members of Congress from you, the owners. (p. 23)

How this story might play out empirically is not as obvious as the deficit story. Clearly, there is a foundational American perspective expressed here that cannot be attributed directly to Perot's agency. Americans like to think of markets as free and government as small and unobtrusive. To get some purchase on the role of this type of story in the voting decision, we find it useful to take advantage of a distinction common in studies of industrial organization, Oliver Williamson's distinction between market and hierarchical governance of economic functions (Williamson 1985). Although the distinction is intended for application in the private sector, it forms a nice basis, at this level of abstraction, on which to group opinions about the appropriate role of government intervention. We would then expect voters who favored management by the market to be more supportive of

Perot than those who favored hierarchical management. Moreover, given the centrality of this divide in forming an idea of American politics as noncommunist and free, it might be reasonable to suspect that an affective or moral orientation might accentuate the impact of the perspective.

Perhaps less central to Perot's message at the time of the election was the theme that wrongheaded and corrupt international trade agreements were costing American jobs and crippling the economy. This story was immortalized with Perot's "great sucking sound" one-liner in the October 15 presidential debate that described what would happen to American jobs under existing trade agreements. Like the other stories, this one was emotionally charged and spoke to patriotism and loyalty as American virtues. He argued that American trade negotiators were disloyal and American corporations were not committed to American jobs:

> We've had American trade negotiators quit on Friday and show up on Monday as consultants for the country they were negotiating with. What has happened to common decency, ethics, and patriotism among the people who are supposed to lead our country?

His position was not straightforward protectionism but warned about the threat to American jobs that the trade agreements represented:

> In Mexico, workers are paid $1/hour. There are no environmental and pollution controls, little or no health care. . . . And if there are no restrictions to shipping the products north, there's no way that a comparable factory making comparable products, paying American standard of living wages can compete.

Perot seemed to have a special relationship to this issue because among the candidates, he was the only one who had direct experience with the temptation to manufacture outside of the United States but had had the opportunity to resist it for moral reasons:

> I could make so much money [by manufacturing outside the United States] in the next five years it would be obscene. You know why I won't do it? It would cost American jobs.

Given that this theme was developed later than the other two and with less consistency, we would expect that it would be less strongly associated with a vote for Perot relative to the other candidates, but nevertheless associated.

A direct concern for the loss of American jobs is perhaps also associated with this position on foreign trade. The recession of 1990–1991 was particularly disruptive of the job structure in the United States along gender lines (Goodman 1994). Jobs were an issue of concern for Perot's target audience, and attention to trade issues might be one way to gauge this. We would expect that independent of trade issues, a concern for jobs and the economy[1] can be understood as part of Perot's story and Perot's support in the 1990s.

Data and Methods

For the empirical portion of this chapter, we explore the relationships between vote choice and the economic themes that characterized Perot's message. For this purpose we employed the general election exit poll data collected by the Voter Research and Surveys (VRS) consortium in 1992 (VRS 1992) and the 1996 equivalent, the Voter News Service (VNS) (VNS 1996). These data have been used extensively in voting studies and are particularly useful for our purposes because there are items that measure the respondents' position on the economic themes. For both elections we examine the direct impact of economic influences and narrative interpretations on vote choice while controlling for standard demographic, organizational, and ideological influences.

Independent Variables

In order to structure our examination of the relationships of interest, we have made use of a four-category typology that groups variables into demographic, political, economic, and narrative influences. For both 1992 and 1996 we have included the following demographic controls: sex, race, educational attainment, and age.[2] Because there is widespread belief and some scientific evidence (Alvarez and Nagler 1995) that Perot was specially appealing to white men, we have included measures on sex and race as dummy variables labelled male and white respectively. This formulation allows for easy interpretation. Educational attainment is divided into three categories: less than college degree, college degree, and postgraduate degree. These break points follow the major divisions on returns to human capital (Mishel, Bernstein, and Scmitt 1999). We have coded the age variable into five categories.[3] In all of the following models, we contrast the following age categories to the age bracket 30–39 years old: 18–29, 40–49, 50–64, and 65 and older.

Political influences were captured in three dummy variables, which we call Democrat, Republican, and Moderate. The variables are largely self-explanatory. The Democrat and Republican variables allow for contrasts between voters who classified themselves as Democratic or Republican party members versus those who classified themselves independents. Respondents were coded Moderate if they chose this response in a choice among liberal, conservative, and moderate options.

The choice of economic influences was a little more complicated. As stated above, there is a large and varied literature developed around economic voting studies. Because of the structure of the VRS and VNS data sets, we were not able to include the standard pocketbook and sociotropic measures in all of the models (Mitofsky and Edelman 1995). These questions were not asked of all respondents.

Therefore, we have included these measures when possible but have substituted another measure when these were absent. This item measures the respondent's long-term perspective on the direction of the economy. Respondents were asked if they believed the economy was in a temporary recession or in a serious, long-term decline. For the purposes of this study this is particularly useful given that we are concerned with the long-term pattern of the redistribution of economic rewards. This question was available only in 1992.

The narrative influences were divided along the lines of the economic themes of the 1992 presidential election. These included measures of the importance of the deficit as a national issue, market versus hierarchy philosophy, and the impact of trade on jobs. In addition, a measure of the importance of jobs as a national issue was included. Similar measures of economic narratives were included for comparison for the 1996 election. Although we had thought to control for the influence of positions on welfare and social security, the explicit goal of this survey was to test for the enduring influence of Perot's more prominent 1992 intervention into the popular discourse. Because the trade issue had already largely been decided at this point, no question was asked in 1996.

In order to capture the moral dimesion of Perot's economic stories, we have employed a distinction between instrumental/strategic and normative/legitimation orientations to the economy. This is important because, if the rhetoric employed bears any relation to the character of the opinions held by the voters, they are clearly not acting solely on purely strategic grounds in their vote decisions. The first type of orientation is strictly instrumental and relies on the respondents' beliefs about the factual basis of the impact of policies. So, for example, respondents who truly believe that a smaller deficit is likely to improve their material opportunities are reacting along this dimension. The second category allows for some purchase on the public's moral or emotional relationship to unjust or illegitimate policies.

The normative/legitimation orientation to the economic or legal system is often left out of accounts of economic voting but has a sound theoretical basis in diverse litcratures (Habermas 1998; Thompson 1971). In thinking about how things ought to be run, individuals have a concern both for the factual effectiveness of a plan in obtaining an objective and the normative validity of the approach vis-à-vis moral commitments. This second dimension should result in emotional responses and moral positions that are commonly reported in views on the course of the economy (Teixeira and Rogers 1996).

To examine for these types of influences we have included three measures of the voters' emotional relationship to the government: anger toward the government, pessimism toward the future welfare of Americans, and indecisiveness toward selection of a candidate. Each variable is coded as a dummy variable. Anger is measured in a straightforward way. A voter is characterized as pessimistic if he or she believes that the future life of Americans will be worse than it is today, and indecisiveness is simply another name for a late decision. If the respondent made the decision in the last week of the campaign, he or she was coded as indecisive.[4] These variables were included only in 1992. In 1996 different questions were asked.

Results

The results presented here are taken from two sets of multinomial regression models applied to the elections of 1992 and 1996. We have selected the multinomial regression method because our dependent variable has three response catgories for both elections. For a binary independent variable, this technique, like binary logistic and log–linear models, produces coefficients that, when exponentiated, represent the odds of choosing either candidate relative to the left out category when the value of the independent variable is equal to one, relative to the odds of voting for the candidate when the value is equal to zero. This multiplicative framework allows for relatively straightforward interpretations relative to alternatives (Agresti 1990; Long 1997). We have employed two sets of models because the data are divided into separate versions, each of which asks slightly different questions.[5] On the basis of listwise deletion, not all relevant questions could be included in the same model.

Tables 5.1 and 5.2 display analyses of the fit of model one and two respectively. The final model in each table represents the model preferred to others on the basis of maximum likelihood estimation. For the second model in 1992, the economic decline and trade interaction term did not definitively improve the fit of the model according to the likelihood ratio test, but was significant on the basis of Wald statistics in all specifications of the model.

Tables 5.3 and 5.4 display the coefficients, standard errors, and exponentiated coefficients of the first and second set of multinomial logistic regressions for 1992 and 1996 respectively. The first portion of each table displays the coefficients that compare the odds of supporting Clinton relative to Perot and the second portion displays the coefficients comparing the Republican candidate to Perot.

Demographic and Political Variables

There has already been a good deal of work done on the general basis of Perot's appeal (Alvarez and Nagler 1995; Greenberg 1993). There are few surprises in the results from these models. Perot had strong support from independents relative to

Table 5.1. Fit Statistics for Model 1

Model	d.f.	-2 log-likelihood	Chi-square	p-value
1992				
Base = Demographic, Political, and Economic Variables	26	5753.267	4226.941	.000
Base + Narrative Variables	4	5270.457	482.81	.000
Above + Interactions	6	5245.124	25.330	.000
1996				
Base = Demographic, Political, and Economic Variables	26	4402.854	3653.627	.000
Base + Narrative Variables	4	4220.306	182.54	.000
Above + Deficit Interactions	4	4209.371	373.17	.000
Above + Jobs Interaction	2	4208.174	1.1970	Above .30

Table 5.2. Fit Statistics for Model 2

Model	d.f.	-2 log-likelihood	Chi-square	p-value
1992				
Base = Demographic and Political Variables	*16*	*3068.411*	*1002.574*	*.000*
Base + Psychological Variables	*6*	*2924.109*	*104.302*	*.000*
Above + Long-Term Economics Variable	*2*	*2773.327*	*150.782*	*.000*
Above + Narrative Variables	*8*	*2622.402*	*150.925*	*.000*
Above + Economic-Trade Interaction	*2*	*2616.971*	*5.431*	*.100*
Above + Anger-Markets Interaction	*2*	*2606.975*	*9.996*	*.010*
1996				
Base = Demographic, Political, Economic Psychological and Narrative Variables	*32*	*2332.646*	*1619.692*	*000*
Base + Young-Markets Interaction	*2*	*2319.631*	*13.01*	*.001*

Table 5.3. Multinomial Logistic Coefficients from the Regression of Presidential Vote on Selected Independent Variables in 1992 and 1996

Variable	Coefficient	Odds of Voting for Clinton vs. Perot	Coefficient	Odds of Voting for Clinton vs. Perot
Clinton vs. Perot	1992		1996	
Demographic Variables				
Male	-.102	.903	-.535**	.585
	(.072)		(.106)	
White	-1.145**	.318	-1.216**	.296
	(.124)		(.169)	
No College Degree	-1.119**	.327	-.859**	.424
	(.124)		(.178)	
College Degree	-.661**	.517	-.414*	.661
	(.124)		(.183)	
Age 18-29	.302*	1.353	-.136	.872
	(.131)		(.171)	
Age 40-49	.157	1.170	.113	1.120
	(.124)		(.173)	
Age 50-64	.170	2.740	.081	1.085
	(.102)		(.148)	
Age 65 and older	.604**	1.829	.169	1.185
	(.179)		(.218)	
Political Variables				
Democrat	1.255**	3.509	1.621*	5.059
	(.083)		(.123)	
Republican	-.921**	.398	-.179**	.836
	(.101)		(.138)	
Moderate	.116	1.123	-.069	.933
	(.072)		(.106)	
Economic Variables				
National economic conditions are good or excellent	-.567**	.567	1.439**	4.217
	(.141)		(.114)	
Personal finances worse than four years ago	.027	1.028	-.650*	.522
	(.074)		(.126)	

Table 5.3 (continued)

Variable	Coefficient	Odds of Voting for Clinton vs. Perot	Coefficient	Odds of Voting for Clinton vs. Perot
Republican vs. Perot		1992		1996
Narrative Variables				
Deficit issue is greatest problem	-1.421**	.241	-1.986**	.137
	(.126)		(.210)	
Jobs issue is greatest problem	.115	1.122	-.378**	.685
	(.084)		(.140)	
Demographic and Narrative Interactions				
No College Degree and deficit	.351*	1.421	.599*	1.820
issue is greatest problem	(.162)		(.263)	
Age 65 plus and deficit issue	.743*	2.101	.704	2.022
is greatest problem	(.303)		(.462)	
Age 18-29 and jobs issue is	-.508**	.602	-.258	.772
the greatest problem	(.169)		(.264)	
Intercept	2.402**		2.720**	
	(.189)		(.270)	

* p < .05   **p < .01 According to Wald Statistics

Table 5.3 (continued)

Variable	Coefficient	Odds of Voting for Bush vs. Perot	Coefficient	Odds of Voting for Dole vs. Perot
Republican vs. Perot	1992		1996	
Demographic Variables				
Male	-.155	.856	-.114	.892
	(.081)		(.107)	
White	-.375*	.688	.181	1.198
	(.155)		(.189)	
No College Degree	-.616**	.540	-.899**	.407
	(.135)		(.181)	
College Degree	-.261	.770	-.223	.800
	(.135)		(.183)	
Age 18–29	.308*	.735	-.216	.806
	(.139)		(.171)	
Age 40–49	.255	1.291	.022	1.022
	(.134)		(.175)	
Age 50–64	.141	1.151	.345*	1.412
	(.113)		(.146)	
Age 65 and older	.417*	1.517	.204	1.226
	(.192)		(.221)	
Political Variables				
Democrat	-.434**	.648	-.175	.839
	(.192)		(.141)	
Republican	1.128**	3.088	1.927**	6.870
	(.093)		(.124)	
Moderate	-.352	.704	-.384**	.681
	(.080)		(.106)	
Economic Variables				
National economic conditions are good or excellent	1.500**	4.483	.355**	1.426
	(.112)		(.115)	
Personal finances worse than four years ago	-1.175**	.309	-.026	.975
	(.093)		(.121)	

Table 5.3 (continued)

Variable	Coefficient	Odds of Voting for Bush vs. Perot	Coefficient	Odds of Voting for Dole vs. Perot
Republican vs. Perot	1992		1996	
Narrative Variables				
Deficit issue is greatest problem	-1.722**	.179	-1.299**	.273
	(.141)		(.195)	
Jobs issue is greatest problem	-.857**	.425	-.960**	.383
	(.094)		(.146)	
Demographic and Narrative Interactions				
No College Degree and deficit	.355	1.426	.421*	1.524
issue is greatest problem	(.184)		(.244)	
Age 65 plus and deficit issue	.511	1.667	.894	2.445
is greatest problem	(.345)		(.430)	
Age 18–29 and jobs issue is	-.029	1.029	-.069	.934
the greatest problem	(.191)		(.280)	
Intercept	2.402**		1.474**	
	(.189)		(.286)	

* $p < .05$ ** $p < .01$ According to Wald Statistics

Table 5.4. Multinomial Logistic Coefficients from the Regression of Presidential Vote on Selected Independent Variables in 1992 and 1996—Model 2

Variable	Coefficient	Odds of Voting for Clinton vs. Perot	Coefficient	Odds of Voting for Clinton vs. Perot
Clinton vs. Perot	1992		1996	
Demographic Variables				
Male	-.359**	.698	-.455**	.635
	(.134)		(.175)	
White	-.985**	.698	-.705**	.494
	(.208)		(.271)	
Age 18–29	-.268	.765	-1.039**	.354
	(.164)		(.299)	
Age 40–49	-.070	.932	.108	1.114
	(.205)		(.308)	
Age 50–64	.135	1.145	-.087	.916
	(.200)		(.236)	
Age 65 and older	.811**	2.249	.316	1.372
	(.293)		(.338)	
Political Variables				
Democrat	1.373**	3.947	1.603**	4.969
	(.148)		(.215)	
Republican	-.284	.753	-.105	.900
	(.184)		(.219)	
Economic Variables				
Economy in long-term decline	.241	1.272	–	–
	(.194)			
Personal finances worse than four years ago	–	–	-1.074**	.309
			(.203)	
Psychological Variables				
Anger	-.452	.636	–	–
Pessimism	-.253	.776	–	–
	(.137)			

Table 5.4 (continued)

Variable	Coefficient	Odds of Voting for Clinton vs. Perot	Coefficient	Odds of Voting for Clinton vs. Perot
Clinton vs. Perot	1992		1996	
Indecision	-.887** (.141)	.412	–	–
Narrative Variables				
Deficit should be national priority	-.619** (.137)	.539	–	–
Trade eliminates U.S. jobs	.393 (.281)	1.482	–	–
Trade creates U.S. jobs	1.544** (.555)	4.684	–	–
Government should leave more to private sector	-.926** (.166)	.396	-1.173** (.220)	.309
Narrative Interactions				
Economy in long-term decline and trade creates jobs	-.562* (.287)	.570	–	–
Angry and government should leave more to private sector	.022* (.283)	1.022	–	–
Age 18–29 and government should leave more to private sector	–	–	1.376** (.411)	3.959
Intercept	2.586** (.532)		2.720** (.270)	

For 1996 model, social security and welfare items were included but are not reported for purposes of comparability

Table 5.4 (continued)

Variable	Odds of Voting for Bush vs. Perot		Odds of Voting for Dole vs. Perot	
	Coefficient	vs. Perot	Coefficient	vs. Perot
Republican vs. Perot	1992		1996	
Demographic Variables				
Male	-.507**	.602	1.375**	.740
	(.149)		(.418)	
White	.024	1.025	-.264	.768
	(.279)		(.288)	
Age 18–29	-.492**	.611	-.725**	.485
	(.186)		(.328)	
Age 40–49	-.200	.819	.502	1.652
	(.233)		(.304)	
Age 50–64	.311	1.365	-.018	.982
	(.213)		(.229)	
Age 65 and older	.183	1.200	.458	1.582
	(.322)		(.331)	
Political Variables				
Democrat	-.521*	.594	.100	1.105
	(.207)		(.236)	
Republican	1.386**	4.000	1.604**	4.973
	(.167)		(.198)	
Economic Variables				
Economy in long-term decline	-1.126** (.211)	.214	–	–
Personal finances worse than four years ago	–	–	-.198 (.188)	.820
Psychological Variables				
Anger	-2.618**	.073	–	–
	(.653)			
Pessimism	-.259	.772	–	–
	(.158)			
Indecision	-.949**	.387	–	–
	(.158)			

Table 5.4 (continued)

Variable	Coefficient	Odds of Voting for Bush vs. Perot	Coefficient	Odds of Voting for Dole vs. Perot
Republican vs. Perot	1992		1996	
Narrative Variables				
Deficit should be national priority	-.217 (.157)	.762	—	—
Trade eliminates U.S. jobs	-.580 (.300)	.560	—	—
Trade creates U.S. jobs	1.113★ (.540)	3.043	—	—
Government should leave more to private sector	.175 (.174)	1.192	.313 (.229)	1.368
Narrative Interactions				
Economy in long-term decline andtrade creates jobs	-.639★ (.304)	.528	—	—
Angry and government should leave more to private sector	1.069★★ (.373)	2.911	—	—
Age 18–29 and government should leave more to private sector	—	—	.647 (.423)	1.909
Intercept	2.609★★ (.575)		1.375★★ (.418)	

For 1996 model, social security and welfare items were included as controls but are not reported partisans, from the young relative to the old, and from whites and men relative to nonwhites and women. Perot's support seems to have declined among women from 1992 to 1996 and to have strengthened among older voters. Given that the redistribution of rewards from the less to the more educated has been a dominant theme in American institutional life, we would expect the less educated to have been particularly supportive of Perot. This was true of the least educated group in both models for both years. However, the strength of the support declined relative to Clinton and improved relative to the Republican candidate from 1992 to 1996.

Support from the young and the poorly educated, although relatively well known, provides some confirmation of the hypothesis that Perot was able to appeal to those adversely affected by economic restructuring. The very young and the poorly educated are among those groups most disadvantaged by the recent economic trends. Similarly, the support of men could fall in the same box, as men have been suffering more from wage erosion and loss of work relative to women (Goodman 1994).

Economic Variables

There are three economic variables included in these analyses: a sociotropic measure, a pocketbook measure, and a long-term decline measure. The first two are traditional in economic voting studies and the last is not. For the first measure, national economic conditions, support for the incumbent relative to Perot remained quite stable. In 1992 a voter who believed that national economic conditions were good or excellent was 4.5 times as likely to vote for Bush as for Perot, all else equal. In 1996 the number was 4.2 times as likely for Clinton as for Perot.

Interestingly, in contrast to 1992, in 1996 Perot was the only beneficiary of economic discontent. The 47 percent of the voters who believed that national economic conditions were fair to poor were 1.4 times as likely to choose Perot relative to Dole, other things being equal. Pocketbook voting against the incumbent was less pronounced in 1996 than it was in 1992. In 1992, a voter whose finances were worse than they had been four years previous was roughly three times as likely to select Perot relative to the incumbent, while in 1996 he was only twice as likely. This decline is doubly important when one considers that the proportion of voters who felt this way had also substantially declined from 1992 to 1996, from 34.3 percent to 20.9 percent respectively.

Even stronger than either of these two measures is the measure of long-term economic decline. In 1992, 54 percent of the voters considered the economy to be in long-term decline. A voter who felt this way was nearly five times as likely to select Perot as Bush. There is no statistically significant difference between Clinton and Perot on this issue. Although this is not definitive support of the long-term perspective on economic voting, it certainly does not disconfirm the hypothesis. At the very least, we can say with certitude that economic conditions explain a significant portion of the variance in voting for Perot.

Narrative Variables

The first order results from the narrative variables tend to confirm the hypothesis that Perot was more successful among those who believed his stories than among those who did not. Moreover, from the three items that were consistent across the two elections, it seems that the impact of these stories carried over from 1992 to 1996. From Model 1 we can see that in 1992, voters who believed that the deficit was the number one problem facing the country were 4.1 times as supportive of Perot relative to Clinton and 5.5 times as supportive of Perot relative to Bush. In 1996, the numbers were 7.3 for Perot relative to Clinton and 3.7 for Perot relative to Dole. Clearly this issue had staying power. It is almost as if these voters had supplanted one abstract idea for another, the image of the deficit for the economy. The markets-versus-hierarchies story is fairly consistent as well. From Model 2, we can see that voters who favored market solutions were only one-third as likely to vote for Clinton relative to Perot in 1992 and even less so in 1996.

With respect to jobs and trade, the story for the main effects is unsurprising as well. Voters who believed that trade creates jobs were less likely to support Perot than they were either of the other candidates. A voter who believed that trade creates U.S. jobs was 4.7 times as likely to support Clinton relative to Perot and 3.0 times as likely to support Bush relative to Perot. One could imagine that this trend would have continued into 1996 if the question had been asked, given the fact that Clinton now claims a commitment to world trade as a cornerstone of his economic policy.

The jobs question was asked in both 1992 and 1996 and so can serve as a basis for comparison. In 1992 concern for jobs did not distinguish the two rivals to the incumbent but did significantly reduce the odds of voting for Bush relative to Perot. A voter concerned about jobs was 2.4 times as likely to vote for Perot relative to Bush than one who was not. In 1996, like the national economic conditions variable, concern for economic distribution worked to Perot's favor against both of his opponents. A voter in 1996 who was concerned about jobs was 1.5 times as likely to vote for Perot relative to Clinton and 2.6 times as likely relative to Dole. Clearly, the economic distribution issue is not working to the traditional parties' advantage in the middle to late nineties.

Table 5.5. Odds of Voting for Perot vs. Opponent from Model 1 Interactions

1992	Jobs Not the Greatest Problem		Jobs Are the Greatest Problem	
	Clinton	Bush	Clinton	Bush
Base Age	*Base Probability*	*Base Probability*	0.89	3.24
Age 18–29	0.74	1.36	1.09	5.99
			(0.66)	(4.41)

1996	Jobs Not the Greatest Problem		Jobs Are the Greatest Problem	
	Clinton	Dole	Clinton	Dole
Base age	*Base Probability*	*Base Probability*	1.55	2.68
Age 18–29	1.25	1.29	1.94	3.46
			(1.94)	(3.46)

1992	Deficit Not the Greatest Problem		Deficit Is the Greatest Problem	
	Clinton	Bush	Clinton	Bush
Base age and education	*Base Probability*	*Base Probability*	4.15	5.59
No College Degree	3.06	1.85	8.93	7.26
			(12.70)	(10.34)
Age 65 and older	0.55	0.66	1.08	2.21
			(2.28)	(3.69)

1996	Deficit Not the Greatest Problem		Deficit Is the Greatest Problem	
	Clinton	Dole	Clinton	Dole
Base age and education	*Base Probability*	*Base Probability*	7.30	3.66
No College Degree	2.36	2.46	9.46	5.67
			(17.22)	(9.00)
Age 65 and older	0.85	0.82	3.05	1.22
			(6.20)	(3.00)

All items in this table are the reciprocal values of the exponentiated coefficients taken from model 1. Items in parentheses represent the product of the two marginal odds ratios, i.e., the value that would have obtained if there were no interaction effect.

Table 5.6. Odds of Voting for Perot vs. Opponent from Model 2 Interactions

1992	Government Should Do More		Leave More to Private Sector	
	Clinton	Bush	Clinton	Bush
Not angry	*Base Probability*	*Base Probability*	2.52	.8935
Angry at federal government	1.57	13.70	3.89	3.95
			(3.96)	(12.24)

1996	Government Should Do More		Leave More to Private Sector	
	Clinton	Dole	Clinton	Dole
Base age	*Base Probability*	*Base Probability*	3.23	0.73
Age 18–29	2.83	2.06	2.30	0.79
			(9.14)	(1.50)

1992	Trade Has No Impact		Trade Causes More Jobs	
	Clinton	Bush	Clinton	Bush
Economy in temporary recession	*Base Probability*	*Base Probability*	0.21	0.33
Economy in long-term decline	0.78	3.09	0.29	1.92
			(0.16)	(1.01)

All items in this table are the reciprocal values of the exponentiated coefficients taken from model 2. Items in parentheses represent the product of the two marginal odds ratios, i.e., the value that would have obtained if there were no interaction effect.

Psychological Variables

The campaign of 1992 was very emotionally charged. In order to see where the thrust of the emotional energy was directed, we have included measures of three emotional orientations: anger toward the government, pessimism toward the future, and indecision toward the vote choice. All three of these worked to Perot's advantage. Angry voters were extremely unlikely to vote for the incumbent in 1992. An angry voter was 13.7 times as likely to select Perot relative to Bush and only 8.7 times as likely to choose Clinton relative to Bush, other things being equal. Pessimism was a significant predictor of support for Perot until the narratives were controlled for, and this might play a role in future studies. Finally, indecisive voters were far more likely to vote for Perot in 1992 than were other voters. This result is interesting for two reasons: on the one hand it might suggest that emotional energy worked to his advantage, and on the other that the strategy he pursued of concentrating his advertising on the last weeks of the campaign may have worked.[6]

Interaction Effects

Perhaps the strongest evidence in favor of the efficacy of Perot's stories to mobilize discontent would be to find interaction effects between the stories and aspects of the suffering groups. In both sets of models there were significant interaction effects. For Model 1, three interactions were significant. In Model 2 two interactions were significant in 1992 and one in 1996. To understand the story that these coefficients tell it is useful to look at a table of exponentiated coefficients. Table 5.5 displays a set of reciprocal values of exponentiated coefficients. The reciprocal value is shown so that comparisons run from Perot to the opponent and not the other way around. Exponentiating the coefficients transforms the meaning from a log-odds to a more readily comprehensible odds ratio. Table 5.6 displays a similar set of values for Model 2.

With respect to the deficit issue we can make two observations with confidence. The deficit story was even more compelling to the better educated than it was to the less educated. Voters who had attained less education than a college degree and believed that the deficit was the greatest problem facing the country in 1992 were 8.93 times as likely to vote for Perot relative to Clinton. Even though this is an extremly strong result and supports the hypothesis that the working poor were moved by Perot's stories, it is less strong than we would have expected from the main effects of the model. That is to say, more educated voters were even more moved by the deficit story than were less educated voters. This result holds for 1996 as well, narrowing the gap between better and less educated voters even more than in 1992. Second, although older voters were unlikely to vote for Perot if they were concerned about the deficit, they were even less likely to support him relative to Clinton in 1992. This effect loses significance in 1996.

We can also say that a concern for distributive issues in the form of jobs worked to Perot's advantage in special measure among the young in 1992 but not in 1996. In 1992, young people who were concerned about jobs turned their support from Clinton to Perot, even though others concerned about jobs did not. We read the 1992 result as a key sign of the kind of energy that Perot was able to generate in 1992 relative to 1996. Young people who faced low-paying and uncertain entry-level jobs in 1992 voted for Perot. In 1996, a slightly changed young cohort had either found more satisfaction in their job prospects or decided that Perot was not a suitable advocate.

On the issue of trade and jobs, there is a potentially confusing result. Those voters who believed that trade creates jobs and who believed that the economy was in a long-term decline were more likely to support Perot relative to Bush than would be predicted by the main effects alone. This is difficult to understand without looking at the frequency tabulations.

What seems to be happening is really a polarization on trade issues that was driven by a respondent's position on economic conditions. A pessimistic Perot voter had strong opinions about international trade. Among Perot voters, the proportion of voters who were neutral with respect to the effect of trade declined dramatically among those who believed that the economy was in long-term decline, but only slightly among those who believed trade creates jobs. This effect was stronger than for either of the other two candidates. This less than obvious phenomenon is what drives the interaction coefficient to significance but must be read in slightly weaker terms than one might normally read it. What we can say is, voters who believed that the economy was in a long-term decline and were neutral on trade issues were less likely to vote for Perot than they were for the other candidates. Put another way, voters who believed in long-term decline and voted for Perot were polarized on the trade issue.

Finally, we can turn to the effect of the markets-versus-hierarchies story. There are three interesting results to note. First, by the 1996 election young Perot voters were less market oriented than were older Perot voters. This might suggest that by 1996 young voters saw Perot as more of a government activist than a privatizer. Although the coefficient from Model 2 in 1996 suggests that young market oriented voters turned to Bill Clinton relative to Perot, in fact, the opposite was true. Young voters who had what has been called here a hierarchical orientation to government intervention were more likely to turn to Perot than would have been expected by the main effects. This drives the coefficient for the interaction between young and market perspective into significance. This result might suggest that the image of Perot and of his interpretation of the economy had changed from 1992 to 1996.

Second, angry voters who voted for Bush were overwhelmingly market oriented, while the bulk of the angry Perot voters were more or less evenly split between markets and hierarchies orientations. Angry Bush voters may have been angry because he had broken his promise not to raise taxes. The markets-versus-hierarchies interactions do not add support to the hypothesis that the stories Perot told were more effective among the less advantaged or morally offended than they were among the more advantaged or less offended, but they do suggest that these dimensions had impacts on respondents' views of the other candidates.

What can we say about the role of long-term economic restructuring and economic stories in the vote decision on the basis of these results? First, it is clear from the long-term decline variable that voters who had a negative long-term vision of economic performance were more likely to support Perot than those who did not. From this result and from the sociotropic and pocketbook measures, we can say that a negative view on the state of the economy improved the chances of voting for Perot in both 1992 and 1996. We can also say that groups who were most affected by the negative impact of the economic restructuring were more likely to vote for Perot than for his opponents. This group includes less educated, white, male and entry-level workers.

We can also say that the stories that we have associated with Perot in 1992 were effective for him in that year and continued to work for him in 1996. Voters who wanted to cut the deficit, move toward domestic market regulation, and yet curtail foreign trade were more likely to support him than those voters who did not. For the first two stories this was true in 1996 as well as in 1992. A concern for the distribution of rewards tended to work in Perot's favor as well. In both elections the jobs issue benefited Perot relative to the Republican candidate and in 1992, which we view as the crucial, open year, the jobs issue worked to Perot's advantage relative to Clinton among one of the most disadvantaged groups, young and presumably entry-level workers. These results represent a moderate confirmation of the major position of this chapter that researchers should pay attention to long-run economic redistribution and a stronger confirmation of the importance of voter interpretations of economic circumstances.

Conclusion

In the above, we have argued three major points:

(1) There are political consequences of long-term changes in the vertical distribution of rewards across groups.
(2) The volatile political environment of the 1990s is, in part, one of those consequences.
(3) The link between the experience of economic decline and political action is provided by interpretive stories about how the economy works.

We believe that it is important to recognize that Ross Perot was a figure made prominent by his ability to speak to the tensions of increasing economic inequality and insecurity. Much of his success in the 1992 and 1996 elections was based on economic issues and particular stories that he told about what could be done. Although Perot's strongest showing was achieved more than seven years ago in a much different economic environment, the conditions of 1992 are not markedly different for many American workers today than they were then. The institutions that once insulated the middle class from external risks have been eroding. The 1990s have been a decade in which personal responsibility has become a watchword. In fat times, such developments might only produce political volatility of the sort we have witnessed this decade, but in lean times it is hard to say exactly how violently the winds might blow.

Notes

1. Another way to treat this concept would be to include it as an economic measure. A focus on jobs might be part of a distributional perspective on economic performance. For our purposes it seems more reasonable to include it as a narrative concept. One reason is that it is part of a battery of issues separate from a direct assessment of respondents' views on the economy and their financial condition.

2. Measures of family income were included in all models as well, but were never found to be a significant predictor in any preferred model, and therefore are not mentioned further.

3. This decision was not arbitrary. We tested many separate formulations in the following models and decided on the basis of likelihood ratio tests that this formulation was as good as any other. In addition, it allowed us to test for interesting interaction effects.

4. We, of course, recognize that a late decision could have been entirely strategic if new information was continuing to appear regarding the candidates' issue positions. Nevertheless, given the extensive nature of campaign coverage, it does not seem unreasonable to label such a respondent indecisive relative to most, while attaching no pejorative status to the term.

5. There are four versions of the questionnaire for each year. In both cases, two versions are virtually identical but have alternative question order. The other two versions allow for special questions to be asked of smaller samples.

6. Although we could not include a measure of indecision in the models for 1996 because it was not asked in the same questionnaire as our other items, it seems that late deciders were also more likely to choose him in that year as well.

References

Agresti, Alan. 1990. *Categorical Data Analysis.* New York: Wiley.

Alvarez, Michael, and Jonathan Nagler. 1995. "Economics, Issues and the Perot Candidacy: Voter Choice in the 1992 Presidential Election," *American Journal of Political Science* 39: 714–744.

Clarke, Harold D., and Marianne C. Stewart. 1995. "Economic Evaluations, Prime Ministerial Approval and Governing Party Support," *British Journal of Political Science* 25: 145–170.

Downs, Anthony. 1957. *An Economic Theory of Democracy*. New York: Harper.

Dresser, Laura, Scott Mangum, and Joel Rogers. 1998. *The State of Working Wisconsin*. Madison: Center on Wisconsin Strategy.

Frank, Robert, and Phillip J. Cook. 1996. *The Winner-Take-All Society: Why the Few at the Top Get So Much More Than the Rest of Us*. Penguin U.S.A.

Giddens, Anthony. 1991. *The Consequences of Modernity*. Palo Alto: Stanford University Press.

Goodman, William. 1994. "Women and Jobs in Recoveries," *Monthly Labor Review* 117.

Greenberg, Stanley. 1993. "The Perot Voters and American Politics: Here to Stay?" Washington, D.C.: Democratic Leadership Council.

Habermas, Jurgen. 1998. *Between Facts and Norms: Contributions to a Discourse Theory of Law and Democracy*. Cambridge: The MIT Press.

Key, V. O. 1966. *The Responsible Electorate*. Cambridge: Belknap Press of Harvard University Press.

Kinder, Donald R., and Roderik Kiewiet. 1979. "Economic Discontent and Political Behavior," *American Journal of Political Science* 23: 495–527.

Kinder, Donald R., and Walter R. Mebane Jr. 1983. "Politics and Economics in Everyday Life." In K. Monroe, ed., *The Political Process and Economic Change*. New York: Agathon.

Kohut, Andrew. 1996. "Class Collisions in Response to Buchanan, Nationwide." Washington, D.C.: The Pew Research Center.

Kramer, Gerald. 1971. "Short-term Fluctuation in U.S. Voting Behavior," *American Poltical Science Review* 65: 131–143.

Lewis-Beck, Michael. 1988. *Economics and Elections: The Major Western Democracies*. Ann Arbor: University of Michigan Press.

Long, J. Scott. 1997. *Regression Models for Categorical Dependent and Limited Dependent Variables*. Thousand Oaks: Sage.

MacKuen, Michael B., Robert S. Erickson, and James A. Stimson. 1992. "Peasants or Bankers? The American Electorate and the U.S. Economy," *The American Political Science Review* 86: 597–611.

Mishel, Lawrence, Jared Bernstein, and John Scmitt. 1999. *The State of Working America*. Ithaca: Cornell University Press.

Mitofsky, Warren J., and Murray Edelman. 1995. "A Review of the 1992 VRS Exit Polls." In Lavrakas Traugott, ed., *Presidential Polls and the Media*. Boulder: Westview Press.

Monroe, Kristen. 1978. "Economic Influences on Presidential Popularity," *Public Opinion Quarterly* 42: 360–369.

Morris, M, Arnette D. Bernhardt, and Mark S. Handcock. 1994. "Economic Inequality: New methods for new trends," *American Sociological Review* 59: 205–219.

Olsen, Craig A. 1995. "Health Benefits Coverage among Male Workers," *Monthly Labor Review*. March 18, #3.

Perot, Ross. 1992. *Not For Sale at Any Price*. New York: Free Press.

Roemer, John E. 1994. "The Strategic Role of Party Ideology When Voters Are Uncertain About How the Economy Works," *The American Political Science Review* 88: 327–335.

Rose, Stephan. 1997. "Declining Job Security and the Professionalization of Opportunity." Washington, D.C.: National Commission for Employment Policy.

Sassen, Saskia. 1990. "Economic Restructuring and the American City," *Annual Review of Sociology* 16: 465–490.

Teixeira, Ruy, and Joel Rogers. 1996. "Volatile Voters: Declining Living Standards and Non-educated College Whites." Washington, D.C.: Economic Policy Institute.

Thompson, E. P. 1971. "The Moral Economy of the English Crowd in the Eighteenth Century," *Past and Present* 50.

VNS. 1996. "Voter News Service General Election Exit Polls." Ann Arbor: ICPSR.

VRS. 1992. "Voter Reserach and Surveys General Election Exit Poll." Storrs, Ct.: The Roper Center for Public Opinion Research.

Walstad, William B., ed. 1994. *An International Perspective on Economic Education*: Kluwer Law International.

Williamson, Oliver. 1985. *The Economic Institutions of Capitalism; Firms, Markets, Relational Contracting*: New York: Free Press.

Yankelovich, Daniel. 1992. "Foreign Policy after the Election," *Foreign Affairs* 71: 1–12.

6

Structural Constraints on Perot Voting Patterns

The Effects of Religious Adherence

Christopher P. Gilbert, Timothy R. Johnson, David A. M. Peterson, and Paul A. Djupe

T he presidential candidacies of H. Ross Perot have forced political scientists to rethink some conventional wisdom surrounding independent presidential bids.[1] As other chapters in this volume detail, the Perot campaigns indeed present many unique facets. By contrast, our chapter examines some important and heretofore neglected continuities between Perot and previous independent presidential candidates. We uncover these connections through a careful focus on the religious factor as it relates to Ross Perot's 1992 and 1996 presidential candidacies.

The existing literature on third party and independent presidential bids is replete with detailed case studies utilizing aggregate and individual data (Mazmanian 1974; Smallwood 1983; Rosenstone, Behr, and Lazarus 1984; Chressanthis and Shaffer 1993; Gould 1993). It is curious to find in all this work scant attention paid to the impact of religious belief, affiliation, or membership patterns. Decades of analysis have established the multifaceted nature of religion's influence on the attitudes and actions of American voters, to the extent that explanations of American voting behavior that omit religion's role are necessarily incomplete (Lopatto 1985; Leege and Kellstedt 1993; Wald 1997).

To date, however, there is little research that extends the findings about connections between religion and traditional two-candidate electoral contests to three-candidate races. In a recent book (Gilbert et al. 1999) we offer four hypotheses about religious factors and independent candidate voting: independent candidates do not develop significant support along denominational lines; social issue positions do not tend to predict voting for independent candidates; the religious composition of a citizen's social environment affects that citizen's likelihood of voting for an independent candidate; and most importantly, the primary effect of religion on third candidate voting is negative—religious factors tend to motivate people not to vote for independent candidates. In effect, religious factors work against independent candidates, because religious factors over time have become salient factors that structure support for the major parties and their candidates, and independent candidates have neither the time nor the resources to break this nexus.

As we will see in the analysis to follow, each of these hypotheses has been confirmed for the 1992 Perot candidacy, and most have been confirmed for 1996. Following a review of the literature on independent candidacies, we will utilize aggregate, county-level data that link 1992 and 1996 Perot voting patterns to those of other independent presidential candidates in the twentieth century, to show an important constant barrier to independent candidate success. We will also develop individual-level models of 1992 and 1996 Perot voting, to examine the impact of religious variables and to offer support for the trends revealed by the aggregate analysis. We then conclude with a look at alternative explanations of Perot's electoral fortunes, and how these alternatives mesh with our own analysis.

Existing Research

The strong tradition and inertia of the two party system, combined with significant institutional factors that make it difficult for more than two parties to remain viable, explain why minor parties and independent candidates have remained little more than curiosities to the vast majority of American voters. Despite a notable lack of success at the ballot box, independent candidates have not been ignored by political scientists. The relatively limited number of viable third party and independent runs for the presidency has generated substantial scholarship that seeks to explain how and why such candidates gain electoral support, with primary focus on demographic and election-specific factors, as well as on certain structural conditions necessary to give rise to independent candidacies (Mazmanian 1974; Smallwood 1983; Chressanthis and Shaffer 1993; Gillespie 1993; Gould 1993; Rosenstone, Behr, and Lazarus 1996).

To understand how we know what we know about independent candidates, we must recognize that this understanding often depends on the historical context in which the researcher resides. For example, in his classic book, *Politics, Parties, and Pressure Groups* (1948), V. O. Key describes third candidacies as "deviations" from the two party norm. Key's descriptive label might well have been different had he written one year later, given the candidacies of Strom Thurmond and Henry Wallace in 1948. With four more significant independent candidacies in the twelve presidential races since 1948, it is no wonder that more contemporary analysts describe such candidacies not as deviant but rather as regular, recurring events, stressing the considerable similarities among independent candidates in widely varying elections.[2] Clearly, there are aspects of the electoral process that frequently provide conditions favorable for these candidacies, and these conditions appear to occur more frequently in contemporary politics.

The most comprehensive treatment of the subject, combining historical background with empirical analysis, is *Third Parties in America: Citizen Response to Major Party Failure,* by Steven Rosenstone, Roy Behr, and Edward Lazarus (1996). The subtitle indicates the primary condition for viable independent candidacies—voters must perceive that the major parties have deteriorated to the point of losing legitimacy. Rosenstone et al. offer two additional factors that could prompt voter support of an independent candidate: an attractive, nationally prestigious third party candidate decides to run; and/or citizens acquire an allegiance to a third party (1996, 126).

The first condition may arise from a variety of sources. Chressanthis and Shaffer (1993) posit that when salient issues are not adequately addressed by either major party, third candidacies almost always occur. Key suggests that independent candidates act as a "safety valve" for the expression of voter discontent with the major parties (1948, 235–246). Similarly, Downs (1957) demonstrates that as the distance between voters and parties increases, so does support for third candidates. Mazmanian (1974) and Gillespie (1993) offer additional historical perspectives that buttress the argument that political crises are at the root of every viable independent candidacy. More recent scholarship on the 1992 and 1996 Perot campaigns does not deviate from these basic conclusions (Abramson, Aldrich, Paolino, and Rohde 1995; Alvarez and Nagler 1995; Gold 1995; Menendez 1996; Gilbert et al. 1999). Third candidate voting can thus be said generally to stem from animosity toward, or disaffection with, the major parties.

The latter two factors also have historical precedent, although the entry of a nationally prestigious independent candidate is more frequent than third party allegiance. Indeed, this final condition is notable for the lack of empirical research on its existence; Rosenstone et al. argue that in the nineteenth century, voter loyalty to minor parties was more substantial, but nearly all twentieth-century third candidacies have been transient and therefore no loyalty could develop nor could loyalty be cultivated (1996, 174–175). By contrast, Rosenstone et al. show that national prestige predicts third candidate support in every case (1996, 170–174).

A more recent investigation of the 1968, 1980, and 1992 elections using National Election Studies data (Peterson, Johnson, and Gilbert 1995) addresses some unexplored questions about the timing of vote decisions and defections from one candidate to another during the campaign. Peterson et al. find that voters in the 1968, 1980, and 1992 elections are willing to choose third candidates even as election day nears, provided there are substantive reasons to do so. A candidate's likely showing is evidently not among these reasons in two of the three elections (1968 and 1992). Peterson et al. conclude that voters do not reject third candidates because of perceptions of their remoteness of winning. Along these same lines, Magleby and Monson (1995) analyze recent independent candidacies in Utah state elections and find that voters who decide late in the campaign favor the independent candidate over the major party candidates, despite the fact that late-campaign polls show independent support slipping badly (1995, 19).

One point must be made concerning the definition of viable third candidacies. The prevailing convention in the literature is that a candidate must receive at least 5 percent of the national popular vote; this is also written into current law as the threshold for receiving federal campaign funds (Rosenstone et al. 1996, 174). From our perspective, however, interesting third candidacies also include individuals who had a substantial impact on the election they contested, even if their final vote total did not reach the conventional 5 percent threshold. We will connect Ross Perot's 1992 and 1996 campaigns to several previous independent candidates: Theodore Roosevelt (Progressive) and Eugene Debs (Socialist) in 1912; Robert LaFollette (Progressive) in 1924; Strom Thurmond (States' Rights Democrat) and Henry Wallace (Progressive) in 1948; George Wallace (American Independent) in 1968; and John Anderson (independent) in 1980. Neither Thurmond nor Henry Wallace received 5 percent, but for reasons that will become obvious below, their candidacies are instructive in helping to understand the context of Perot's bids.

Finally, in using county-level data for both our aggregate and empirical analysis, we make some assumptions about the importance of social environments, or contexts, in determining citizen attitudes and behaviors. Contextual theories of political behavior posit that political attitudes and actions are a function of individual beliefs and characteristics interacting with awareness of surrounding environments (Huckfeldt and Sprague 1995). Much of the contextual literature on religion and individual political behavior utilizes the church as the unit of context (Wald, Owen, and Hill 1988, 1990; Jelen 1992; Gilbert 1993; Huckfeldt and Sprague 1995). Others have found modest contextual effects using the blunter instrument of county measures (Gaustad 1976; Newman and Halvorson 1980; Salisbury, Sprague, and Weiher 1984; Lieske 1993; Gilbert, Johnson, and Peterson 1995). We will make connections between the aggregate and individual-level analysis, to show how basic factors work at different levels to impede the chances of independent candidates such as Perot.

Data Sources

Data for this paper are drawn from several sources that require some explication. First, the aggregate data on independent candidacies in the twentieth century combine two sets of two important data sources. County vote totals can be found in the set compiled by Clubb, Flanigan, and Zingale (ICPSR 8611) as well as the *America Votes* series (Scammon 1995, Scammon et al. 1997). These data give percentages for all candidates in each election, including the major party candidates, independents, and a summary total for all other minor candidates.

We combine the county vote totals with religious adherence data that come from two places: the U.S. census surveys of religious membership conducted in 1890, 1906, 1916, 1926, and 1936 (ICPSR 0008); and post–World War II surveys of church membership compiled by the National Council of Churches of Christ (NCCC) in 1952, 1971, 1980, and 1990. Because the church census years do not coincide with three-candidate presidential election years (except in 1980), and because there is no reason to assume that change in denominational totals between censuses is linear, we choose to match up the years as closely as possible and append the appropriate religious adherence data to the corresponding county vote data for each election. The explanation of data sources below results in the following scheme for analysis:

Election	Church Membership	Population Data
1912	1916	1920
1924	1926	1930
1948	1952	1950
1968	1971	1970
1980	1980	1980
1992	1990	1990
1996	1990	1996

Population data from the U.S. census are used to calculate religious membership by counties in terms of their share of the population.

Individual-level data for 1992 and 1996 come from the National Election Studies. NES surveys provide by far the richest individual-level data source to study citizen motivations and draw comparisons across elections. We append information from the 1990 NCCC survey to the 1992 and 1996 NES, to test the effects of county contextual measures on individual voter decisions. We also incorporate county presidential vote totals. Warren Miller (1956) finds that Democrats living in highly Democratic counties are more likely to vote Democratic—an amplification effect—than Democrats living among high concentrations of Republicans. Such effects are tested in the Perot voting model.

Modelling Strategies

With the county as the unit of analysis for the aggregate models, all variables used are expressed as percentages from 0 to 100,[3] and the dependent variable is the percentage of the county vote for the third candidate(s) being studied. We estimate OLS regression models to account for the impact of county religious adherence on county vote for the third candidate(s). Models are constructed for the strongest third candidates (Roosevelt, Debs, LaFollette, Thurmond, Henry Wallace, George Wallace, Anderson, Perot), as well as models for all minor candidates combined. In the aggregate models a *negative sign* on a coefficient indicates that county vote for the third candidate decreases with each unit change of the independent variable; this is the effect we hypothesize with county religious adherence. Occasional controls for region also appear in some models.

For the 1992 and 1996 individual-level models, the dependent measure is vote choice, operationalized as a dichotomous variable: 1 if a citizen chooses Perot, and 0 if a citizen chooses any other candidate. Because of this coding scheme, the models show the specific factors that cause voters to choose or reject Perot, but the models do not reveal much about how major party voters choose between the candidates.[4] The regression technique for this dependent variable is logistic regression,[5] and the models attempt to account fully for the factors affecting Perot voting, and to examine in detail the effects of religious factors.[6] Moreover, specification of both individual- and contextual-level effects ameliorates the oft-cited criticism of contextual analysis, that it fails to account for individual factors that are the true agents of causality (Hauser 1974). In each model, a positive coefficient indicates a greater likelihood of choosing Perot while a negative coefficient indicates less likelihood of choosing Perot.

Continuities: Religious Adherence and Third Candidate Voting

What does it mean to state that religious adherence, or church membership, serves to impede the electoral fortunes of independent presidential candidates? This question motivates the aggregate analysis in this section, and it demonstrates that in one fundamental respect, Ross Perot's campaigns faced a barrier common to nearly all independent candidacies.

Since the publication of Robert Putnam's influential 1995 essay "Bowling Alone: America's Declining Social Capital," scholars have given renewed attention to what Putnam terms "the norms and networks of civic engagement" (Putnam 1995, 66). Despite evidence of a modest decline in weekly churchgoing and church-related group membership since the 1960s, religious affiliation remains the most common associational membership of Americans, helping to foster civic engagement and the utilization of social capital (1995, 69–70). Social connectedness—the means by which citizens manipulate the links between democracy and civil society—clearly depends on strong institutions such as churches.

One facet of the social connections that churches provide in U.S. civil society is their essential role in strengthening the two party system. Religious institutions sustain major parties through the development of long-term attachments between certain denominations and one of the two major parties (Lopatto 1985; Kellstedt and Noll 1990). The parties themselves reinforce these connections through elite-level cue giving or through the influence of mass movements with religious ties (Lopatto 1985). These linkages lead directly to the hypothesis that higher levels of church membership should work against independent candidates. Independent candidates are not privy to the ties that bind Democratic and Republican voters to their parties over time; one factor that creates and strengthens such ties is religion; therefore independent candidates should do best where party loyalties are least strong (counties with fewer church members) or where the third candidate has an underlying base of his own (for example, George Wallace in the south in 1968).

This hypothesis is empirically tested through simple models that regress independent candidate vote on religious adherence, for each independent presidential candidacy of the twentieth century. The results are reported in Table 6.1.

In many respects, one would expect that the most distant elections should demonstrate an even stronger inverse relationship between county religious adherence and third candidate voting. If Putnam is correct that religious vitality has waned modestly in the last thirty years, then higher church membership numbers should correlate with higher levels of major party voting, thus providing a greater obstacle to minor party candidates in 1912, 1924, and 1948. Moreover, there is substantial evidence to indicate the presence of robust denominational ties to major parties prior to the New Deal realignment of the U.S. electorate (Kellstedt and Noll 1990), another factor that would serve to strengthen the adherence-major party link.

Table 6.1 reveals a consistent and robust inverse relationship between county religious adherence and voting for independent candidates. With the exception of the 1924 and 1996 elections,[7] increasing levels of religious adherence lead to

Table 6.1. Independent Candidate Vote Regressed on County Religious Adherence (OLS regression estimates)

		Adherence Coefficient	Adjusted R^2
1912	T. Roosevelt	-0.05 (0.01)***	.15
	Debs	-0.08 (0.00)***	.10
	All minor candidates	-0.15 (0.01)***	.32
1924	LaFollette	0.01 (0.01)	.04
	All minor candidates	0.00 (0.01)	.26
1948	Thurmond	-0.27 (0.04)***	.04
	H. Wallace	-0.01 (0.00)*	.10
	All minor candidates	-0.12 (0.02)***	.29
1968	G. Wallace	-0.13 (0.02)***	.02
1980	Anderson	-0.03 (0.01)***	.02
1992	Perot	-0.03 (0.01)***	.57
1996	Perot	0.01 (0.01)*	.57
	Other minor candidates	-0.01 (0.00)***	.34

Source: County presidential vote totals from ICPSR 8611 and *America Votes* series; church membership figures from ICPSR 0008 and NCCC church membership studies; see text for full discussion of these data sources.

Note: Standard errors in parentheses. Control variable coefficients not included.

* = Significant at 0.10 level.
** = Significant at 0.05 level.
*** = Significant at 0.01 level.

lower levels of independent candidate voting. The same relationship is observed when the third candidate has bolted from the Republicans or the Democrats (Roosevelt, H. Wallace and Thurmond, G. Wallace, Anderson), when the third candidate represents a true minor party (Debs), and when the third candidate simply decides to enter the political fray (Perot 1992). Control variables such as region introduced into several models do not alter the fundamental results.[8]

Perhaps most intriguing, the 1924 and 1996 elections have something in common: the third candidate was not running for the first time. Robert LaFollette had sought the presidency for nearly a decade, while Perot was of course repeating his 1992 bid. Further, both LaFollette and Perot had the backing of a political party, not just a set of voters converted temporarily to minor candidate voting. We will explore this facet of Perot's 1996 support in more detail below. But Table 6.1 does suggest that the perception of party status attached to a minor candidate helps to overcome the adherence-minor party inverse link found in all other twentieth-century cases.

The most recent independent bids deserve some further consideration. George Wallace's campaign was based almost entirely in southern states; John Anderson received a smattering of votes from all regions; and in 1992 Perot similarly did well in all regions and tripled Anderson's overall vote total in the process. Perot's 1996 patterns more closely resemble Anderson's in magnitude and distribution; in addition, although his vote share declines by twelve points, in 1996 Perot does do comparatively better in the same places where he did well in 1992 (Gilbert et al. 1999, 128). These three candidates could not be more different in terms of political orientation, background, and results. Yet in 1968, 1980, and 1992—the first presidential bids for each candidate—the structural effects of religious adherence operate in the same manner for each candidate. In the case of Wallace and Perot in 1996, the structural effect is strong enough to appear as a causal factor in individual-level vote models (Gilbert, Johnson, and Peterson 1995); this is not true for Anderson or Perot in 1992. Clearly, however, there is a powerful continuity running through these elections. The rather blunt instrument of religious adherence, which does not account for strength of individual beliefs and does not indicate strong concentrations of particular denominations, nevertheless works against independent candidates consistently and predictably.

Moreover, there are clues about individual voters that can be inferred from this aggregate data. While traditional methods for making inferences about individuals from aggregate or ecological data are problematic, a new method developed by King (1997) helps to overcome these long-standing problems.[9] Using King's ecological inference program, EzI, we estimate nationwide percentages of the 1992 Perot vote for two sets of voters: citizens who belong to a church and citizens who do not. EzI estimates do not distinguish between the major candidates, but they do offer a measure of how religious adherents voted versus non-adherents, in other words a way to link the aggregate results from Table 6.1 with the survey data to be analyzed in the next section. We control for the differential turnout rates of adherents and non-adherents by dividing the estimated rate of support by the estimated rate of turnout. Using this method we estimate that 15.6 percent of church members nationwide voted for Ross Perot in 1992; by contrast, we estimate that 23.1 percent of non-church members voted for Perot, a rate nearly 50 percent higher than the rate for adherents.[10]

The EzI estimates for 1996 offer similar results. Controlling for turnout rates, Ross Perot receives 6.9 percent of the votes of church members, and 9.8 percent of the votes of nonmembers (standard errors not reported). The difference, in terms of percent, is slightly less than what we found in the 1992 EzI estimates of Perot voting. For all minor candidates combined, the figures are 7.5 percent support among church members and 12.6 percent among non-church members.

Thus, the spread among the larger set of minor candidate voters is larger than the spread among Perot voters.

These findings are estimates, and care must be taken not to overemphasize the literal percentages. However, they shed light on the individual decision patterns responsible for the aggregate results shown in Table 6.1, and the results are striking. Ross Perot's support in both elections comes disproportionately from people who do not attend church, a confirmation of both the aggregate findings and our hypotheses about the negative nature of the relationship between religious factors and independent candidate voting. We turn now to individual factors using the 1992 and 1996 NES data, to further explain Perot voting and the constancy of religious factors over time.

Connections: Individual Models of 1992 Perot Voting

We begin the systematic analysis by restating the initial hypotheses concerning religious factors and independent candidates: voting along denominational lines should be rare; social issues should not be good predictors of independent candidate voting; religious factors are likely to work against independent candidates; and religious contexts may play a role, though the full nature of that role is unclear.

To assess the second and third hypotheses above, Table 6.2 presents a simplified look at religious variables and Perot voting. The table displays a series of bivariate logit models, demonstrating religious links to Perot voting in the absence of other causal factors. Few of these variables appear in the fully specified Perot vote model to follow (as noted in right hand column of Table 6.2), because other causal factors override the effects of these religious measures. We present Table 6.2 to show that connections between religion and Perot voting do exist, and their impact confirms our initial hypotheses in all respects.

Based on the development of improved measures of religiosity, the 1992 NES incorporates more detailed questions about religious practices and beliefs than previous surveys (Leege, Kellstedt, and Wald 1990). Table 6.2 shows a striking consistency in how these factors affect Perot voting. For every variable included, the effect on Perot voting is negative. Higher levels of any religious activity—praying, reading the Bible, attending church—make voters less likely to choose Perot. Further, the same attitudes that were negatively related to Anderson voting in 1980 (Gilbert, Johnson, and Peterson 1995) also turn up as negative influences on Perot voting—pro-life abortion views, belief in biblical inerrancy, support for school prayer. These religious effects fall out of the full Perot vote model (Table 6.3 below), with the sole exception of church attendance. As a well-known salient

Table 6.2. Impact of Religious Variables on Voting for Ross Perot, 1992 (Bivariate logit estimates)

Independent Variable	Coefficient	Significant in full vote model?
Church attendance	-0.17 (0.06)***	Yes
Attitude toward abortion	-0.19 (0.06)***	No
View on authorship of Bible	-0.22 (0.10)**	No
Born-again Christian	-0.18 (0.15)	No
Support for prayer in public schools	-0.08 (0.04)*	No
Guidance religion gives for daily living	-0.23 (0.09)**	No
Importance of religion to one's life	-0.59 (0.15)***	No
Frequency of prayer	-0.13 (0.05)***	No
Frequency of Bible reading	-0.20 (0.07)***	No

Source: 1992 National Election Study.

Note: Standard errors in parentheses.

    * = Significant at 0.10 level.

    ** = Significant at 0.05 level.

    *** = Significant at 0.01 level.

factor in explaining major party voting patterns (Knoke 1974), the significance of church attendance (and its anti-Perot effect) is no surprise. Clearly, the more important a person's personal religious views are, the less likely that person is to vote for Ross Perot. This conclusion depends to an extent on the denominational adherence of individuals; however, there do not appear to be any overwhelmingly or even modestly pro-Perot denominations among the American electorate (1992 NES, results not shown).

Bivariate models are necessarily limited in scope and explanatory power. A full model attempts to incorporate all potentially relevant factors and thus to sort out what really drives individual behavior. The results of our effort appear in Table 6.3. Where relevant, we will draw parallels with other research on the individual determinants of independent candidate voting; this limits comparisons to only the candidacies of Wallace and Anderson, since no survey data exists on earlier independent candidates.

With the notable exception of a considerable personal fortune to support his campaign, the Perot candidacy fits many of the familiar patterns observed in prior

Table 6.3. Estimated 1992 Vote for Ross Perot (Logit Estimates)

Independent Variable	Coefficient
Constant	*-0.74 (0.95)*
Pentecostal	*-1.28 (0.67)★*
Church attendance	*-0.14 (0.08)★*
Importance of religion to one's life	*-0.13 (0.16)*
Percent mainline Protestant in county	*-0.03 (0.07)*
Age	*-0.01 (0.01)★*
Nonwhite respondent	*-2.17 (0.62)★★★*
Male	*0.40 (0.21)★*
Follows public affairs	*-0.52 (0.14)★★★*
Discusses politics frequently with friends and family	*0.17 (0.10)★*
Folded party identification	*-0.27 (0.12)★★*
Bush job approval	*-0.35 (0.12)★★★*
Positive feelings toward federal govt.	*-0.02 (0.01)★★★*
Positive feelings toward feminists	*0.01 (0.00)★★★*
Has reasons to vote for Clinton	*-0.18 (0.07)★★*
Dissatisfied with choices among presidential candidates	*0.56 (0.14)★★★*
Believes Perot will better handle economy	*0.57 (0.22)★★★*
Favors new limits on imports	*0.47 (0.23)★★*
Percent Perot vote in county	*0.04 (0.02)★★*
Weighted number of cases	*820*
Percent of cases correctly predicted	*76.7*

Source: 1992 National Election Study; 1990 NCCC Church Census.
Note: Standard errors in parentheses.
         ★ = Significant at 0.10 level.
         ★★ = Significant at 0.05 level.
         ★★★ = Significant at 0.01 level.

independent bids. Perot supporters are displeased with the political status quo, expressed through dissatisfaction with the major party candidates and George Bush's job performance. Perot voters tend to be young, white, and male, believing that Perot can rescue the nation's economy. More frequent political discussion with friends and family increases the likelihood of Perot voting, but Perot voting is negatively related to following public affairs—the more a voter follows what goes on in politics, the less likely she is to vote for Perot. Being independent (measured through folded partisanship) is also a statistically significant predictor of Perot voting. These findings are somewhat parallel to factors predicting Wallace voting, though the impact of race as seen through issues is far less significant in 1992 than it is in 1968 (Gilbert, Johnson, and Peterson 1995). Further, a modest contextual amplification effect is found: Perot does better in places with more Perot voters, suggesting that he can benefit from connections to community, but significantly not from religiously oriented connections.

Some other variables delineate marked differences between Perot voters and third candidate voters in 1968 and 1980. Voters who find favorable reasons to vote for Bill Clinton do so, and are less likely therefore to vote for Perot. Unlike 1968 and 1980, the third candidate is not the sole alternative for voters who are unhappy with status quo politics and traditional choices. The findings in Table 6.3 suggest that the Clinton "new Democrat" appeal to disaffected voters mitigates the pro-Perot effects of anti-major party and anti-Washington attitudes.[11] Hence dislike for the parties or the federal government does not automatically translate into support for Perot; large numbers of Clinton voters show similar attitudes.

Many of these same factors that explain Perot voting also account for the paucity of significant religious factors in Table 6.3. Younger males are less frequent churchgoers and less certain believers. The seeming antireligious character of Perot voters was borne out by the results in Table 6.2, and it can be found again in Table 6.3. Some researchers have observed that white Protestants constitute the overwhelming majority of Perot voters (Kosmin and Lachman 1993, 168); others find evidence of Catholic support (Leege 1993). But in Table 6.3, no dichotomous denominational variable is found to be a positive influence on Perot voting. Pentecostals vote against Perot (they support Bush in large numbers), and frequent church attendance also decreases the probability of a Perot vote. This points to the conclusion that 1992 Perot voters are primarily secularist in orientation (Leege 1993).

Perot Voting in 1996: Dissimilar Patterns, Fewer Votes

As we argued above in discussing Table 6.1 and the EzI results, the 1996 aggregate Perot results indicate the existence of modest connections between religious institutions and patterns of Perot voting. This demonstrates the advantages of running a second presidential campaign with a nascent party organization in place. Clearly, Perot is not picking up substantial support in 1996 from religious groups or through religious institutions. But he is certainly not losing as much in these places as he did in 1992 (Gilbert et al. 1999, 125–129). Hence we expect that individual-level models of Perot voting in 1996 should show modest contextual effects in a positive direction; that is, Perot should gain votes from voters who live among other Perot voters, and Perot should not lose as many votes from religious Americans. In fact, our models will show these patterns, and we present models for other minor candidates in 1996 as well, to demonstrate further the adherence-minor party link and to explain the differences in support for Perot from 1992 to 1996.

The analysis of causal factors related to 1996 Perot and minor candidate voting begins with Table 6.4, which displays the results of bivariate models testing the influence of religious affiliation, beliefs, and practices on Perot voting (no similar tests are done for other minor candidates). Table 6.2 showed that individuals holding stronger religious beliefs, or engaging more in various religious practices, were less likely to vote for Perot in 1992. This same basic pattern holds in Table 6.4, with one caveat. In 1992 nearly all religious factors were statistically significant when examined in isolation, but lost statistical significance (except church attendance) in the full Perot vote model (Table 3). By contrast, in 1996 only two religious factors are statistically significant predictors of Perot voting when examined in isolation: church members and more frequent church attenders are less likely to vote for Perot. All other religious factors except one have no relationship with 1996 Perot voting, either alone or in full models. The exception is a question asking how important religion is in an individual's life. This variable is not significant on its own, but becomes significant and positive in the full 1996 Perot vote model (Table 6.5).

The preliminary results in Table 6.4 suggest few connections between religious factors and Perot support in the 1996 election. This conclusion raises additional questions, for in 1992 we did find at least a consistent pattern of inverse relationships, while in 1996 no pattern is found at all. If one emphasizes the lack of any pattern, it would seem that religion simply does not matter in understanding Perot voting. But if one emphasizes the lack of the negative-connection pattern that was found in 1992, it could be argued that the Reform Party's organizational efforts have begun to pay dividends. Had Perot not formed a party organization in 1993, the only lingering effect of the 1992 campaign would have been Perot himself, who appears to have little appeal among religious institutions or their members. But party organizations, working in cities and towns with churches and church-sponsored groups, among other social institutions, can begin to build networks in these communities that can be utilized to support campaigns for political office. Thus, the *absence* of a negative relationship between religious factors and Perot voting in 1996 could signal the weakening of the barriers to Perot voting that were in part reinforced by religious institutions and the beliefs of congregation members.

Table 6.4. Influence of Religious Variables on 1996 Presidential Vote for Ross Perot (Individual-Level Data, Bivariate Logit Estimates)

Independent Variable	Coefficient	Significant in full vote model?
Attitude toward abortion	*-0.03 (0.11)*	*No*
Born-again Christian	*-0.03 (0.26)*	*No*
Church attendance	*-0.15 (0.07)***	*No*
Church member	*-0.90 (0.23)****	*Yes*
Clergyperson urged congregation to vote for a candidate	*-0.21 (0.61)*	*No*
Contacted by religious or moral groups	*0.33 (0.29)*	*No*
Frequency of Bible reading	*-0.06 (0.11)*	*No*
Frequency of prayer	*-0.04 (0.09)*	*No*
Guidance religion gives for daily living	*-0.12 (0.16)*	*No*
Importance of religion to one's life	*0.05 (0.29)*	*Yes*
Political information available at respondent's church	*0.20 (0.35)*	*No*
Support for prayer in public schools	*0.09 (0.08)*	*No*
View on authorship of Bible	*-0.06 (0.17)*	*No*

Source: 1996 National Election Study.
Note: Standard errors in parentheses.
  * = Significant at 0.10 level.
  ** = Significant at 0.05 level.
  *** = Significant at 0.01 level.

Table 6.5 examines factors that affect Perot vote choice and vote choice for all minor candidates in the 1996 election. By estimating identical models and comparing coefficients, we can infer how the addition of other minor candidates alters the relationships found in the Perot model.[12] The Perot model is of most interest, however, and we expect to find more evidence of connections between societal institutions and Perot voters in 1996 than were found in 1992.

Examining Perot voting in Table 6.5, only church membership and the importance of religion are holdovers from Table 6.4; church attendance has no significance and is dropped from the final model. Recall that the 1992 NES Perot vote model

Table 6.5. Estimated 1996 Presidential Vote for Ross Perot and All Minor Candidates (Individual-Level Data, Logit Estimates)

Independent Variable	Perot Coefficient	All Minor Candidates Coefficient
Constant	-11.51 (2.36)★★★	-9.31 (2.06)★★★
Church member	-1.10 (0.42)★★★	-0.99 (0.36)★★★
Importance of religion to one's life	0.94 (0.52)★	0.15 (0.40)
Age	-0.01 (0.01)	-0.01 (0.01)
Male respondent	0.81 (0.42)★	0.35 (0.37)
Union	-1.23 (0.57)★★	-0.47 (0.44)
Income	-0.07 (0.04)★★	-0.08 (0.03)★★
Southern resident	1.04 (0.50)★★	0.87 (0.44)★★
Follows public affairs	-0.87 (0.28)★★★	-0.66 (0.24)★★★
Nonwhite respondent	-1.06 (0.98)	-0.71 (0.79)
Folded partisanship	0.47 (0.23)★★	0.75 (0.21)★★★
Folded liberal-conservative scale	0.40 (0.24)★	0.28 (0.21)
Positive feelings toward Dole	-0.02 (0.01)★★	-0.02 (0.01)★★
Gave money to a candidate	1.31 (0.51)★★★	1.08 (0.44)★★
Positive feelings toward NOW	0.03 (0.01)★★★	0.02 (0.01)★★
Decided late to vote for minor candidate	0.09 (0.02)★★★	0.10 (0.04)★★
Feels own beliefs not similar to others	0.85 (0.32)★★★	0.79 (0.28)★★★
Wants growth of other parties to challenge major parties	0.79 (0.26)★★★	0.81 (0.24)★★★
Believes Perot would better handle deficit	0.89 (0.27)★★★	0.87 (0.24)★★★
Watched presidential debates	-0.41 (0.21)★	-0.17 (0.18)
Believes jobs, living standards more important than protecting environment	0.41 (0.15)★★★	0.23 (0.13)★
Government should provide more services	-0.30 (0.14)★★	-0.19 (0.13)
Willing to serve on a jury	1.25 (0.44)★★★	0.79 (0.37)★★
Married, widowed, living with a partner	1.81 (0.53)★★★	1.26 (0.43)★★★
Percent 1996 Perot vote in county	0.22 (0.08)★★★	0.19 (0.06)★★★
Percent other minor candidate vote in county	0.08 (0.15)	0.26 (0.11)★★
Number of cases	771	771
Percent of cases correctly predicted	91.7	89.7

Source: 1996 National Election Study; 1990 NCCC Church Census; America Votes, 1996 presidential vote.

Note: Standard errors in parentheses. ★★ = Significant at 0.05 level.
    ★ = Significant at 0.10 level. ★★★ = Significant at 0.01 level.

also had few religious variables. The importance of religion was not significant in a bivariate model, but after numerous other salient factors are incorporated in Table 6.5, there is a barely significant and positive relationship to Perot voting in 1996.

Apart from religious factors, a contextual amplification effect—Perot voting is positively affected by rising levels of Perot voting in an individual's county—is present in 1996, just as it was in 1992. Contextual effects by definition involve the transmission of information within a defined frame of reference. If Perot gains more votes from individuals who live and work among relatively more Perot voters, then it is plausible to suggest that minor candidates can tap into existing social networks and use these to their advantage.

The Perot model in Table 6.5 has other continuities with the 1992 Perot model. Men in general and individuals who pay less attention to public affairs are still more likely to support Perot, as are political independents and ideological moderates. Respondents who believe Perot to be a good choice for handling economic policy, or who have no positive inclinations toward the major party candidates, also show greater propensity to support Perot. On the flip side, union members are less likely to vote for Perot, and as individual income rises a Perot vote becomes less likely.

The greatest differences in the 1996 Perot model come from variables assessing individual attitudes toward the political system and public officials. Perot voters in 1996 appear much less disaffected than 1992 Perot voters; this time the support for Perot has positive dimensions, rather than simply stemming from negative attitudes toward the major candidates and the political system in general. One example is a variable asking whether an individual gave money to any candidate; this variable does not appear in the 1992 model. Voters who did so are more likely to vote for Perot. Perot voters in 1996 are also more likely to be living with a significant other, and to say they would perform jury duty if asked.

To be sure, these relationships do not indicate that Perot voters are firmly grounded in the political mainstream. Yet no positive attitudes toward the political system are found in the 1992 Perot vote choice model. The 1996 Perot model therefore represents an evolutionary trend moving Perot (and perhaps his party in future elections) into the political mainstream, such that their support no longer comes from a disaffected and disconnected segment of the electorate. Perot voters in 1996 have some community attachments, evidence that the Reform Party has managed to carve out some base of support within communities.

Other modest differences include the salience of age, which we found in most presidential and state-level elections to be a consistent indicator of minor candidate voting. Although younger voters are still more likely to support a minor candidate, the variable does not achieve statistical significance in the 1996 Perot model.

Table 6.5 also presents a second model (right hand column) that estimates 1996 voting for any minor candidate, including Perot. We present this model to assess differences between support for Perot and other minor candidates at the individual level. After considerable testing of model specifications, we have chosen to estimate a model identical to the 1996 Perot model; with identical cases and variables, changes in coefficients may indicate that some factors have a distinctive impact when all minor candidates are covered in the dependent variable.

Table 6.5 indeed reveals some differences in factors that predict voting for all minor candidates versus factors predicting Perot voting only. Gender and race do not affect support for all minor candidates, nor does a moderate personal ideology, union membership, or viewing the presidential debates. In addition, the variable measuring the importance of religion loses significance. The shift of these factors from statistical significance to insignificance indicates that other minor candidates gain support from a different set of citizens, whose political views are diverse compared to one another and distinct when compared to the views of Perot voters. The other minor candidates in 1996 range across the ideological spectrum, hence we should not be surprised that mixing other minor candidate voters with Perot voters yields mixed results. As we have shown elsewhere, other minor candidates find electoral support from a different segment of the minor candidate market than the segment from which Perot draws his support (Gilbert et al. 1999, 130).

The variable measuring the county vote for other minor candidates is not significant in the Perot model but is significant for all minor candidate voters in the Table 6.5 model. Like Perot voters, other minor candidate voters show a greater propensity to choose outside the political status quo when they live among other like-minded citizens. Without the ability to differentiate further between Perot voters and other minor candidate voters, we conclude that the non-major party vote in 1996 is divided among a portion of the electorate that in some ways validates our theory about the sources of minor candidate support. In other ways the findings demonstrate a new facet—the idea that repeat minor candidates do begin to forge connections to religious and other social institutions that might pay off in greater electoral support in future elections.

Conclusions

Pulling together the evidence from this chapter, the logical conclusion about the electoral appeal of Ross Perot in 1992 is that it had next to nothing to do with organized religion. Instead, analysis of the 1992 Perot campaign with particular emphasis on religious factors reveals a strong continuity with previous independent bids. The differences are indeed crucial to remember: Perot did much better than his recent predecessors, in fact better in terms of vote share than any truly independent candidate. Some researchers have emphasized the unique aspects of the Perot phenomenon and concluded that his candidacy is best understood as unique (Gold 1995). Yet our analysis finds that support for Perot in 1992 was clearly not based on idiosyncratic factors, but rather was structured in predictable and logically coherent ways. The heavy media blitz Perot was able to mount (Feigert 1993) clearly contributed to his ability to gain 19 percent of the total vote. But the unique aspects of Perot's campaign crystallized into decisions made by voters, and in these decisions we assert there was more that was constant than was variable, especially (but not exclusively) the negative role of religious factors.

However, our analysis also indicates that the nature of electoral support for Ross Perot shifted not only in magnitude, but also in substance, from 1992 to 1996. The negative impact of religious adherence on Perot voting changed into a modest positive relationship in 1996. We have only observed this previously in 1924, which also included a minor candidate (LaFollette) who was well known to the general public as the leader of a nascent party organization, and whose support varied by region. We believe the change in the familiar adherence–minor candidate vote relationship indicates that party building activities, even relatively unsuccessful efforts, can begin to attenuate the inherent bias of community networks and institutions toward major party candidates and against upstart challengers. Such efforts are not strong enough to show up in denominational voting patterns (Gilbert et al. 1999, 126); Perot made no particular inroads into any one denomination, nor did any other minor candidate make such a connection.

The results of the 1996 election show that while the Perot phenomenon was not dead as an electoral force in U.S. politics, its significance had stabilized but decreased in magnitude since the 1992 campaign. Our analysis for 1992 and 1996 also shows again that the factors structuring support for Perot and other minor candidates are quite consistent with those for previous minor presidential candidates, more so than other analysts have asserted (Gold 1995). One key difference, availability of resources, helps explain why Perot received so many votes in 1992. But a second difference—the fact that Perot ran a second campaign and created a party organization to assist this effort—explains why in 1996 the institutional factors were either nominal or positive sources of support for Perot, while the usual factors such as political independence and a lack of connections to religious institutions or beliefs are the primary explanations for other minor candidate voting.

These assertions are worthy of further exploration. We stress their importance because we believe they can tell us something meaningful and novel about the relationships between American religious life and American politics. The results here focus on independent candidates, Perot in particular, but lead us back to the major parties and the nature of their persisting support among voters. If most Americans profess belief in God and at least membership in some church, they have drawn themselves in (often unwittingly) to a long-lasting, cultivated network of attachments between the secular and sacred aspects of U.S. society. These bonds may not be as strong as they once were, and the empirical research on the decline of strong partisanship since the 1960s provides an individual-level correlate. Moreover, the increasing mobility of Americans' church attachments might correspond to their mobility in terms of electoral choices and partisan leanings. Because churches are much more than mere extensions of the civic culture, such religious or church-based ties to patterns of political behavior will remain essentially indirect; such ties produce echoes (to use Key's metaphor) of individual-level processes that bring personal beliefs and group-generated cues to bear on vote decisions and issue attitudes.

Writing on the growth of religiously conservative church bodies, Dean Kelley argues that furthering a sense of distinctiveness from society at large is a primary aspect of strong religion-fuelling growth (Kelley 1972). Distinctiveness and strictness are critical salient factors in explaining the success of upstart sects, according to the religious markets paradigm (Finke and Stark 1992). A parallel could certainly be drawn to Ross Perot, whose entry into the political scene of 1992 provided distinctiveness, if not strictness. When it comes to politics, however, churches and churchgoers clearly find it advantageous to abandon distinctive, upstart political figures and strict movements or ideologies at the polling booth; witness the differential support for Perot among churchgoers and nonmembers. Instead, organized religion—represented by established (and declining) mainline denominations, ancient and enduring faith traditions, or growing offshoots in transition from sect to church—can best be viewed as a key sustaining source of Putnam's social capital, adopting new forms and furnishing institutional histories that help to foster the social connectedness necessary to a vibrant civil society. The reinforcement of a central tenet of America's political faith—support for and competition between two and only two political parties—is but one byproduct of this process. Any independent candidate who would break through this structural and historical nexus faces a daunting challenge indeed.

Notes

National Election Studies data utilized in this chapter were made available by the Inter-University Consortium for Political and Social Research (ICPSR) to Washington University in St. Louis. The data for the *Electoral Data for Counties in the United States: Presidential and Congressional Races, 1840–1872* (ICPSR 8611) were originally collected by Jerome M. Clubb, William H. Flanigan, and Nancy H. Zingale. Additional data were obtained by the authors from public sources described in the text. Neither the collectors of the original data nor the Consortium bear any responsibility for the analyses or interpretations presented here.

An earlier version of this chapter was delivered at the 1996 Annual Meeting of the Midwest Political Science Association, The Palmer House Hilton, Chicago, April 18–20, 1996.

1. The terms *independent candidate, third candidate, minor candidate,* and *third party* are used interchangeably in this chapter. These terms refer to candidates not running as Republicans or Democrats. In practice, scholars who study such candidates have asserted with considerable justification that there is little use distinguishing among candidates running under some minor party label and candidates running unattached to any party (Rosenstone et al. 1996); we support and emulate this convention.

2. Not coincidentally, perhaps, 1948 is the same year political scientists began collecting national survey data on voter preferences.

3. Some counties have a religious adherence percentage that exceeds 100; this is partly a function of the population data that does not precisely match with the counting of church members, but it is also an artifact of the membership counting procedure. Both the Census Bureau back in the early twentieth century, as well as the NCCC through the present, use the membership totals of specific church congregations as the unit of analysis from which county totals are calculated. Since individuals can and do attend church in counties other than the ones where they reside, county church membership can (and still does, even in the 1990 NCCC data) exceed the total population of the county.

4. If the questions of interest here necessitated differentiations among all three candidates in 1992, the appropriate modelling strategy involves a multinomial probit technique; for such an analysis see Alvarez and Nagler (1995).

5. When a dependent variable is dichotomous, ordinary least squares (OLS) regression does not produce efficient or reliable estimates. Hence a logit model, which calculates probabilities based on the relationship between the independent variables and the dichotomous dependent variable using the equation $P = 1/(1+e^{-Xb})$, is the appropriate choice (Hanushek and Jackson 1977, 187–203).

6. Coding schemes for all variables are available from the authors.

7. In 1924, Robert LaFollette, an unsuccessful Republican candidate for three prior elections, gained some significant union endorsements and worked through existing parties such as the Progressives and Socialists (Rosenstone et al. 1996, 96–97). Party systems in disarray may well produce electoral outcomes that do not reflect normal patterns; the Democrats' chaos, the GOP split, and the eclectic nature of the LaFollette alliance all contributed to the disorder that marked the 1924 race and the impending end of the fourth U.S. party system. The strong Socialist support for LaFollette might have been a factor, yet 1912 Debs voting declined as adherence rose, and there is no a priori reason why 1924 patterns should have differed so starkly. Alternatively, we might expect county LaFollette and Republican (Coolidge) voting to be strongly correlated; in fact, the simple correlation between the two measures is not significant. A more satisfying explanation would connect the county LaFollette voting patterns to some specific denominational alliances grouped around issues such as Prohibition.

8. Results for control variables are not reported in Table 6.1.

9. For a detailed explanation of King's solution to the ecological inference problem, see King 1997.

10. Full results from the EzI analysis are not reported but are available from the authors.

11. For a contrary conclusion, see Alvarez and Nagler 1995.

12. For the Perot model in Table 6.5, we have added other minor candidate voters to the 0 category in the dependent variable, thus the samples are identical in the two models displayed in Table 6.5.

References

Abramson, Paul R., John H. Aldrich, Phil Paolino, and David W. Rohde. 1995. "Third-Party and Independent Candidates in American Politics: Wallace, Anderson, and Perot," *Political Science Quarterly* (Fall): 349–367.

Alvarez, R. Michael, and Jonathan Nagler. 1995. "Economics, Issues, and the Perot Candidacy: Voter Choice in the 1992 Presidential Election," *American Journal of Political Science* 39: 714–744.

Bradley, Martin, et al., eds. 1992. *Churches and Church Membership in the United States.* Atlanta: Glenmary Research Center.

Chressanthis, George, and Stephen Shaffer. 1993. "Major-Party Failure and Third-Party Voting in Presidential Elections, 1976–1988," *Social Science Quarterly* 74: 264–273.

Downs, Anthony. 1957. *An Economic Theory of Democracy.* New York: Harper.

Feigert, Frank B. 1993. "The Ross Perot Candidacy and Its Significance." In William Crotty, ed., *America's Choice: The Election of 1992.* Guilford, C.t: The Dushkin Publishing Group.

Flanigan, William, and Nancy Zingale. 1994. *Political Behavior of the American Electorate.* 8th ed. Washington, D.C.: Congressional Quarterly Press.

Finke, Roger, and Rodney Stark. 1992. *The Churching of America, 1776–1990: Winners and Losers in Our Religious Economy.* New Brunswick, N.J.: Rutgers University Press.

Gaustad, Edwin. 1976. *Historical Atlas of Religion in America* (revised edition). New York: Harper & Row.

Gilbert, Christopher P. 1993. *The Impact of Churches on Political Behavior: An Empirical Study.* Westport, Ct.: Greenwood Press.

Gilbert, Christopher P., Timothy R. Johnson, and David A. M. Peterson. 1995. "The Religious Roots of Third Candidate Voting: A Comparison of Anderson, Perot, and Wallace Voters," *Journal for the Scientific Study of Religion* 34 (4): 470–484.

Gilbert, Christopher P., and David A. M. Peterson. 1995. "Minnesota: Christians and Quistians in the GOP." In Mark J. Rozell and Clyde Wilcox, eds., *God at the Grassroots: The Christian Right in the 1994 Elections.* Lanham, Md.: Rowman and Littlefield.

Gilbert, Christopher P., David A. M. Peterson, Timothy R. Johnson, and Paul A. Djupe. 1999. *Religious Institutions and Minor Parties in the United States.* Westport, Ct.: Praeger Publishers.

Gillespie, J. David. 1993. *Politics at the Periphery: Third Parties in Two-Party America.* Columbia, S.C.: University of South Carolina Press.

Gold, Howard J. 1995. "Third Party Voting in Presidential Elections: A Study of Perot, Anderson, and Wallace," *Political Research Quarterly* 48: 751–773.

Gould, Lewis L. 1993. *1968: The Election that Changed America.* Chicago: Ivan R. Dee.

Hanushek, Eric, and John E. Jackson. 1977. *Statistical Models for Social Scientists*. New York: Academic.

Hauser, Robert M. 1974. "Contextual Analysis Revisited," *Sociological Methods and Research* 2: 365–375.

Huckfeldt, R. Robert, and John Sprague. 1995. *Citizens, Politics, and Social Communication*. Cambridge: Cambridge University Press.

Jelen, Ted. 1992. "Political Christianity: A Contextual Analysis," *American Journal of Political Science* 36: 692–714.

Johnson, Douglas W., et al., eds. 1974. *Churches and Church Membership in the United States, 1971*. Washington: Glenmary Research Center.

Johnson, Timothy, David A. M. Peterson, and Christopher P. Gilbert. 1995. "Religious Adherence and County Voting Patterns: Evidence From the States, 1994." Presented at the Society for the Scientific Study of Religion annual meeting, St. Louis.

Karl, Barry. 1983. *The Uneasy State: The United States from 1915 to 1945*. Chicago: University of Chicago Press.

Kelley, Dean M. 1972. *Why Conservative Churches Are Growing; A Study in Sociology of Religion*. New York: Harper & Row.

Kellstedt, Lyman, and Mark Noll. 1990. "Religion, Voting for President, and Party Identification, 1948–1984." In Mark Noll, ed., *Religion and American Politics: From the Colonial Period to the 1980s*. New York: Oxford University Press.

Key, V. O. 1948. *Politics, Parties, and Pressure Groups*. 2nd ed. New York: Thomas Crowell Company.

———. 1949. *Southern Politics in State and Nation*. New York: Random House.

King, Gary. 1997. *A Solution to the Ecological Inference Problem: Reconstructing Individual Behavior from Aggregate Data*. Princeton: Princeton University Press.

Kosmin, Barry, and Seymour Lachman. 1993. *One Nation Under God: Religion in Contemporary American Society*. New York: Harmony Books.

Leege, David C. 1993. "The Decomposition of the Religious Vote: A Comparison of White, Non-Hispanic Catholics with Other Ethnoreligious Groups, 1960–1992." Presented at the American Political Science Association annual meeting, Washington.

Leege, David C., and Lyman Kellstedt, eds. 1993. *Rediscovering the Religious Factor in American Politics*. Armonk, N.Y.: M.E. Sharpe.

Leege, David C., Lyman Kellstedt, and Kenneth D. Wald. 1990. "Religion and Politics: A Report on Measures of Religiosity in the 1989 NES Pilot Study." Presented at Midwest Political Science Association annual meeting, Chicago.

Lenski, Gerhard. 1961. *The Religious Factor*. Garden City, N.Y.: Doubleday-Anchor.

Lieske, Joel. 1993. "Regional Subcultures of the United States," *Journal of Politics* 55: 888–913.

Lopatto, Paul. 1985. *Religion and the Presidential Election*. New York: Praeger.

MacKay, Kenneth. 1947. *The Progressive Movement of 1924*. New York: Columbia University Press.

Magleby, David, and Joseph Quin Monson. 1995. "If You Can't Win, Change the Rules: Strategic Voting, Expressive Voting, and a Proposed Runoff Election in Utah." Presented at the Western Political Science Association annual meeting, Portland.

Mazmanian, Daniel. 1974. *Third Parties in Presidential Elections*. Washington: Brookings Institution.

Menendez, Albert J. 1996. *The Perot Voters and the Future of American Politics.* Amherst, N.Y.: Prometheus Books.

Milkis, Sidney M. 1993. *The President and the Parties.* New York: Oxford University Press.

Miller, Warren. 1956. "One-Party Politics and the Voter," *American Political Science Review* 50: 707–725.

Newman, William, and Peter Halvorson. 1980. *Patterns in Pluralism: A Portrait of American Religion, 1952–1971.* Washington: Glenmary Research Center.

Peterson, David A. M., Timothy R. Johnson, and Christopher P. Gilbert. 1995. "Voter Preference Conversions in American Presidential Elections: A Comparison of Two-Candidate and Three-Candidate Races." Presented at Midwest Political Science Association annual meeting, Chicago.

Putnam, Robert. 1995. "Bowling Alone: America's Declining Social Capital," *Journal of Democracy*: 65–78.

Quinn, Bernard, et al., eds. 1982. *Churches and Church Membership in the United States, 1980.* Washington: Glenmary Research Center.

Rosenstone, Steven, Roy Behr, and Edward Lazarus. 1996. *Third Parties in America: Citizen Response to Major Party Failure.* 2nd ed. Princeton: Princeton University Press.

Salisbury, Robert, John Sprague, and Gregory Weiher. 1984. "Does Religious Pluralism Make a Difference? Interactions Among Context, Attendance, and Political Behavior." Presented at the American Political Science Association annual meeting, Washington.

Scammon, Richard A. 1995. *America Votes: A Handbook of Contemporary Election Statistics* (volume 21). Washington, D.C.: Congressional Quarterly.

Scammon, Richard M., Alice V. McGillivray, and Rhodes Cook. 1997. *America Votes 22: A Handbook of Contemporary American Election Statistics.* Washington, D.C.: Elections Research Center, Congressional Quarterly, Inc.

Schlesinger, Arthur. 1973. *History of U.S. Political Parties.* New York: Chelsea House.

Smallwood, Frank. 1983. *The Other Candidates: Third Parties in Presidential Elections.* Hanover, N.H.: University Press of New England.

Sorauf, Frank, and Paul Beck. 1988. *Party Politics in America.* New York: Harper Collins Publishers.

Wald, Kenneth D. 1997. *Religion and Politics in the United States.* 3rd ed. Washington: Congressional Quarterly Press.

Wald, Kenneth D., Dennis E. Owen, and Samuel S. Hill. 1988. "Churches As Political Communities," *American Political Science Review* 82: 531–548.

———. 1990. "Political Cohesion in Churches," *Journal of Politics* 52: 197–215.

7

Understanding
Perot's Plummet

Jeremy D. Mayer
Clyde Wilcox

When Ross Perot received nearly 20 percent of the popular vote in the 1992 elections, many observers believed that he was destined to become an important, permanent fixture in American politics. Perot had led both major party nominees at one point in the campaign, and finished strong despite the absence of a party organization to help mobilize his supporters. He had spent nearly $70 million in his quest for the White House, mostly his own money, and it was clear that he had the means to do so again. Throughout Clinton's first term, pundits pondered a possible Perot candidacy in 1996, and political strategists worried about how to attract Perot's supporters to their party (Luntz 1993; Dionne 1996). Observing a Perot rally in 1995, David S. Broder, perhaps the most respected political journalist of his generation, claimed that the Perot voters were "the radical middle, the most significant and fastest-growing element in our politics" (Broder 1995).

Yet in the 1996 presidential election Perot was not a factor in the campaign, and his share of the popular vote was less than half that of 1992. In 1992 Perot was a major part of the story of the election, but in 1996 he was a mere footnote. Why did the same candidate, running on largely the same platform, experience such a precipitous plummet in support? We begin our account by briefly discussing the changes in Perot's public image, resulting from events before and during the 1996 campaign. We next examine changes in the electoral context, including public evaluations of the state of the economy and of the major party candidates. Finally, we use aggregate and survey data to explore the sources of the decline in Perot's support.

The Texas Titan Topples: Changing Images of Ross Perot

Early in the 1992 presidential campaign, Ross Perot captured the imagination of the American electorate. Republican pollster Frank Luntz argued it was Perot's position as a nonpolitician that attracted many of his supporters. "Thank God he has no political experience," said one participant in a Luntz focus group (Luntz 1993). Not only was Perot a new face on the political scene, he also relied heavily on nontraditional media to communicate his message, including television talk shows and half-hour infomercials, to the near-exclusion of traditional campaign devices such as rallies and thirty-second ads (Menendez 1996). His low-tech broadcasts attracted high ratings from a supposedly cynical and alienated public (Posner 1996: 291–292). Perot peddled a mythic account of his successful rise and personal fortune, and consistently implied that political problems could be easily fixed by a leader with the will to get things done. However, by 1996, Perot's image had undergone a thorough metamorphosis. In 1992 Perot was novel, a white knight prepared to rescue the government from politicians, a Cincinnatus reluctantly entering politics only to save the republic, but by 1996 Perot was seen as an eccentric, cranky politician. Between 1992 and 1996, media coverage was generally negative, and this led the public to a more critical view of Perot the man. As pollster Andrew Kohut put it, "His image is at best that of an eccentric, and at worst, an egomaniac," (Kalb 1996). Perot was also seriously damaged by events in 1996 that suggested he was willing to bend the rules to win nomination in the very party he created (Greenblatt 1996). Moreover, although Perot had emphasized in 1992 that he was not campaigning with public funds, in 1996 Perot accepted public funding. Accepting public funds created two problems for Perot's campaign: it made him appear to be a regular politician, and it limited the amount he could spend in the campaign. Perhaps the most important difference between the 1992 and 1996 campaigns was the exclusion of Perot from the 1996 debates. In 1992, Perot was declared by a number of pundits to be the winner of at least one of the three clashes among the nominees (Nagourney 1996). Without the automatic stature and attention that come with participation in a presidential debate, Perot was never able to make campaign finance salient as he had the equally complex issues of recessions and budget deficits four years before. Perot's image in 1996, while bearing a surface resemblance to the Texas titan of 1992, was in actuality radically different on a number of key points. At the same time, the America of 1996 was starkly dissimilar in important respects from the America of four years before.

Changes in the Nation and the Electorate

If Perot was not as attractive a candidate in 1996 as he had been in 1992, it is also true that changes in the state of the economy and in the choices facing the electorate created difficulties for his campaign. The repetitive slogan of the inner circle of the Clinton campaign in 1992 was, "It's the economy, stupid,"[1] and according to any number of analysts, the economy was the fundamental factor in Clinton's 1992 victory (Lipset 1993; Levine 1995). The election seemed to fit perfectly the retrospective economic evaluation model of presidential politics (Fiorina 1981; Markus 1988) in which voters reward or punish the president's party for economic performance. While some (Alvarez and Nagler 1995) question whether negative economic evaluations produced many votes for Perot, it is clear that his campaign theme—the dangers of budget deficits—found some receptive ears in 1992. In debates and in his commercials, Perot explained how badly the economy was doing, and how serious were the problems facing the nation. With a budget deficit of roughly $200 billion and the nation slowly emerging from a sharp recession, Perot struck a nerve.

By 1996 the nation was in the midst of a fourth year of solid recovery and growth, and the deficit had fallen dramatically. Polls showed much greater optimism about the economy and the state of the nation in general (Alvarez and Nagler 1997). Part of Perot's appeal in 1992 was his business acumen, and his vow to "get under the hood" of the U.S. economy and fix it, but in 1996 the economy appeared to many voters to be running smoothly. The greatest focus of Perot's 1992 campaign was the budget deficit, which Perot characterized as "the crazy old aunt in the attic" that none of the professional politicians wanted to talk about. By 1996, Clinton and congressional Republicans had made a real dent in the deficit, and were publicly agreed that the deficit would disappear in the near future. The greater confidence in the economy is clearly seen in the Consumer Confidence Index, which stood at 47.3 in Feb, 1992 and had increased to 109.4 in August, 1996. In early 1992 57 percent of the public perceived that the economy was getting worse; in August 1996 the figure was 23 percent. Moreover, voters were simply happier in 1996; Gallup data show that voters were twice as likely in 1992 to indicate that they were dissatisfied with the way their lives were going as they were in 1996.

Perot's other issues in 1992 were also less effective in 1996. Perot had championed term limits, but with congressional Republicans now enjoying the benefits of seniority the GOP was no longer pushing this issue. Moreover, the GOP takeover of Congress in 1994 showed that elections can serve as term limits when voters demand it. Perot's grab bag of reform proposals—eliminating the Electoral College, shortening the electoral cycle, limiting congressional retirement packages, controlling exit polling, a national referendum covering every future tax increase, campaign finance reform, and the balanced budget amendment (*Not For Sale* transcript 1996)—did not capture the voters' imagination in 1996.

On a number of occasions, Perot demonstrated that he still had the ability to attack his opponents with simple but elegant language. After bringing up the mushrooming fund-raising scandals, Perot then alluded to Clinton's rumored sexual harassment, when he asked a crowd in San Antonio immediately prior to the election which candidate they would be comfortable having their daughter work for just out of college (Tollerson 1996). On the question of Whitewater pardons, Perot stated on *Meet the Press,* "Surely if our President has the moral and ethical base necessary to send our troops into combat, he would be strong enough to look the American people in the eye and say, 'I will not pardon those people'" (*Meet The Press,* transcript 1996). In a single sentence, Perot cogently made a case against Clinton's silence on Whitewater pardons, something that Dole had waffled, fumbled, and stammered about for weeks. But although Perot could still adeptly attack the incumbent, he lacked an issue that could connect with the electorate.

Perot in 1992 also benefited from an electorate that found both candidates to be unacceptable. A majority of voters had decided not to renew George Bush's contract because he had failed to quickly end the recession, and appeared not to care about the suffering of those who had lost their jobs. Yet many were uneasy with Bill Clinton, a southern governor burdened by many rumors of questionable conduct. Although the public also did not trust Bill Clinton in 1996, he no longer appeared to be a risky choice for president—indeed, many believed that under his presidency the economy and the country more generally had improved. It is always easier to challenge an unpopular incumbent than one that is acceptable to voters, thus the electoral context in 1996 was far less favorable to Perot. In September, 1992, 54 percent of the public told Gallup that they disapproved of Bush's handling of the presidency; the figure for Clinton in 1996 was only 31 percent.

Thus, many factors may have influenced the drop in Perot's support. We now turn to an empirical investigation of the sources of the decline. We begin with an examination of aggregate state results, to see if Perot lost support disproportionately in one or more regions or states. We then turn to survey data from 1992 and 1996 to see if different demographic or attitudinal groups were more likely to change their evaluation of Perot.

Perot in 1992 and 1996: A View from the States

Although Perot ran a national media campaign in 1992 and 1996, he nonetheless divided his staff into state organizations (Posner 1996). Presidential candidates campaign state by state seeking to assemble an electoral college majority (Wayne

1992), and although this is less true of Perot than for Bush, Dole, or Clinton, it is nonetheless important to understand the geography of Perot's support.

Perot did dramatically better in some states than in others in both 1992 and 1996. In 1992, aggregate statewide Perot percentages ranged from a low of 9 percent (Mississippi) to 30 percent (Maine), with an average of 20 percent. Perot even managed to come in second in 1992 in two states, Utah (to Bush) and Maine (to Clinton). In 1996, Perot was not even close to second place in any state: his support ranged from 6 percent (Georgia, Mississippi, Tennessee, South Carolina, Alabama, and New Mexico) to a high of 14 percent (Montana and Maine), with a mean of 9 percent.

The average drop in Perot support from 1992 to 1996 was just over 10 percent, and his decline ranged from a high of 18 percent in Kansas to a low of 2 percent in Arkansas. Both states had favorite sons in the race: Dole undoubtedly pulled Perot voters to his candidacy, as Clinton had done in 1992 and again in 1996. Overall, Perot's support declined in every state, and fell most sharply in those states where he had fared the best in 1992. In states where Perot received 24 percent or more of the popular vote in 1992, his vote total declined by 57 percent, while in those states where Perot received 15 percent or less in 1992 his vote fell off by only 42 percent. Yet there was considerable continuity in Perot's support in the states; the correlation between aggregate Perot support in 1992 and 1996 is .74. Thus, the geography of Perot's support was relatively constant from 1992 to 1996, but his decline was steepest in those states that had given him the greatest support in 1992.

Table 7.1 shows the statewide vote for Perot in 1992 and 1996, along with the absolute decline and the percentage decline. Table 7.2 shows statewide vote for Perot in 1992 and 1996, with states classified several different ways. Perot did markedly worse in his home region of the South in both 1992 and 1996, but proportionately his support fell by half in every region. He did best in states with moralistic political cultures in 1992 and worst in traditionalistic states (which are mostly southern), and a similar pattern held again in 1996. Yet once again Perot's support declined similarly in states with all three types of political cultures. Perot did better in both 1992 and 1996 in Republican states, and his support declined slightly more in GOP states.

Somewhat surprisingly, Perot did not do significantly better in states with large numbers of independent voters in 1992 or 1996, although his very best states included two that have elected independent governors—Maine and Alaska. Finally, there was little relationship between state ideology (Erikson, Wright, and McIver 1993) and Perot vote in 1992 or 1996. This may be due to Perot's decidedly nonideological appeal. Perot argued that we should simply "fix" problems, without providing a comprehensive account of how these problems relate to larger issues of social and economic life. Frank Luntz, early in 1993, argued, based on his focus group research, that Perot voters were nonideological.

Table 7.1. Perot Vote by State, 1992–1996

	1992	1996	Absolute Drop	% Drop
AL	11	6	-5	44
AK	28	11	-17	61
AZ	24	8	-16	66
AR	10	8	-2	23
CA	21	7	-14	66
CO	23	7	-16	70
CT	21	10	-12	54
DE	20	11	-9	46
FL	20	9	-11	55
GA	13	6	-7	55
HI	14	8	-6	44
ID	27	13	-14	52
IL	17	3	-14	52
IN	20	10	-10	49
IA	19	9	-10	52
KS	27	9	-18	67
KY	14	9	-5	34
LA	12	7	-5	41
ME	30	14	-16	54
MD	14	7	-7	50
MA	23	9	-14	60
MI	19	9	-10	53
MN	24	12	-12	50
MS	9	6	-3	31
MO	22	10	-12	54
MT	26	14	-12	46
NB	24	11	-13	53
NV	26	9	-17	66
NH	23	10	-13	56
NJ	16	9	-7	42
NM	16	6	-10	63
NY	16	8	-8	49
NC	14	7	-7	50
ND	23	12	-11	48
OH	21	11	-10	48
OK	23	11	-12	52
OR	24	11	-13	55

Table 7.1 (continued)

	1992	1996	Absolute Drop	% Drop
PA	18	10	-8	45
RI	23	11	-12	53
SC	12	6	-6	50
SD	22	10	-12	54
TN	10	6	-4	41
TX	22	7	-15	68
UT	27	10	-17	63
VT	22	12	-11	47
VA	14	7	-7	50
WA	24	9	-15	62
WV	16	11	-5	31
WI	22	10	-12	53
WY	26	12	-14	53

It is also significant that in the 70-odd pages of focus-group transcripts, not once did a Perot supporter identify either Perot or himself as liberal or conservative. This suggests that ideology is irrelevant to Perovians, and that the word "conservative" may not be very useful in attracting the Perot constituency. (Luntz 1993)

States that were demographically diverse also differed in their level of Perot support. Perot did better in "whiter" states in both years. This is not surprising, since his level of support among African Americans and other minorities was quite low. Perot, unlike some previous third party candidates (Thurmond, George Wallace) had very little to say about the issue of race.[2] Although in both years, Perot would occasionally mention prominent African Americans as potential running mates, the Perot movement was largely a white phenomenon.

Overall, Perot's support in 1992 varied significantly by state. In 1996, Perot did better in those states where he had been strongest in 1992, but his support also declined the most in those states. Perot's plummet was mainly a national phenomenon, however, for his vote totals declined sharply in all fifty states.

Perot's Plummet among Voters

Data from the National Election Study confirm that voters were far less interested in Ross Perot in 1996 than they had been in 1992. More than half of voters in

Table 7.2. Patterns of Statewide Vote for Perot, 1992–1996

	1992	1996	Average
Region			
Northeast	21	10	16
Midwest	22	10	16
West	24	10	17
South	14	8	11
State Political Culture			
Moralistic	24	11	18
Individualistic	21	10	16
Traditionalistic	15	8	12
State Partisanship			
More Republican	24	10	17
Middle	21	10	16
Less Republican	15	8	12
Independent Identifiers			
Low	18	9	14
Medium	19	9	14
High	22	10	11
State Ideology			
Liberal	20	9	15
Moderate	21	10	16
Conservative	18	9	14
State Black Population Level			
High	23	11	17
Medium	22	10	16
Low	15	7	11

1992 reported that they could think of at least one reason to vote for Perot; by 1996 the figure had dropped to 27 percent. Table 7.3 shows other evaluations of the candidates in 1992 and 1996. Note first that respondents rated Perot less warmly in 1996 than in 1992, and this was true even among the smaller core of 1996 Perot voters. In 1996, respondents were far less likely to report emotional reactions of any kind to Perot than to Clinton or Dole. Perot was less likely to make citizens feel proud or hopeful but also to feel angry and even afraid, a clear indication that the electorate didn't seriously consider Perot in 1996. When asked to rate candidates on character traits, Perot finished second (ahead of Clinton) as honest and moral, but was a distant third on inspiring and cares about people like

Table 7.3. Evaluations of Candidates, 1992–1996

Evaluations of the Candidates, 1992			
	Clinton	Bush	Perot
Feeling Thermometer			
0	*3*	*5*	*7*
1–49	*19*	*26*	*23*
50–69	*20*	*32*	*42*
70–100	*49*	*37*	*28*
Candidates Rated by Own Voters	*80*	*79*	*76*
Extremely Liberal/Liberal	*35%*	*8%*	*18%*
Slightly. Liberal/Conservative/Moderate	*58%*	*42%*	*52%*
Extremely Conservative/Conservative	*7%*	*50%*	*30%*
Evaluations of Candidates, 1996			
Feeling Thermometer			
0	*7*	*3*	*10*
1–49	*20*	*28*	*34*
50–69	*23*	*39*	*43*
70–100	*50*	*30*	*13*
Candidates Rated by Own Voters	*80*	*70*	*69*
Extremely Liberal/Liberal	*40%*	*6%*	*16%*
Slightly Liberal/Conservative/Moderate	*51%*	*42%*	*50%*
Extremely Conservative/Conservative	*9%*	*52%*	*33%*
	Clinton	Dole	Perot
Angry	*53%*	*35%*	*27%*
Hopeful	*59%*	*36%*	*31%*
Afraid	*32%*	*25%*	*27%*
Proud	*51%*	*39%*	*23%*
Fits Candidate Quite Well or Extremely Well			
Moral	*39%*	*79%*	*66%*
Inspiring	*53%*	*37%*	*34%*
Strong leader	*60%*	*60%*	*38%*
Cares about people like you	*58%*	*42%*	*38%*
Knowledgeable	*84%*	*84%*	*70%*
Honest	*43%*	*69%*	*58%*
Gets things done	*58%*	*64%*	*54%*

Table 7.3 (continued)

Evaluations of the Candidates, 1996				
Which Candidate Would:	*Clinton*	*Dole*	*Perot*	*None*
Protect environment	*50%*	*14%*	*4%*	*33%*
Reduce deficit	*30*	*25*	*23*	*22*
Improve education	*50*	*21*	*6*	*23*
Campaign reform	*20*	*15*	*26*	*39*
Raise taxes	*41*	*29*	*7*	*23*
Cut Social Security	*19*	*45*	*9*	*25*

you. Moreover, the candidate whose 1992 theme was that his personal strong leadership could get things done was seen as far less able to get things done than either Dole or Clinton, and as less likely to be a strong leader.

Although Perot tried to appeal to the "radical middle" Clinton was again more likely to be perceived as representing the political center than Perot—a testimony to the success of Clinton's efforts to capture the middle ground on issues such as crime, violence on television, school discipline, and welfare. On specific issues, Perot was seen as far less likely to protect the environment or to improve education, and was actually seen as less likely than either Clinton or Dole to reduce the deficit. Only on campaign reform did Perot have a narrow advantage over Clinton, perhaps because of Perot's handling of his own convention and his acceptance of federal campaign funds.

Perot's vote totals declined across all states, and they also declined across social and political groups. Table 7.4 shows Perot's vote in 1992 and 1996 among selected social groups. What is remarkable about the data in this table is the constancy of Perot's decline. Perot's vote declined by 11 percent among all voters, and the only deviation from this decline is among those groups that did not support Perot in significant numbers in 1992—blacks, born-again Christians, Democrats, and the oldest Americans. If, as some theorized, Perot's loss in support had to do with a judgment in elite and media circles that he was not a substantial or credible candidate, then we would expect support to have declined most among respondents with moderately high levels of education, who could process the information and therefore be influenced by it (Zaller 1992; Converse 1964). There is some evidence of this happening; Perot's decline in support from 1992 to 1996 among those with college degrees was twice as great as the fall among those without high school diplomas.

In Table 7.5 we show the results of logistic regressions estimated with data from the 1992 and 1996 NES, predicting first a Perot vote overall, and then separate

Table 7.4. Perot Vote Among Select Political and Social Groups, 1992-1996

	1992	1996	Drop
Overall	*19%*	*8%*	*11%*
Men	*21%*	*10%*	*11%*
Women	*17%*	*7%*	*10%*
Whites	*20*	*9%*	*11%*
Blacks	*7%*	*4%*	*3%*
Married	*20%*	*9%*	*11%*
Unmarried	*18%*	*9%*	*9%*
18–29 years old	*22%*	*10%*	*12%*
30–44	*20%*	*9%*	*11%*
45–59	*19*	*9%*	*10%*
60+	*12%*	*7%*	*5%*
Not HS graduate	*17%*	*11%*	*6%*
HS	*20%*	*13%*	*7%*
Some college	*21%*	*10%*	*11%*
College graduate or more	*18%*	*7%*	*11%*
White Protestant	*21%*	*10%*	*11%*
Catholic	*20%*	*9%*	*11%*
White Born-Again Christian	*15%*	*8%*	*7%*
Union household	*21%*	*9%*	*12%*
Income less than $15,000	*18%*	*11%*	*7%*
$15,000–29,000	*20%*	*9%*	*11%*
$30,000–49,000	*21%*	*10%*	*11%*
$50,000+	*18%*	*7%*	*11%*
Republicans	*17%*	*6%*	*11%*
Independents	*30%*	*17%*	*13%*
Democrats	*13%*	*5%*	*8%*
Conservatives	*17%*	*8%*	*11%*
Moderates	*21%*	*9%*	*12%*
Liberals	*18%*	*7%*	*11%*

Source: *New York Times*, November 10, 1996, 28.

Table 7.5. Multivariate Analysis of Perot Vote, 1992 and 1996

1992	Perot v. All	Perot v. Bush	Perot v. Clinton
Strength of Partisanship	-.54**	-.72**	-.23
	(.14)	(.18)	(.17)
Ideology	.13	-.29*	.45**
	(.11)	(.14)	(.14)
Government Services/Spending	-.13	.29*	-.52**
	(.10)	(.14)	(.14)
Abortion	.26	.35@	.15
	(.17)	(.20)	(.21)
Evaluation of Economy	-.19	.00	-.40**
	(.11)@	(.13)	(.14)
Education	-.05	.02	-.09
	(.06)	(.07)	(.07)
Church Attendance	-.08	-.15	-.04
	(.09)	(.11)	(11)
South	-.48	-.40	-.55
	(.38)	(.49)	(.42)
Age	-.01	-.00	-.01
	(.01)	(.01)	(.01)
Male	-.53*	-.81*	-.53@
	(.27)	(.35)	(.32)
White	6.65	5.15	8.50
	(10.25)	(13.9)	(16.39)
Constant	-4.88	-3.61	-4.36
	10.35	(14.00)	(16.48)
-2 Log Likelihood	355.361	224.876	249.689
Percent predicted correctly:			
Overall	79%	75%	75%
Perot	12%	60%	46%
Not Perot	97%	83%	88%

Table 7.5 (continued)

1996	Perot v. All	Perot v. Dole	Perot v. Clinton
Strength of Partisanship	-.85**	-.69**	-.78**
	(.15)	(.17)	(.19)
Ideology	-.05	-.58**	.43**
	(.13)	(.14)	(.14)
Government Services/Spending	-.06	.12	-.34**
	(.11)	(.13)	(.13)
Abortion	.03	.17	-.27
	(.16)	(.17)	(.17)
Evaluation of Economy	.15	-.05	.35**
	(.10)	(.11)	(.11)
Education	-.14*	-.14@	-.03
	(.07)	(.08)	(.07)
Church Attendance	-.09	-.14	-.03
	(.09)	(.11)	(.10)
South	.10	.01	.14
	(.31)	(.34)	(.35)
Age	-.02*	-.02*	-.02*
	(.01)	(.01)	(.01)
Male	-.08	-.00	-.15
	(.28)	(.32)	(.31)
White	1.71	.71	2.21
	(1.05)	(1.78)	(1.06)
Constant	.64	4.34	-1.05
	1.85	(2.43)	(2.04)
-2 Log Likelihood	393.050	279.387	281.689
Percent predicted correctly:			
Overall	92%	87%	87%
Perot	2%	28%	22%
Not Perot	99%	98%	98%

pairwise comparisons of Perot with the two major party candidates. Although some voters may have considered a vote for all three candidates, many undoubtedly eliminated one or the other major party candidate from their deliberations because of partisanship, ideology, or some other factor. Our results confirm those of Miller and Shanks (1996) that Perot voters were often positioned between those of Bush and Clinton in 1992, and the same result is somewhat true in 1996.

We experimented with a variety of estimations, and found that some results were quite sensitive to model specification. In particular, several models showed that Perot voters were less likely to attend church than GOP voters, and were more liberal on abortion. Moreover, models that did not include an indicator of attitudes on government services produced large and significant coefficients for race. In some models Perot voters in 1992 were younger, and were especially more likely to be young men. The models we present include the most important demographic and attitudinal predictors of support for Perot across several models. In 1992 and especially in 1996, the models do a poor job in predicting actual Perot voters compared with both other candidates, but do significantly better in predicting Perot vote in pairwise comparisons with the other candidates.

In the 1992 equations, strength of partisanship predicted Perot support in all three equations, and in all equations Perot voters were significantly more likely to be men. Perot voters were significantly more liberal than those who voted for Bush, and more conservative than those who voted for Clinton. Similarly, Perot voters were more likely to want to cut spending on services in order to reduce the deficit than were those who cast ballots for Clinton, but less likely to favor this position than Bush voters. Perot voters were somewhat more pro-choice than Bush voters, and somewhat more positive in their evaluations of the national economy than those who voted for Clinton.

It may seem surprising that the candidate whose central issue was the budget deficit would attract voters who were less willing to cut government services to reduce the deficit than were Bush voters. Other models showed that Perot voters were slightly more concerned with the budget deficit than Bush voters, and somewhat more willing to increase taxes (although less willing than Clinton voters). This suggests that even on his central issue Perot remained a Rorschach figure for his supporters, subject to multiple interpretations on nearly any point. Some saw Perot as likely to reduce the deficit by cutting spending, others by increasing taxes. But a significant portion of Perot voters who listed the deficit as a central concern did not favor sharp cuts in spending *or* increases in taxes—presumably they wanted Perot to put his head under the hood and just *fix it* somehow, painlessly.

The 1996 equations produce similar results—once again Perot voters are consistently more likely to be political independents, to identify themselves as moderate, and to be more moderate on spending on government services than voters who backed either major party nominee. They were significantly less favorable in their assessment of economic performance than were Clinton voters, and were less educated and younger than voters who supported the major party candidates. We estimated additional equations that included controls for recalled 1992 vote for Perot, and found very similar results. Not surprisingly, Perot's 1992 supporters provided most of his 1996 votes—fully 70 percent of Perot's 1996 voters cast ballots for him also in 1992. Yet Perot managed to hold onto less than a third of his 1992 voters in the NES data, with the rest splitting 55-45 percent in favor of Dole. In contrast, Clinton held onto more than 90 percent of his 1992 voters, and Dole won about 80 percent of those who recalled voting for Bush.

We reestimated the equations in Table 7.5 for those voters who recalled casting a ballot for Perot in 1992 (not shown). Those who remained loyal to Perot in 1996 overall were younger and more likely to be independent, those who defected to Bill Clinton less likely to favor cuts in social spending, and those who defected to Dole were older, more conservative, and more male than those who remained with Perot. But these coefficients were not especially large, and the differences were not substantial.

Untangling the dynamics of candidate evaluations and vote choice is a tricky business, especially with a brief two-point panel. Yet our analysis suggests that the greatest source of defection from Perot was evaluations of Perot himself. In the preelection survey those who would eventually defect from Perot rated him significantly cooler (forty-eight degrees on average) than those who would eventually stick with him. Moreover, Perot's defectors were less likely in the preelection poll to say that Perot was a strong leader or inspiring than were those who stuck with Perot, and were less likely to cite any reasons for voting for Perot. The most common reasons cited by his defectors for voting against Perot were that he was a quitter, he was unstable, and he could not win. Those who defected to Dole were decidedly more negative toward Perot than those who defected to Clinton; the data suggest that the Perot-Dole voters were more likely to have become disillusioned with Perot himself, while the Perot-Clinton voters were somewhat more likely to be attracted to Clinton and satisfied with the state of the economy, although there are too few cases to be certain.

Overall, though, our conclusion from individual-level data is that Perot's decline was remarkably uniform, and was due primarily to two factors—a dissatisfaction with Perot himself, and the belief that he could not win. Voters do not appear to have been significantly more satisfied with the choices offered them by the two major parties in 1996—indeed, Clinton's average feeling thermometer rating was lower in 1996 than in 1992 and Dole's was only incrementally warmer than that for Bush. They do appear to have been satisfied with the state of the economy, and dissatisfied with the man who headed the Reform Party.

Conclusion: A Uniform Drop from an Unnatural High?

Perot's showing in 1992 was a surprise to established pundits and politicians. Unlike many previous third party and independent candidates, he had no regional base for his support (as had Thurmond, George Wallace, and LaFollette), nor did he represent a strong disgruntled faction within one of the major parties (Roosevelt, Thurmond, and Henry Wallace). Finally, he did not have an established record as a successful political leader, as had Anderson, Roosevelt, and most other candidates. Perot, compared to previous challengers to the two party system, came from nowhere, or more specifically, he emerged from the *Larry King Show* to bedevil the two major candidates. And it is in the origin of his strong 1992 showing that an explanation for his 1996 drop may be found. Perot, who lacked many of the traditional aspects of third party or independent candidates in the past, had three attributes that made up for these considerable desiderata: money, media savvy, and novelty.

Using his money and his access to free and paid media, Perot constructed a nonpartisan, nonideological assault upon the current state of national politics. Indeed, he ran as much against politics as he did for political office. In many ways, Perot represents the apotheosis of the candidate-centered campaigns that have flourished since the founding of modern American political science in 1960. Partisan labels and party endorsements have been less and less central to American politics (Nie, Verba, and Petrocik 1979), perhaps making it easier for a candidate without a label to have wide appeal. Perot's campaigns in both years avoided difficult specifics, which would have alienated particular social groups. Even on his core issue, the budget deficit, Perot was vague on where and how he would cut government spending. On abortion, one of the only issues on which he took a clear position, he would routinely downplay the issue as less important than the economy and the deficit. The 1992 candidacy of Ross Perot was therefore first and foremost about H. Ross Perot.

Perot attracted the attention of an electorate unhappy with its choices, nervous about its economic future, and deeply dissatisfied with partisan politics. He attracted significant free media and spent generously from his own fortune to portray himself as a nonpolitician. How does this help explain Perot's transformation from the titan of 1992 to the titmouse of 1996? Peddling roughly the same vague policy prescriptions, Perot did much worse in 1996 because the nation itself had changed, from the economic recession of the early 1990s to the strong recovery of the mid-1990s. Perot himself now seems to recognize the contingent nature of his mass support, and its reliance on external events of a catastrophic nature. Long after the debacle of 1996, in his first interview in almost a year, Perot argued that his future political success would depend on some type of calamity, such as a major scandal, a recession, or perhaps even a war (Verhovek 1997).

Perot's message, which had always lacked ideological clarity, partisan edge, or tough divisive issue positions, had never acquired a distinctive demographic look, other than white, young, and somewhat male. Thus, in the changed national economic situation of 1996, Perot's support was bound to drop. With less money to spend, and lacking the legitimacy of participation in the televised debates, Perot did not project the image of a credible candidate. Yet perhaps most importantly, Perot's own image had changed, from a can-do businessman who was willing to sacrifice his time for the good of the nation and speak to issues the other candidates were afraid to address, to a petulant politician out for publicity, who had rigged his own party's convention and whose doomsday predications were wide of the mark. In hindsight it is not remarkable that Perot's support was so low in 1996—rather it was remarkable that the electorate took him seriously in 1992.

That the electorate did seriously consider Perot in 1992 is an indication of a lingering political dissatisfaction in America. In 1997, with unemployment and inflation at long-time lows, with crime, teenage pregnancy, drug use, and the welfare rolls all dropping in concert, a sizable majority of Americas told pollsters that America is off on the wrong track. The source of this unhappiness is not entirely clear—perhaps the long-stagnant wages of working Americans, perhaps unawareness of recent social trends—but it is clear that the electorate is not anchored in the major parties, distrusts most politicians, and is deeply cynical about electoral politics. Other Western democracies have encountered remarkable electoral instability in the aftermath of the end of the Cold War, with governing parties all but eliminated from parliaments in a single election. It seems unlikely today that Ross Perot will ever again be a factor in American politics,[3] but it is clear that the electorate is willing to listen to new voices that speak to them outside the traditional communication channels, and who promise them an end to politics as usual.

Notes

1. This oft-repeated phrase was actually a greatly shortened version of a Carville quote, which included a reference to national health care.

2. There is some evidence to suggest that Perot support in 1992 among whites was affected by state black population levels. Whites were apparently less likely to vote for Perot in states where the electorate contained significant numbers of African Americans. This effect was not present in 1996. For a fuller discussion of this, see Mayer 1996, 1997.

3. It also seems unlikely that Perot will go away anytime soon. In late 1997, Perot ended a year of uncharacteristic silence with an appearance on *Larry King* and an aggressive speech at the Reform Party's convention in Kansas City. A year off had not damaged Perot's ability to pungently criticize politics-as-usual. Of the ongoing campaign finance

hearings, Perot observed, "This is like having Willie Sutton and Jesse James investigate one another for bank robbery." However, the Reform Party gathering garnered little media attention (Verhovek 1997).

References

Abramson, Paul R., John H. Aldrich, Phil Paolino, and David W. Rohde. 1995. "Third Party and Independent Candidates in American Politics: Wallace, Anderson, and Perot," *Political Science Quarterly* 110(3): 349–367.

Abramson, Paul R. John H. Aldrich, and David W. Rohde. 1994. *Change and Continuity in the 1992 Elections.* Washington, D.C.: Congressional Quarterly.

Alvarez, R. Michael and Jonathan Nagler. 1995. "Economics, Issues, and the Perot Candidacy: Voter Choice in the 1992 Presidential Election," *American Journal of Political Science* 39(3): 714–744.

———. 1997. "Economics, Entitlements, and Social Issues: Voter Choice in the 1996 Presidential Election." A paper presented at the 1997 American Political Science Association's Annual Meeting, Washington, D.C.

Associated Press. 1996. "Perot Takes Debate-Exclusion Challenge to Federal Court," *Kalamazoo Gazette,* Oct 1, A3.

Broder, David. 1996. "Debate system needs a fix-up," *Kalamazoo Gazette,* Sept. 25, A8.

Cook, Rhodes. 1996a. "Panel Suggests Barring Perot from Presidential Debates," *Congressional Quarterly,* Sept. 21, 2693.

Cook, Rhodes. 1996b. "Perot Finds It's Not as Easy the Second Time Around," *Congressional Quarterly,* October 5, 2879–2885.

Cook, Rhodes, Juliana Gruenwald, and Alan Greenblatt. 1996. "Reform Party's Convention Dominated by Perot," *Congressional Quarterly,* Aug. 17, 2304–2305.

Dedman, Bill. 1997. "Embracing Perot's Message Without Perot," *New York Times,* Oct 5, A10.

Dionne, E. J. 1996. *They Only Look Dead: Why Progressives Will Dominate the Next Political Era.* New York: Simon and Schuster.

Elazar, Daniel J. 1994. *The American Mosaic: The Impact of Space, Time and Culture on American Politics.* Boulder: Westview.

Erikson, Robert S, Gerald C. Wright, and John P. McIver. 1993. *Statehouse Democracy.* New York: Cambridge University Press.

Fiorina, Morris P. 1981. *Retrospective Voting in American National Elections.* New Haven: Yale University Press.

Gold, Howard J. 1995. "Third Party Voting in Presidential Elections: A Study of Perot, Anderson, and Wallace," *Political Research Quarterly* 48(4): 751–773.

Greenblatt, Alan. 1996. "Reform Party's Chief Rivals: David and Goliath?" *Congressional Quarterly,* July 27, 2134.

Kalb, Deborah. 1996. "Perot Gets Reform Party Nod, Will Take Matching Funds," *Congressional Quarterly,* Aug. 24, 2396–2397.

Levine, Myron A. 1995. *Presidential Campaigns and Elections: Issues and Images in the Media Age. 2nd ed.* Itasca, Ill.: F. E. Peacock Publishers.

Lipset, Seymour Martin. 1993. "The Significance of the 1992 Election," *PS*. XXVI: 7–16.

Luntz, Frank I. 1993. "Perovian Civilization: Who Supported Ross, and Why," *Policy Review* (Spring): 18–23.

Markus, Gregory B. 1988. "The Impact of Personal and National Economic Conditions on the Presidential Vote: A Pooled Cross-sectional Analysis," *American Journal of Political Science* 32: 137–154.

Mayer, Jeremy D. 1996. *Critical Mass: Black Population Levels and White Voting Behavior in the 1988 and 1992 Presidential Elections.* PhD dissertation, Georgetown University.

———. 1997. "White Voters and Racial Context: The Influence of Black Population Levels on White Voting Behavior in the Presidential Elections of 1988, 1992, and 1996." A paper presented at the Southern Political Science Association's Annual Meeting, Nov. 5–7, Norfolk, Virginia.

Menendez, Albert J. 1996. *The Perot Voters and the Future of American Politics.* Amherst, N.Y.: Prometheus Books.

Nagourney, Adam. 1996. "Perot Has His Say on a Familiar Stage, but Not the One He Wanted to Be On," *New York Times,* Oct. 8, A17.

NBC News' *Meet the Press.* 1996. Transcript for October 27.

New York Times. 1996. Editorial, October 25, A14.

Nie, Norman H., Sidney Verba, and John R. Petrocik. 1979. *The Changing American Voter.* Cambridge: Harvard University Press.

Not For Sale At Any Price. 1996. Perot Infomercial Transcript. Broadcast October 6.

Posner, Gerald. 1996. *Citizen Perot: His Life and Times.* New York: Random House.

The Public Perspective, October/November 1996, 38.

Tollerson, Ernest. 1996. "Perot Keeps Up Attacks on Clinton's Integrity," *New York Times,* Nov 5, A12.

Verhovek, Sam Howe. 1997. "Perot Set to Re-Enter Politics," *New York Times,* Oct. 30, A9.

Wayne, Stephen J. 1992. *The Road to the White House: The Politics of Presidential Elections.* New York: St. Martin's Press.

Zaller, John R. 1992. *The Nature and Origins of Mass Opinion.* New York: Cambridge University Press.

8

From Ross the Boss
to Jesse the Body

Did the Perot Phenomenon Spawn
the Ventura Victory?

Christopher P. Gilbert
David A. M. Peterson

J esse Ventura's remarkable victory in the 1998 Minnesota gubernatorial race thrust the Reform Party back into the national spotlight. In many ways the Reform Party was an unlikely beneficiary of Ventura's implausible success in besting two well-known and experienced major party challengers. In the wake of the Reform Party's first victory for any high statewide or national office, the Ventura phenomenon offers some clear continuities to and some startling departures from Ross Perot's presidential campaigns. In this chapter we take a multifaceted look at the 1998 Minnesota campaign, examining the reasons why Jesse Ventura won and what it means for the future of the third party movement created by Perot in his 1992 and 1996 presidential bids.

The Context of Minnesota Politics

Throughout the twentieth century Minnesota's political scene has witnessed numerous electoral and social movements operating through and around the two party system to win elections and govern effectively. The Democratic Farm-Labor Party is one byproduct of this trend, forming just after World War II, when significant electoral successes by the Farmer-Labor Party led Democrats to the merger table (Key 1948; Gilbert et al. 1999: 46).[1] In recent years the DFL has held control of the state legislature and most major offices, although several moderate Republicans have been successful.

Minnesota's Republican Party is best understood as two distinct entities, whose differences were for many years captured in the party's name. The old label Independent Republican, or IR (adopted during the Watergate years and dropped in 1995), stood for two competing political ideologies—a primarily secular constituency advocating moderate to progressive social policies combined with fiscal restraint (the "I" side), and the increasingly Christian conservative-dominated "R" wing that stressed a social agenda centered on opposition to abortion and the restoration of traditional values and family structures. The conflict between the party's two wings has remained intact, though a few notable Republicans have successfully melded or have successfully overcome the schism (Gilbert and Peterson 1997).

The Reform Party in Minnesota, 1992–1996

Given Minnesota's tradition of social movements forming political parties outside the two party norm, it is not surprising to discover that Minnesota's Reform Party actually predates the 1992 Perot presidential campaign. In 1992, several moderate activists led by a Twin Cities lawyer, Dean Barkley, founded the Independence Party and began to contest numerous elections around the state. Barkley was the most successful, receiving 20 percent of the vote in the 1992 Sixth Congressional District race, thus denying victory to incumbent Democrat Gerry Sikorski (Gilbert and Peterson 1995).

Ross Perot's United We Stand movement paralleled the local Minnesota effort in 1992, with similarly impressive results. Perot received 24 percent of the presidential vote in 1992, making Minnesota his second-best state. Perot fared especially well in rural counties, where his anti–free trade stance resonated with distressed agricultural interests (Gilbert and Peterson 1995).

The 1994 elections again found Dean Barkley carrying the Independence Party banner, this time in a U.S. Senate race for the open seat vacated by Republican David Durenberger. Barkley managed just over 5 percent, again siphoning more votes from the DFL candidate and helping to leverage a GOP victory (Gilbert and Peterson 1995). An analysis of Barkley voting using Voter News Services exit polls shows two major factors at work: a previous vote for Ross Perot in 1992; and a pro-choice position on abortion, which Barkley had promoted heavily in his 1992 congressional bid (Gilbert et al. 1999, 103–106).

The Seven Percent Solution: 1996 Results

By 1996 Ross Perot's fortunes in Minnesota had dropped off considerably, as he received only 12 percent of the presidential vote. By this time the Minnesota Independence Party had voted to change its name and cast its future with the national Reform Party. Barkley led the change and became the party's chief strategist, running one more time himself for U.S. Senate. In what turned out to be a crucial factor for Jesse Ventura in 1998, Barkley garnered 7 percent of the vote (Frank and Wagner 1999, 9).

That 7 percent maintained the Reform Party's status within the Minnesota electoral system. In Minnesota, if a party's candidate receives at least 5 percent of the vote for a statewide office (state or federal), the party receives major party status. This means it has automatic ballot access, public funds for campaigning, and even a box on state tax returns for donations (Frank and Wagner 1999, 9). Thus did Dean Barkley singlehandedly carry the Reform Party to an established position under Minnesota law. Such institutional endorsements of the party's status assisted in creating the perception that Minnesota had three major parties, not just two, opening critical doors to debate invitations and public funding from the state's campaign finance system. Moreover, Minnesota allows voters to register at the polls on election day, making possible voter mobilization efforts at the last minute behind candidates with momentum, another factor that turned out to benefit Jesse Ventura greatly (Gilbert and Peterson 1995; Frank and Wagner 1999, 10).

The Candidate

Navy SEAL, Vietnam veteran, college dropout, professional wrestler, talk show host, small city mayor—not the resume entries one would expect to find in a credible contender for governor of one of the nation's most progressive states. Yet Jesse Ventura managed to pull off the most remarkable upset of the 1998 electoral season in defeating St. Paul mayor Norm Coleman and state attorney general Hubert "Skip" Humphrey III to win the governor's seat. Political analysts will spend decades sorting out the multiple factors that led to Ventura's victory. Most relevant to the themes covered in this volume, it must be pointed out that while the Reform Party was the vehicle through which Ventura entered the gubernatorial race, in the eyes of most voters the candidate—not the party—held the appeal.

Jesse Ventura first entered electoral politics in 1991, when he decided to run for mayor of Brooklyn Park, a large suburb located northwest of Minneapolis. Claiming that city officials were unresponsive to public concerns, Ventura swept to victory by bringing large numbers of new voters to the polls—20,000 total votes were cast, compared with 2,600 votes in the previous municipal election (Frank and Wagner 1999, 10). Brooklyn Park has a weak mayoral system, and Ventura had difficulty generating support from a hostile city council. Late in his single four-year term, critics charged that he no longer even lived in the city; in fact he maintained a vacant apartment while residing in another suburb outside town.

Ventura's political leanings can best be described as populist and libertarian, and he understood the advantages of his celebrity and played the role skillfully (Frank and Wagner 1999, 13–14). He shunned all contact with and donations from lobbyists and political action committees, representing himself as an ordinary Minnesotan (despite his considerable wealth accrued through a long career in professional wrestling). As a talk show host on a prominent Twin Cities station during the mid-1990s, Ventura honed both his philosophy and his communication skills. He also struck up a friendship with frequent radio guest Dean Barkley, which ultimately led to Ventura's Reform candidacy for governor (Frank and Wagner 1999, 14).

Thus, in Jesse Ventura, Dean Barkley and the Reform Party found a candidate who immediately broadened the party's visibility among the Minnesota electorate. Ventura announced his candidacy in August 1997, and was formally named the party's choice at its June 1998 convention (Frank and Wagner 1999, 15). From the beginning of his candidacy, Ventura capitalized on two crucial factors: first, his own charisma and name recognition, which made him a hit on the campaign trail; and second, the fact that neither major party paid him any attention whatsoever, a situation that did not change until very close to election day.

The Campaign

Most of the attention in the first nine months of 1998 centered on the DFL and Republican nomination races for governor. The Republican Party quickly rallied behind one of its newest members. Norm Coleman, a New York City native and lawyer by training, had served as mayor of the state's capital city since 1993. In that first election Coleman emerged from a crowded field of DFL candidates, running on a platform of economic development and crime control. In many respects he was not a typical Democrat, certainly not a Democrat in the usual Minnesota mold—liberal and government-oriented. Coleman was also an outspoken opponent of abortion rights and stood against most state and local initiatives for gay rights. In early 1997, after a draft-Coleman campaign orchestrated by the mayor's own political operatives, Coleman surprised no one by finally publicly switching his allegiance to the GOP.

Republicans considered Coleman ideal in many respects—young, charismatic, energetic, a tireless advocate for St. Paul, and most important someone able to win as a conservative candidate in a liberal, DFL-dominated city. Opposition within the party withered quickly and Coleman was anointed from the outset as the GOP nominee to replace retiring Republican governor Arne Carlson.

In retrospect, Coleman's easy ride to the party nomination may have hurt his electoral chances, for nearly all the pre–general election attention switched to the DFL race. Five well-known candidates stepped forward to seek the DFL nomination, wide open in the wake of a disastrous 1994 bid by state senator John Marty, who received only 32 percent of the vote (worst in party history). This field included prominent conservative state senator Doug Johnson from the vital Iron Range of northeastern Minnesota; former state auditor Mark Dayton, an heir to the Dayton's department store fortune; and three sons of Minnesota political legends: former state senator Ted Mondale (son of Walter); Hennepin County Attorney Mike Freeman (son of Orville, governor and U.S. agriculture secretary); and attorney general Hubert Humphrey III, known as Skip and heir to the considerable legacy of his father Hubert Humphrey.

While Mike Freeman emerged as the choice of party leaders at the state convention in June, Humphrey possessed a tremendous advantage in name recognition due to his four terms as attorney general, and a previous (though unsuccessful) run for U.S. Senate in the 1980s. Most observers predicted a tight race in the September primary, but in the end Humphrey won a comfortable victory with 37 percent of the primary vote. The first post-primary poll in mid-September put Humphrey twenty-one points ahead (50–29) of Norm Coleman (Frank and Wagner 1999, 21).

Almost lost in the coverage of Coleman's conversion and Humphrey's decisive primary win, Jesse Ventura registered 10 percent support in the September poll. From this point through election day almost without exception, Ventura's support was noted by analysts and major party leaders strictly in the context of which major party candidate would be hurt more by Ventura. The consensus was that Coleman stood to lose more if Ventura did well, and all three candidates seemed to structure their campaigns around the assumption that Humphrey was the favorite and that Ventura voters could and would be enticed to return to the major party fold on election day.

These assumptions of course proved to be a major mistake, for they grossly underestimated the magic of Jesse Ventura, the candidate. Third candidates must show they stand outside the status quo of the major parties, but rarely do major party candidates offer such a lackluster campaign that plays into the hands of the third candidate. It is essential to remember that Ventura's triumph rested on his own wise decisions and effective campaigning, but that these took place in the context of weak debate performances and poor campaigning by Coleman and Humphrey.

Jesse Ventura's victory points out the obvious: a minor party candidate in U.S. politics can only win if everything goes right for his campaign, and almost nothing goes right for his opponents. Despite their long track records of electoral success and strong records of achievement in office, neither Humphrey nor Coleman said or did much to excite Minnesota voters about their candidacies. By contrast, Jesse Ventura became a phenomenon: his plain speaking resonated with the public; his contrasting background to two career public servants appealed especially to disaffected nonvoters as the perfect example of what ailed modern politics; and his campaign advertising team developed a brilliant series of television spots using "Jesse Ventura action figures" and scenes of the candidate touring the state in a motor home.

With each succeeding poll Ventura's standing grew, Humphrey's lead shrank, and Coleman's percentage moved slowly upward to parity with Humphrey. Most preelection polls had the race too close to call between the major party candidates, but on November 3 Ventura emerged with 37 percent of the vote, to Coleman's 34 with Humphrey fading badly to third with 28 percent (Belluck 1998).

The immediate postelection analysis, based on exit polls, concluded that Ventura won for three major reasons. First, he capitalized on a base built by Ross Perot and other Reform Party candidates in previous elections, good for about 10 percent of the vote. Second, he undercut the bases of support for both major party candidates, running even with Humphrey among women (the Minnesota gender gap mirrors the national advantage that women have given Democrats in recent years) and even with or ahead of Coleman among voters stressing economic growth and tax relief (Coleman's main issues). Finally, an estimated 12 percent of voters showed up only to vote for Jesse Ventura. This remarkable turnout boost made the difference in what would otherwise have been a narrow Coleman victory over either opponent (VNS Exit Poll 1998).

These first impressions deserve closer attention, particularly in comparison with what is known about predictors of Perot support nationally and in Minnesota specifically. In the next section we detail aggregate and individual-level comparisons between Ventura and Perot, in order to show more clearly how Ventura won, whether Ross Perot and the Reform Party had any role to play in Ventura's victory, and what implications his victory has for the Reform Party's future.

Campaign Resources and Their Uses: An Underrated Factor

Having forsworn all support from established political interests, Jesse Ventura relied entirely on the Reform Party's modest public subsidy (about $300,000) and individual donations. Ventura spent $626,067 on his campaign, compared with more than $2.1 million each for Coleman and Humphrey (Frank and Wagner 1999, 23). Additionally, the state GOP and Democratic parties spent a total of $8.3 million to promote their candidates, versus $14,148 for the Reform Party (Frank and Wagner 1999, 24).

These figures suggest an overwhelming disadvantage for Ventura. In order to overcome the resource gap and win, he relied on four principal factors: his skillful use of the media; his debate performances; his use of the Internet as a campaign tool; and the careful husbanding of resources for the final push to election day.

Media Use and Coverage

Ventura used his platform as a talk show host to establish a political persona, not just a celebrity image, with Minnesota voters prior to the fall 1998 campaign. It was determined by all involved with the Reform Party that Ventura's appeal rested on "Jesse being Jesse"—that the candidate's plainspokenness and irreverence were his key asset. Accordingly, Ventura spent the entire campaign saying whatever he wished and gaining free media attention as a result. The consensus among election observers was that Ventura's campaign and statements received far less critical scrutiny than did his opponents', and that this media "free ride" contributed to Ventura's ability to pull even as election day approached (Frank and Wagner 1999, 27–28).

Having gained ground on his opponents, Ventura's television advertising was brilliant in execution and timing. Bill Hillsman, who had masterminded Paul Wellstone's upset 1990 U.S. Senate victory in Minnesota, conceived of a series of ads showing the candidate as an action figure doll, beating up on "Evil Special Interest Man" and keeping government free from corrupt influences (Frank and Wagner 1999, 27). In the final days ads showing Ventura in the pose of Rodin's "The Thinker" and touring the state in a recreational vehicle also spurred Ventura's momentum. These ads were inspired, fitting the candidate to perfection and contrasting his persona with the pedestrian advertisements and speeches of Coleman and Humphrey.

The Debates: An Equal Platform

A series of nine debates among the major gubernatorial candidates was established for the 1998 campaign; three were televised statewide. By virtue of the Reform Party's standing as a major party under state law, and Ventura's standing in preelection polls, Ventura found himself with a free, equal platform against Coleman and Humphrey. He used this platform to great effect, presenting stereotypical views of his opponents—Coleman the Republican as too conservative and a tool of the rich, Humphrey the DFLer as too government-oriented and liberal—and then allowing his opponents by their own statements to breathe life into his stereotypes. Thus, Ventura made credible his assertion that the major parties offered nothing new, and his own performance stood out against the low-key Humphrey and Coleman (Frank and Wagner 1999, 19–21).

After the election, many major party activists bemoaned the decision of the Humphrey campaign to insist on having Ventura included in every debate. The Humphrey camp followed the conventional wisdom that Ventura would pull more votes from Coleman (Frank and Wagner 1999, 19–21). Two comments should be made regarding this aspect of the campaign. First, due to debate organizers' criteria and to the Reform Party's status, it is unclear whether Humphrey or Coleman could have excluded Ventura even if they wished to do so. Second, the Humphrey camp was probably correct: Ventura did take more votes away from Norm Coleman in the end, but Humphrey's real problem turned out to be his failure to gain any votes through his debate or his campaign appearances. The conventional wisdom was not incorrect; it simply failed to account for how well the minor party candidate could do in taking votes away from the major party candidates.

The Internet as a Tool for Organizing

Political campaigns have created web sites since the Internet was developed in the late 1980s. The difference between earlier efforts and Ventura's Web presence, according to Ventura webmaster Phil Madsen, was that Ventura used the Internet not just to get his positions known but to organize and mobilize support during the campaign. Thus Ventura turned a passive tool into an active one. The Internet turned out to be cheap, attractive to younger voters who were more likely to use the Web in the first place, and effective in a state that is more "wired" than other places in the United States (Frank and Wagner 1999, 25–26).

Resource Gap to Resource Edge

All of these factors combined by the end of October to put Ventura in an enviable position, with more cash on hand than either Coleman or Humphrey. Third candidates without personal fortunes rarely have resources, and normally such resources must be expended early on ballot access and name recognition (Rosenstone et al. 1996). Without these concerns, Ventura could save what he had until it mattered. Coleman and Humphrey, having spent their funds on attacking each other, could not respond in kind, and their failure to ignite partisans meant that the election day mobilization would only help Ventura.

Figure 8.1 Minnesota County-Level Voting for Ross Perot, 1992, and Jesse Ventura, 1998

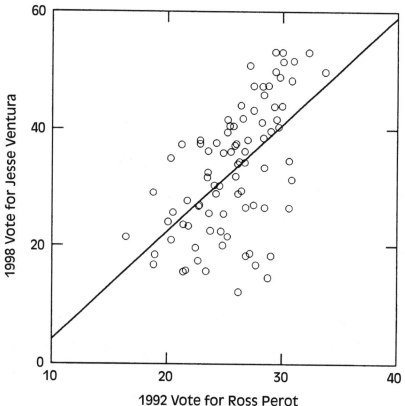

Sources: *America Votes 21* (Scammon 1995); authors' compilation of 1998 county election results.

Aggregate Data: Perot Vote Patterns and Support for Ventura

To investigate how previous electoral support for third candidates affected support for Jesse Ventura, we present a series of scatterplots showing county level voting patterns. These plots reveal how Ventura capitalized on an existing base of minor party support, and how his support differs in one important way from predecessors.

Figure 8.1 presents county support for Ventura against 1992 county support for Ross Perot. It seems clear that Perot's strong 1992 showing in Minnesota opened the door for future third candidates, hence Figure 8.1 can reveal whether strong

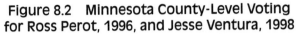

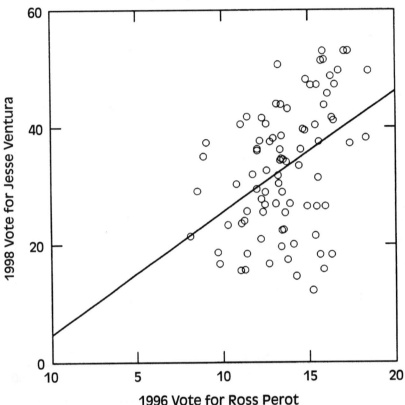

Figure 8.2 Minnesota County-Level Voting for Ross Perot, 1996, and Jesse Ventura, 1998

Sources: *America Votes 22* (Scammon et al. 1997); authors' compilation of 1998 county election results.

third candidate support in specific places is repeated in later elections. In fact there is a strong positive correlation between 1992 Perot voting and 1998 Ventura voting (r = .58, p<.001)—Ventura does well in the same counties where Perot thrived.

Figure 8.2 compares Ventura voting with 1996 Perot voting. Although Perot fared much worse in 1996, he still outpolled Dean Barkley and all other minor candidates that year. Thus, Figure 8.2 is a snapshot of the Reform Party's nascent bases of support in the election just prior to Ventura's breakthrough. Once again we observe a strong positive correlation (r = .42, p<.001).

The critical conclusion here is that unlike nearly all minor party candidates, in 1998 Jesse Ventura and the Reform Party could count on a significant (by

Figure 8.3   Minnesota County-Level Religious Adherence, 1990, and Voting for Jesse Ventura, 1998

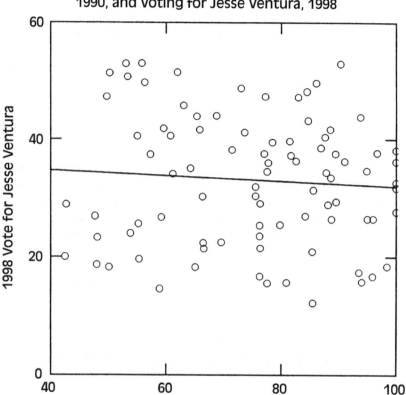

Sources: NCCC church census, 1990 (Bradley et al. 1992); authors' compilation of 1998 county election results.

minor party standards) existing level of support among Minnesota voters. Unlike John Anderson or even Ross Perot—both of whom had to start from scratch in building an organization and voter loyalties—Ventura started the 1998 race with at least 10 percent of the vote. Highlighting only the fact that Ventura won the election obscures the fact that anyone the Reform Party put forward in 1998 was likely to do well relative to the usual dismal showing of minor party candidates.

Figure 8.3 examines one other facet of aggregate support for the Reform Party in Minnesota. Our previous research, described in this volume and elsewhere (Gilbert et al. 1999), has revealed that minor candidates receive more votes in counties with lower religious adherence, and fewer votes in counties with higher religious adherence. We have argued that this result demonstrates how minor candidates must mobilize unlikely voters and citizens less connected to the local institutions that knit communities together. Given his populist, "not part of the system" campaign message, we would expect Jesse Ventura to fit this general pattern. On the other hand, our research has also shown that when minor candidates run again, or when they represent minor parties that have endured past one election cycle, the adherence-voting link is attenuated due to party-building efforts and emerging voter loyalty to the minor party (Gilbert et al. 1999, 121–137). The primary evidence for this argument comes from Ross Perot's 1996 electoral support; thus, we might expect Ventura support to reflect Perot 1996 (no link) rather than Perot 1992 (a strong link in Minnesota and nationwide).

Figure 8.3 demonstrates that no link exists in 1998 between levels of religious adherence and levels of Ventura voting in Minnesota counties (r = -.07, $p<.537$). This fits the second pattern described above: religious adherence does predict 1994 Barkley vote in the usual inverse manner, but it is not significantly related to 1996 Perot support within Minnesota (in fact the correlation is positive) (Gilbert et al. 1999, 103–106). We conclude from these three figures that Jesse Ventura and the Minnesota Reform Party are clear beneficiaries of a six-year electoral record that positioned the Reform Party as a valid alternative to the DFL and the GOP in the eyes of Minnesota voters.

Individual Data: Ventura Voting Compared with Perot Support

In comparing the individual-level correlates of Ventura voting with prior studies of Perot voting, we are limited in two ways. First, exit polls—the only source of individual voter beliefs and behaviors for 1998—do not contain the range and depth of questions that exist for presidential elections, which are analyzed using National Election Studies (NES) data. Second, we do not have direct access to the 1998 exit poll data, thus we have not estimated multivariate models of Ventura support.

Having said that, what we can do is to compare the behavior of specific sets of Ventura voters with the known correlates of Perot voting in 1992 and 1996. This comparison reveals how Ventura parallels Perot and how Ventura differs markedly from Perot in terms of electoral support.

These comparisons appear in Table 8.1. For several independent variables, we show percentages of support for Jesse Ventura, and a summary of how the independent variable related to 1992 and 1996 national voting for Ross Perot. The comparisons are best understood in terms of demographic factors and issue-oriented factors.

Table 8.1. 1998 Voter Support for Jesse Ventura, Compared with 1992 and 1996 National Support for Ross Perot

Factor	Support for Ventura	How factor worked for Perot
TOTAL VOTE SHARE	37%	1992 – 19%, 1996 – 8%
Gender	39% of men**	1992 – more support among men, significant
	35% of women	1996 – more support among men, significant
Age	39% of 18–64 yrs.**	1992 – more support among young, significant
	21% of 65 and over	1996 – not significant
Income	39% of under $50K**	1992 – not significant
	41% of $50–75K**	1996 – more support from lower incomes, significant
	32% of $75K and up	
Education	44% of no college degree**	1992 – not significant
	29% of college grads	1996 – not significant
Party ID	33% of DFL	1992 – strong support from independents, significant
	28% of GOP	
	52% of independents**	1996 – more support from independents, significant
Ideology	44% of liberals	1992 – not significant
	40% of moderates**	1996 – more support from moderates, significant
	29% of conservatives	

Table 8.1 1998 Voter Support for Jesse Ventura, Compared with 1992 and 1996 National Support for Ross Perot (continued)

Most Important Issues		Most Important Issues (significant findings only)
Abortion	14% (3rd)	1992 – favors limits on imports
State taxes	40% (2nd)	disapproval of President Bush
Education	27% (2nd)	Perot can better handle economy
Economy/jobs	45% (1st)	
		1996 – wants more political parties
Opposes taxes to pay for stadium	37% (1st)	Perot can better handle deficit
		government should be smaller
State's economic condition		jobs more important than protecting
Excellent	35% (1st)	environment
Good	36% (1st)	
Not so Good	52% (1st)	

Sources: Voter News Service exit poll, 1998; Gilbert et al. 1999: 87, 133, estimated from 1992 and 1996 National Election Studies data.

Note: ★★ — indicates Ventura led in this category of voters.

As this volume and numerous other publications have demonstrated, age, gender, and political independence are critical correlates of Perot support, especially in 1992. In his first presidential bid Perot received more support from younger voters, men, and political independents/moderates. Age was not significant for Perot voting in 1996, and income does matter, with lower income voters giving more support to Perot.

Jesse Ventura's support in 1998 shows marked parallels to Perot on the demographic factors. Ventura was relatively more popular among men, although his strength among women was crucial in undercutting DFL candidate Humphrey's chances. Ventura also won a plurality of votes from voters under age sixty-five, with even greater strength in lower age brackets. Ventura also was the choice of lower income and less educated voters. Moderates and independents comprise strong Ventura categories as well.

Issue-oriented factors should differ between Perot and Ventura, for the context of their campaigns differ markedly. The 1992 presidential election marked a rejection of incumbent George Bush, and both Bill Clinton and Ross Perot gained among voters eager for change or unhappy with the nation's economy. Perot scored specifically in 1992 with voters who opposed free trade and who believed Perot offered the antidote to the nation's budget difficulties (Gilbert et al. 1999, 86–88). In 1996 Perot's support reveals primarily an antigovernment bent, rather than any positive indicators that favor Perot.

By contrast, Ventura ran for office in a state with very low unemployment and a massive budget surplus. Minnesota voters tend to like their state government and perceived no great problems with the state of the state. Two issues stood out as most contentious with the Minnesota electorate, and Ventura managed to manipulate voter loyalties to his benefit on both. First, the existence of the $4 billion state surplus led many voters to conclude that taxes were too high. Ventura gained 40 percent of the vote among voters who felt state taxes were the most important issue; this placed him second to Norm Coleman but in effect Ventura's strength on the surplus issue (he had promised to return all of it to taxpayers; Frank and Wagner 1999, 19) undercut the GOP platform and base of support. Second, voters did worry that Minnesota's economy had left out many sectors of the public and might not be sustainable. Ventura won 45 percent from voters who felt the economy and jobs were most important. Most noteworthy, Ventura won among voters who felt the state's economy was excellent, and among those who felt it was good or not so good.

In short, both Perot (especially in 1992) and Ventura appealed to voters who were less than enthused about economic circumstances, but the crucial difference benefiting Ventura is that he gained broad support among all segments of the electorate. Ventura was not simply a protest candidate. In the end he defeated his more highly regarded opponents because, when compared with them, a slim plurality of

Minnesotans thought that Ventura was the best person for the job—so much better, in fact, that one in eight Minnesota voters came to the polls solely to support Jesse. This 12 percent segment—mainly men, younger and less well educated, eager to see the surplus ("their money," as Ventura constantly reminded them) returned—turned a probable Coleman triumph into an election that "shocked the world" (Belluck 1998).

Limitations on the Revolution

Excluding Ventura's victory, 1998 proved to be a strong Republican year in Minnesota. The GOP regained control of the state House of Representatives for the first time since 1986. Analysis of aggregate voting patterns shows that Ventura voters made a decisive difference in helping the GOP to their state House victories. Using ecological inference, we have shown elsewhere that GOP state House candidates received 40 percent of the votes from non-Ventura voters, and an astounding 72 percent from Ventura supporters—enough to tip a closely balanced election decisively to the GOP (Gilbert and Peterson 1999). Our district level estimates indicate that had the Ventura vote been unrelated to Republican House vote, the Republicans would have won eight fewer seats than they did win, which would not have been enough to take control of the House.

Beyond the state House, the status quo prevailed: all eight of the state's incumbent U.S. representatives won reelection easily, and no Reform candidate hit double digits in any U.S. House race. The statewide offices also went to the major parties, although Reform candidates did relatively better. Clearly, to the extent that Jesse Ventura's victory was a protest against the political status quo, it is obvious that the protest was focused on one office only. Moreover, the turnout boost generated by Ventura's candidacy served to boost GOP fortunes markedly.

The Bottom Line: How Did Perot Help Ventura?

Our analysis reveals that Jesse Ventura and Ross Perot share some important similarities. Both candidates overcame the usual name recognition problem facing third candidates—Perot through sheer expenditure of resources and Ventura by being well known in the first place. Perot and Ventura also capitalized on antigovernment sentiment. In retrospect, Perot did not gain as much as he could in 1992 from those voters who were unhappy with the political status quo, because Bill Clinton wisely co-opted this strategy for himself. By contrast, Jesse Ventura had the perfect setup from which to level the "throw the bums out" charge, with two career politicians as his opponents, neither of whom could pull off an antigovernment campaign motif as well as Bill Clinton.

Ventura also parallels Perot in having campaign resources available at critical junctures in the race. Perot's deep personal pockets obviously kept him going, but Ventura had to rely on his own skills as a campaigner to pull himself close enough to the leaders to become a credible candidate by late October 1998. Once Ventura had established his electoral support at close to 30 percent, his campaign ended up with more resources than the opposition for the final push to election day.

The differences between the two are also significant to recall. Had Perot faced as lackluster a major party lineup as Jesse Ventura, the U.S. electorate may have been shocked before 1998. There is no question that the inability of Humphrey and Coleman to distance themselves from Ventura's portrayal of them as out of touch and out of ideas—an unfair characterization, to be sure—contributed to their lack of success.

Just as important, Ventura started his campaign with a base of support for the Reform Party. Even a 10 percent share is better than any minor party can normally count on receiving, and from this modest start the candidate succeeded in swelling the ranks effectively. The Reform Party in Minnesota is far too weak to win an election on its own; its grass-roots organization is virtually nonexistent and its name recognition pales in comparison with Ventura's (Smith 1999; Hamburger and Von Sternberg 1999). Yet the party gave Ventura a ballot position and its painstaking 5 and 7 percent showings earlier in the 1990s became the foundation on which Ventura rose up to defeat his opponents.

What Does This Mean for the Reform Party's Future?

After all the party strategizing and sophisticated market research is concluded, in the end good candidates tend to win elections, and Jesse Ventura turned out to be a far better candidate than anyone (himself included) could have imagined. Does Ventura's victory mark the beginning of a trend toward a true three party system in Minnesota or the entire United States? Unfortunately for Governor Ventura and his supporters, history and the evidence suggest that the answer is no.

First and foremost, Minnesota 1998 must be regarded as a victory for Jesse Ventura, who ran for the Reform Party, rather than a victory for the Reform Party itself. The distinction is not purely semantic. No other figure in Minnesota politics could have pulled off this feat, and surely the major parties are most unlikely to repeat their own mistakes from 1998. Further, since the major parties swept all other state and federal offices (no Reform candidate won more than 16 percent), the grassroots weakness of the Reform Party becomes all the more apparent (Smith 1999).

Second, in the wake of Ventura's win the state Reform Party has gained unprecedented publicity, but to date has done little to build a lasting organization. In fact the party will still not be able to field a full slate of candidates for the 2000 legislative races. Advertising executive Bill Hillsman, who masterminded the Ventura television spots, summed up the state of the party almost a year after its breakthrough: "I'm totally frustrated with the party, in Minnesota and nationally, that they've done nothing in the wake of Jesse Ventura to build a party structure. Ever since Jesse's election, all sorts of people have come to me wanting to help the party—but there's nowhere to send them, there's no there there" (Hamburger and Von Sternberg 1999).

Finally, despite a high approval rating as governor, Jesse Ventura may have done more to hurt than to help the Reform Party's future. The internal power struggle between Perot forces and Ventura supporters does not benefit the party's real work, which is organizing at all levels throughout the nation. Moreover, many Reform Party activists seem to have concluded that celebrity candidates should be the preferred choice. But most political analysts would not characterize Donald Trump as the Reform Party's best bet to be taken seriously in 2000 and beyond.

Perhaps most telling is how Jesse Ventura perceives his status within the party. In the wake of a successful legislative session that saw a massive tax rebate for Minnesotans (though not all the surplus was returned, as candidate Ventura had promised), Ventura has promoted himself as the party's new "kingmaker," supplanting Ross Perot. The Reform Party will probably benefit from having Ross Perot in its past and not its future, yet Ventura is a less than ideal successor. He lacks a clear agenda, has poor relations with the media, and generally has confused his own popularity with that of the party. Additionally, the Reform Party seems unable to escape being the empty vessel into which a disparate set of political figures wishes to pour its electoral fortunes. Libertarians, social conservatives, celebrity liberals—all see the Reform Party as a potential vehicle, but taken together no coherent third party platform is possible with these ingredients.

Without a set of principles, presumably based on reform in a broad or specific sense, the Reform Party is handicapped versus the major parties as the twenty-first century arrives. Despite the rhetoric from Ventura and others, there are significant philosophical and policy differences between the major parties, and the major parties retain a virtual monopoly on partisan elective office in the United States. In order for Jesse Ventura to win in Minnesota in 1998, all had to go right for his campaign and all had to go wrong for his opponents. Until the Reform Party is seen by a large segment of the U.S. electorate as a viable alternative to Democrats and Republicans—a situation that clearly does not now exist—the risk of disappearing into traditional third party oblivion still arises with each succeeding election cycle. Ventura's victory did indeed shock the world; should the Reform Party never win a U.S. election again, no one should be at all surprised.

Notes

1. In 1948, the state Democratic Party merged with the Farmer-Labor Party to form the DFL, a name that reflects the traditional coalition supporting Democratic candidates statewide. In terms of issue positions and candidate appeal today, the Minnesota DFL stands in the liberal wing of the national Democratic Party. We will use the local terminology throughout this chapter.

References

Abramson, Paul R., John H. Aldrich, Phil Paolino, and David W. Rohde. 1995. "Third-Party and Independent Candidates in American Politics: Wallace, Anderson, and Perot," *Political Science Quarterly* (Fall): 349–367.

Belluck, Pam. 1998. "A 'Bad Boy'Wrestler's Unscripted Upset," *New York Times*, November 5, A1.

Bradley, Martin, Norman M. Green Jr., Dale E. Jones, Mac Lynn, and Lou McNeil, eds. 1992. *Churches and Church Membership in the United States.* Atlanta: Glenmary Research Center.

Clubb, Jerome M., William H. Flanigan, and Nancy H. Zingale. 1986. *Electoral Data for Counties in the United States: Presidential and Congressional Races, 1840–1972* (ICPSR 8611). Ann Arbor: Inter-University Consortium for Political and Social Research.

Frank, Stephen I., and Steven C. Wagner. 1999. *"We Shocked the World!" A Case Study of Jesse Ventura's Election As Governor of Minnesota.* New York: Harcourt College Publishers.

Gilbert, Christopher P., David A. M. Peterson, Timothy R. Johnson, and Paul A. Djupe. 1999. *Religious Institutions and Minor Parties in the United States.* Westport, Ct.: Praeger Publishers.

Gilbert, Christopher P., and David A. M. Peterson. 1995. "Minnesota: Christians and Quistians in the GOP." In Mark J. Rozell and Clyde Wilcox, eds., *God at the Grassroots: The Christian Right in the 1994 Elections.* Lanham, Md.: Rowman and Littlefield, 169–189.

———. 1997. "Minnesota: Onward Quistian Soldiers? Christian Conservatives Confront Their Limitations." In Mark J. Rozell and Clyde Wilcox, eds., *God at the Grassroots 1996: The Christian Right in the 1996 Elections.* Lanham, Md.: Rowman and Littlefield, 187–205.

———. 1999. "Minnesota 1998: Christian Conservatives and the Body Politic." In Mark J. Rozell and Clyde Wilcox, eds., *God at the Grassroots 1998: The Christian Right in the 1998 Elections.* Washington, D.C.: Georgetown University Press.

Gold, Howard J. 1995. "Third Party Voting in Presidential Elections: A Study of Perot, Anderson, and Wallace," *Political Research Quarterly* 48: 751–773.

Hamburger, Tom, and Bob Von Sternberg. 1999. "If Buchanan Jumps, Expect Waves," *Minneapolis Star Tribune,* September 26, B3.

Key, V. O. 1948. *Politics, Parties, and Pressure Groups.* 2nd ed. New York: Thomas Crowell Company.

Rosenstone, Steven J., Roy Behr, and Edward Lazarus. 1996. *Third Parties in America: Citizen Response to Major Party Failure.* 2nd ed. Princeton: Princeton University Press.

Scammon, Richard M. 1995. *America Votes 21: A Handbook of Contemporary American Election Statistics.* Washington, D.C.: Elections Research Center, Congressional Quarterly, Inc.

Scammon, Richard M., Alice V. McGillivray, and Rhodes Cook. 1997. *America Votes 22: A Handbook of Contemporary American Election Statistics.* Washington, D.C.: Elections Research Center, Congressional Quarterly, Inc.

Smith, Dane. 1999. "With New Clout, Reform Party Looks to Build," *Minneapolis Star Tribune,* June 13, A2.

Voter News Service. 1994. *1994 Exit Poll Dataset.* Storrs, Ct.: Roper Center for Public Opinion Research, University of Connecticut.

———. 1998. *1998 Exit Poll Dataset.* Storrs, Ct.: Roper Center for Public Opinion Research, University of Connecticut.

Index